T0113359

Queer

Spirits

QUEER

A Gay Men's

SPIRITS

Myth Book

Will Roscoe

BEACON PRESS

BOSTON

Beacon Press
25 Beacon Street
Boston, Massachusetts 02108-2892

Beacon Press books are published under the auspices of
the Unitarian Universalist Association of Congregations.

99 98 97 96   8 7 6 5 4 3 2

Text design by Christine Taylor
Composition by Wilsted & Taylor

Library of Congress Cataloging-in-Publication Data

Roscoe, Will.
    Queer spirits : a gay men's myth book / [edited by] Will Roscoe.
      p.   cm.
    Includes bibliographical references and indexes.
    ISBN 0-8070-7938-3 (cloth)
    ISBN 0-8070-7939-1 (paper)
        1. Homosexuality, Male.   2. Homosexuality—Mythology.
    3. Homosexuality—Religious aspects.   4. Homosexuality in
    literature.   5. Archetypes in literature.   I. Roscoe, Will.
    HQ76.25.Q39   1995
    305.9'06642—dc20   94-30970
                                                              CIP

For my queer spirits—Prissy, Andy,

Nona, Pony, Mrdr, Mitch, Tede—

I will never forget you—

and especially for Brad, Harry,

John, and Mark

Contents

This way   gentle men
to the Ineffable Lollapalooza
We offer you the niftiest Half & Half in captivity
Get your tickets now
See the Original Indivisible

This way   boys and boygirls
to the Ideal Impossible
Here is the Matchless Catchall alive and kicking
All twosomes imaginable
in one humdinger package

Step inside   misses and misfits
Acknowledge your symptoms
Prepare for travesties and profound transvestitures
This is the morality-shaking magician
Androgyne the Great

Behold the unseemly hermaphrodite
as he really seems
Is he the master of your questionable solutions?
Is he the mistress of
your insoluble questions?

Warning
He is addicted to effrontery
He can mess up the neatest arrangements
He can make certain that
your squirmings engulf you

He is a harmless rascal
He is a revolutionary harlot
He offers you nothing less than
    the risk of everything
He desires all your desires
He prickles with fecundity

Cunningest of cunts
cockadoodle of all cocks
he will dive for treasure in your deep vaginas
he will grasp your testes
and play ball with heaven

What more could you want?
What are you afraid of?
Does no one here wish to embrace
    the Celestial Totality?
Does no one want to live out
the whole holy story?

James Broughton, "At the Androgyne Carnival"

Preface

This collection was compiled to inspire, guide, and challenge gay men who are seeking a deeper understanding of their sexuality and identity, of the community they live in, of their history and place in society and culture. For many gay men today, the questions posed in 1950 by the Mattachine Foundation, the first grassroots gay organization in the United States, are just as urgent now as they were then: Who are we? Where do we come from? What are we for? The harsh realities of HIV and rampant homophobia have awakened us to the fact that being gay is a serious matter. It's time to ask ourselves, What does it all mean? This intense eroticism that pervades our lives and pulses through all our gatherings—this instinct for reversal, for improvising roles and identities—this sense of flair that shows up in the leatherman no less than the queen? Instinctively seeking to become, in the words of American Indian writer Clyde Hall, "persons of substance," we hunger for clues to the meaning of our lives.

Don't we lead mythical lives? Even the most unassuming of us can tell amazing stories of victory against overwhelming odds, self-respect forged out of mind-boggling hate, invention and wit mothered by inescapable necessity. When Joseph Campbell spoke of the hero's journey, he should have used *us* as his example—although he never did. *We're* the ones who arrive at wholeness after an oblique journey to the margins of the social order and back again, who suffer inordinate wounds and are healed, who win the gift of "insider-outsider" vision and can therefore speak with authority to men and women alike. But you would never know this from a reading of contemporary Western culture. Where are the myths, the adventures, the legendary and semilegendary heroes, the symbols and images that portray the real drama of gay men's lives?

When I was a queer boy growing up in a small town in Montana in the 1960s, myths to me weren't stories about violent, all-powerful male gods and their female (and occasional male) victims—the gods of the Greeks and Romans. In any case, my local school board did not consider knowledge of classical literature an important part of my education, so the gods of Olympus remained remote to me. Rather, the images that captured my imagination came from the culture I grew up in. Batman and Robin, for example, always coming to each other's rescue or tied up together by some villain was mysteriously exciting to me. I also had a crush on Will Robinson, the boy hero of the television series *Lost in Space*, who used brains instead of brawn to meet the challenges of worlds as alien to him as the heterosexual world was to me. I avidly collected comic books like the *X-Men*, rebellious youths with superhuman powers who had been rejected by society as mutants and freaks. They banded together under the guidance of a brilliant but physically handicapped scientist. His mental and moral powers offset their physical powers and rebelliousness, channeling them toward the cause of good.

Jules Verne and science fiction opened my imagination to the possibility of other worlds. I've been an idealist ever since, given to daydreaming and utopianism. My musical tastes were limited to my parents' small collection of classical and jazz albums, but I remember playing Gershwin's "Rhapsody in Blue" over and over again while I danced about the living room wearing a sheet. I still have a hard time sitting still whenever I hear that piece. When it came to erotic appeal, nothing turned me on more than the dark red body-hugging costume of the comic book character the Flash. (A gay friend of mine tells me that he used to masturbate with comic books of the Green Lantern.) Then there were the Hardy Boys. I had no idea what it would be like to have a close brother relationship, but I always dreamed of having a special friend with whom to share adventures.

Isn't this where most of us first encounter those vivid images that inhabit our dreams and fantasies—in children's stories, folktales, nursery rhymes, television series, and comic books and later, when we are adults, in films, novels, drama, and opera? Popular art forms are where archetypal themes and characters thrive, no less than in our dreams. The way in which gay children relate to these popular forms is often revealing. Here, for example, is Samuel Delany's description of his childhood in Harlem in the 1950s from his autobiography, *The Motion of Light in Water* (New York: Arbor, 1988):

> I wrote plays and tried to write novels and was stunned, at eight, when a classmate, a girl named Gabby, wrote a beautiful letter from the hospital in the form of a rebus, illustrated with words and pictures cut from magazines . . . then died; and learned how to do splits and cartwheels from Wendy and memorized "The Raven" and "Jabberwocky" and Gilbert and Sullivan lyrics with Priscilla; and—after seeing a high school production of it one week and the next an Old Vic presentation at the ancient Metropolitan Opera House, with Robert Helpmann as Oberon and fiery-haired Moira Shearer as Titania, with impossibly ornate sets and a wonderfully obscene homoerotic Puck—learned long slabs of *A Midsummer Night's Dream* with Peter; and *The Waste Land* and "The Love Song of J. Alfred Prufrock"—because Sue-Sue, in the

high school division, told me Eliot was impossible to understand and I'd show them—and read science fiction with Robert and Johnny; and borrowed Priscilla's *Mad* comic book to read in the boys' john, cover to cover, and called her nightly to ask her how were things in Afghanistan; and drew maps of imaginary lands; and listened to Tom Lehrer records with my friend Mike, who, like Johnny and Robert, was an inveterate nail-biter. . . .
(p. 10)

My white, middle-class, small-town background could hardly have been more different than Delany's childhood in Harlem . . . yet there are so many themes in this passage that I can identify with that it's hard to know where to begin: from the books, poetry, and plays Delany mentions, to his indifference to appropriate boy-girl behavior, his friendships with girls and other unconventional boys, his attraction to social protest, his budding homoerotic awareness, and the beginning of a pattern of secrecy that charges gay sexuality with the thrill of danger. Of course, each of us could draw a similar map of our childhood imaginations—I would recommend it as a useful exercise. These memories represent the origin points of values, ideals, and desires from which we seldom stray as adults.

I lost touch with many of these early memories during the repressive years of adolescence. In the frantic period following my coming out in 1975, culminating in my move to San Francisco three years later, there was little time or reason to think back to the roots of my personality as a gay man. Within a few months of arriving in the Bay Area, however, I found myself holding a candle in a memorial march for Harvey Milk and George Moscone, then six months later a brick as I joined the riots following the trial of Dan White. By the fall of 1979, I was ready to take stock of my life and the gay world I was living in. That was when I saw an announcement for the first "spiritual conference for radical faeries," held in Arizona, where I met Harry Hay, one of the original founders of the Mattachine Foundation, and many other gay men who've become lifelong friends. More than anything, it was my encounter with Harry's idea of subject-SUBJECT consciousness that has enabled me to reconnect with the imaginary roots of my gayness.

As Harry defines it, subject-SUBJECT is a way of relating in which each person treats the other as an equal, thinking of him or her as we think of ourselves, as subjects, not objects. Same-sex relationships, in which differences are minimized, have a unique potential for fostering this way of relating and escaping the objectification on which Western consciousness is based. When I heard Harry describe these ideas under the starry skies of the Arizona desert, I was overwhelmed by a rush of memories. I, too, had had the dream of finding another boy who mirrored me and equaled me in every respect, with whom I could freely share my thoughts and interests, who would join me on the long walks I liked to take into the hills outside the city. And now I understood how this dream had always guided my life.

In this collection, I've tried to return to these roots, to find the myths behind these memories. For this reason I've included not only "myths" in the traditional sense but also excerpts from literature, poems, anthropological accounts, children's books, and even newspaper clippings. Although they come from faraway and unlikely places, I think that these stories offer insight and inspiration for telling our own stories today. These are not merely documents of same-sex love—its practice, its roles, its presence in other times and places. They are keys to a deeper understanding and appreciation of gayness—the reasons for being gay, the ways of being gay, how we can nurture and foster these ways to discover the deeper meaning of our lives.

This book originated as a handout for a workshop I held in 1990 called "Reclaiming Our Myths/Inventing Our Lives." I put together about fifty examples of gay myths and archetypes, focusing on accounts from non-Western cultures. I decided not to retell the myths in my own words or to edit the original material more than slightly, with the exception of those selections that I translated myself. Because I wanted to allow each myth to speak with its own distinct voice, I reproduced the material in most cases exactly as I found it. Sometimes this preserved the voice of the original narrator. Stories like "I Alone Keep Up Life" and "There Was Great Rejoicing" convey much of the style of traditional Native American oratory. In other cases, however, it meant preserving the distorted and biased commentary of the (usually) Western heterosexual male writer who recorded it. It would be tempting to edit this out, but in many cases we would be left with only fragments. It is possible, however, to learn how to read through the judgments and misconceptions often woven into gay material. In fact, these aspects of the texts can be treated as myths in and of themselves—the myths of homophobia that Western societies have been telling themselves for centuries.

For my workshop, I edited each selection to fit on the front and back of a single page and gave the unbound pages to the participants with the suggestion that they use them to make their own "myth book." They could throw out selections they didn't like and arrange the ones that appealed to them in whatever order made sense. Obviously, to create this book I had to give up my original format. I decided to arrange the stories according to the way in which they reflected various phases of our lives as gay men, from childhood through coming out, our exploration of the gay life and the discovery of our path in it, and, finally, old age and death.

The introductions to each selection provide information that I hope will enable readers to better appreciate the stories.

This is a somewhat arbitrary arrangement since many myths and stories include several themes, sometimes telling a whole life story in themselves. Further, it would be presumptuous to speak of there being a single, ideal life course for gay men. The image of a tree might be more appropriate, with its central trunk ending in a variety of different branches and leaves, or simply the notion of a path that diverges into alternative routes with unexpected detours. *But there is no single path for gay men.* I have tried to include diverse material in this collection, from many different cultures and historical periods, but don't let this or any other book or pronouncement tell you whether you belong to the gay community, whether your particular way of being gay is "really" gay, or whether the path you're following is correct or popular.

A myth book is not only for reading; it's a tool for self-exploration, a place to return to whenever you need a new dream or a new connection. Many of the stories in this collection have immediate appeal. Others take time and repeated readings. Yet others require an ability to visualize the elements of the story rather than to follow a plot line. If the meaning and relevance of a selection is not always clear at first, come back to it later. I hope at least that this book will encourage you to begin the process of exploring your gayness, that it will be for you a golden key, like that found by the boy in the story that follows.

Will Roscoe
June 1994
San Francisco

Acknowledgments

Thanks are due, first of all, to the participants in my 1990 workshop, whose enthusiasm through a long, hot day in a stuffy south of Market warehouse encouraged me to continue collecting and sharing gay myths. Along the way, many friends provided helpful suggestions, without which this would be a much slimmer volume—Bob Barzan, Stephen O. Murray, Mark Thompson, Harry Hay, John Burnside, Robert Hopcke, Wilfred Koponen, Mitch Walker, and Hubert Kennedy. I am especially grateful to those who read early versions of the book: Mark Thompson, Dennis S. Miles, Bob Barzan, and my editor, Deborah Chasman, all made important and valuable suggestions. But, above all, I am indebted to my partner, Bradley Rose, who not only suggested material, read and edited several versions of the manuscript, and translated German sources—he did all this with a T-cell count somewhere around zero. The contribution of his precious time and energy makes this myth book for me, and I hope for readers, too, a very, very special treasure.

➤   ➤   ➤

Note concerning dates: I have used the more recent conventions of C.E. for *common era* and B.C.E. for *before the common era*, instead of A.D. and B.C.

Introduction

There are at least three ways in which a myth book for gay men can be read. Myths offer, above all, confirmation of our *presence* in history and culture. For many that is enough. One friend who reviewed an earlier version of this collection urged me to acknowledge that "this book can be read simply as a historical connector for us few who do not seek religiosity in living." For others, however, a collection of gay myths will offer insight into the *archetypes* of gay experience, psychological and social. By helping us discover connections between these archetypes and our own lives, myths become tools for *transformation*.

PRESENCE

Same-sex love has been present in families and tribes all over the world. Myths tell us of its enduring presence, especially those from cultures in which homosexual patterns had a recognized place. These stories in particular reveal the skills, the personal traits, and, sometimes, the powers of same-sex love. They counter the silence of the Western tradition, offering invaluable wisdom—once we learn how to read them. They are also a source of inspiration and encouragement. Many of the stories in this collection have a theme of triumph over adversity. They feature protagonists powerless in physical or social terms (the terms in which men define power) but strong in character, cunning, and principle. The female opera and movie stars whom gay men so often idolize also have this quality. The non-Western counterparts of these figures reveal an additional dimension to their character, however—the *spiritual* nature of their social and personal powers.

Of course, myths are not recipes to be followed literally. Theirs is the language of metaphor and symbol. A male figure dressed as a woman may symbolize an inner psychological state as well as the trappings of a social role. In my own self-exploration, for example, I found that my ability to form friendships with both men and women has nothing to do with the clothes I wear but is related to my overall attitude toward gender—that of a male who does not identify with the heterosexual male role and is able to identify with women. The fact that I have dressed up from time to time on gay occasions, on the other hand, probably helped me reach this insight a little faster.

ARCHETYPES

Although myths can be read simply for confirmation of our presence, they can also guide us to the archetypal images that shape our psychic lives as gay men.

My understanding of archetypes comes largely from the work of C. G. Jung. Jung defined archetypes as unconscious psychic structures. When they enter the conscious mind, they do so in the form of characteristic images and figures. Jung found these images in the dreams of diverse individuals and in mythology and art from around the world. For this reason, Jung and others have concluded that archetypes are collective, a part of everyone's psyche, and therefore universal.

The concept of core images that represent psychological dynamics has been an important one in guiding my work with mythology. The basic types underlying the gods and traditional stories of diverse peoples are often strikingly similar. At the same time, I have always been uncomfortable with the readiness of Jungians to make sweeping generalizations about very different times and places. In my view, archetypal images are collective to the extent that they are widely shared among communities united through language and culture, but there are important differences in their form and emotional tone cross-culturally. In the introductions to the selections that follow, I try to point out these differences.

In selecting material for this collection, I have relied most of all on my own instinctive reactions. I looked for passages and descriptions that seemed especially vivid and larger than life, that *show* rather than *tell*, that seem to have a deeper meaning, even if that meaning isn't always clear. Ultimately, what makes a motif archetypal is the reaction that it triggers in people. People rarely react in a neutral way to genuinely archetypal figures. Indeed, the myths in this book will take you to strange worlds filled with scary, two-sexed monsters and heroes who undergo radical transformations of the body. Be prepared to experience irresistible attraction or instinctive repulsion—or, perhaps, a disturbing combination of the two.

The ambivalent reactions that archetypes provoke point to another common feature. The gods and goddesses of mythology have an unnerving way of straying back and forth across the boundaries we normally draw between good and evil. They come from a part of the mind/body continuum that isn't capable of making moral distinctions, and, as such, they encompass everything humans are capable of, every human potential. For me, this combination of positive and negative, good and evil, attractive and scary elements in a single figure or image is a good indicator of archetypal content.

Myths are especially rich sources of archetypes because they are collective productions. Their form and content are the result of having been passed through many hands and having been given many retellings. Whatever is extraneous, inessential, or individual in these stories has been sifted out until only the most memorable and essential material remains. All this occurs collectively and by unconscious rules. For this reason, myths with gay themes and characters are a source of insight into the wellsprings of our sexuality and identity.

Indeed, the very existence of gay-related myths and archetypes is proof of an independent basis for gay personality and evidence against all those theories that define gay men (and lesbians) as products of a failed psychological development. Freud, for example, considered homosexuals to be stuck between male and female identity, with sexual desires, in the case of gay men, that "normally" belong to women. One of the assumptions behind this theory is that there are only two sexes, male and female, and that heterosexuality is, therefore, both logical and natural. In this view, which leaves little room for the Native American third-gender role and its counterparts around the world, anything that is not male has to be female. Therefore, men who are different are automatically described as trying or wanting to be women.

Freud was interested in myths, too. He believed that the Greek myth of Oedipus could be used to understand *everyone's* psychology, male and female, heterosexual and homosexual. Oedipus killed his father and married his mother, and, in the end, faced with his incredible blindness, he blinded himself literally. Of course, in the original story, Oedipus does these terrible things unknowingly. Freud believed, however, that it was the secret wish of Oedipus and of all male infants to kill their fathers in order to marry their mothers. In the view of both Freud and Jung, male infants grow up to become homosexuals when they repress their desire for their mothers and identify with them instead, adopting their feminine traits to attract their fathers. Homosexual men are "stuck" on their mothers, whereas psychological maturity requires emotional separation.

I believe that, for many gay boys, our first love, our first romance, is with our fathers—or some other close, charismatic adult male—not our mothers. As the gay poet Rimbaud wrote,

> —For a father is troubling!—and the things
>   conceived! . . .
> His knee, sometimes coaxing; his trousers
> Whose fly my finger longed to open . . . oh! no!—
> To have the swollen dick, dark and hard, of my father,
> Whose hairy hand cradled me! . . .

This doesn't always mean that we identify with our mothers to attract our fathers, however. Sometimes, we are able to identify with *and* desire our fathers at the same time. The myths in this collection provide evidence of the variety of patterns and experiences that can lead us to gay identity in adulthood. Many of them are distinctly nonoedipal. Further, our psychology never consists solely of gay-related images and dynamics. Each of us has, within our psyche and our powers of imagination, all the archetypes. What makes us different from each other, psychologically speaking, are our relationships to these images—we identify with some but repress others, and so on.

TRANSFORMATION

I've described how myths can inform and inspire. A final value of myths is their power to transform.

Working with myths can open channels between the conscious and the unconscious parts of the mind. After all, archetypal images are created by the unconscious to express itself to the conscious mind, and myths are filled with archetypal images. It is these *images*, not the words of the myths, that engage the creative processes of our unconscious mind when we read or hear them.

Of course, by *working with myths* I mean something more than collecting and analyzing them, although these are important projects. I mean *living* the myths, something that can happen only after contemplating, questioning, and imagining them over a period of time. As Lévi-Strauss points out, if religious ceremonies can be considered "acted myths," then myths can be viewed as "thought rituals"—mental enactments of ritual, with the same potential for fostering psychological transformation and growth. The technique that I have developed for this involves visualizing the myth not so much as a narrative film but as a series of tableaux or still pictures or even mandalas (an image of wholeness in which diverse elements are organized symmetrically around a central point) that can be held in the mind and minutely examined. Each tableau can be compared and questioned: What is the point of view of the various figures? What are the relationships between them? Often, I will visualize these images while meditating or as I am falling asleep.

Above all, it is in our dreams that we encounter myths and their images. Because of the personalized forms that archetypes can take when they occur in dreams, however, it's not always easy to see the connections. Dream work requires a long-term commitment to recording and reflecting on one's dreams, whether done on one's own or with a therapist. Rather than looking for logical connections as you read the myths that follow, pay attention to the spontaneous feelings and reactions that you have. Genuine insights typically come in moments of sudden recognition. When my lover dreamed that he was an Indian woman and that he climbed up a telephone pole in order to be "in communication" with the spirit world, there was no doubt that the archetype of the Two-Spirit, exemplified by the Native American third-gender role, had an inner meaning for him. Recently, I dreamed that I stole money from the purse of an unpleasant woman I once worked for. As I was writing the introduction to the myth of Asushunamir, who descends into the underworld, confronts the powerful and angry goddess of the dead, and then recovers the body of Ishtar, which has been turned into a water skin (a kind of purse) and hung on the wall, I suddenly understood at least one meaning of my dream: I was trying to bring back something of "value" from a negative side of the image of the feminine that I had buried deep within me.

As Jung wrote, "Even the best attempts at explanation are more or less successful translations into another metaphorical language. . . . The most we can do is to *dream the myth onwards* and give it a modern dress. And whatever explanation or interpretation does to it, we do to our own souls as well, with corresponding results for our own well-being." When we allow ourselves to "dream the myth onwards," we begin to speak the language that the unconscious understands, and we begin that slow, glacial process of transformation whose goal is the alignment of the total psyche that Jung termed the Self.

GAY IDENTITY AND GAY DIVERSITY

What makes a myth gay? Is it just a story with gay sex in it? Or are there other themes and elements that might make a myth relevant to gay men today? In other words, is *gay* just a synonym for *homosexual*? Or do gay men share traits besides sexuality? What about gender? So many of us don't identify with the dominant definitions of masculinity and femininity. Then again, some of us do. One gay man's myth might be another's stereotype.

Over twenty-five years after Stonewall, we still have little consensus about the meaning of the terms we use to define ourselves and our community. We can agree on negative images of gayness—the closeted McCarthyite lawyer, Roy Cohn, for example, has become a kind of gay antihero—but we rarely agree on which images portray us as we wish to be seen. While feminists have produced a small library of books on the subject of women and mythology, the shelves in the gay men's section are nearly empty. Many gay writers are beginning to cite mythology, including Harry Hay, Judy Grahn, Mitch Walker, Mark Thompson, Robert Hopcke, Arthur Evans, Randy Connor, and others, but *Queer Spirits* is the first readily available collection of myths and tales for gay men. Why is this?

Of course, no single myth or image can speak equally to gay African Americans, Chicanos and Hispanics, Asians, Native Americans, Anglo Americans, and all the other people who get lumped together under that deceptively simple term *gay community*. But this should be no excuse for failing to explore ourselves, whatever our starting point. Instead, I find that merely bringing up the subject of *gay patterns* triggers heated objections. Many refuse even to discuss the subject. If a generalization about gay men is offered, it is quickly countered with an exception. The whole conversation grinds to a halt.

Why? Perhaps because the process involves the telling of almost forgotten episodes of humiliation and loneliness that are just too painful to recall. Perhaps, too, we are afraid of what we might find, afraid that the whole picture of ourselves might yet reveal something we hate.

Yet how can we say that our self-image is positive if we're unable actually to describe what that image includes?

I know many people dislike the idea of defining themselves. They find labels and categories limiting and even dehumanizing, and they complain about being ghettoized. There's a tendency now to dismiss the whole question of gay consciousness by labeling it an example of "identity politics." But this is only a higher form of closetry. It is society's homophobic reaction to our identities that is limiting, not the labels we freely assume. As much as we might like to, we can't do an end run around oppression. Given the death-dealing consequences of homophobia, I believe we have no choice but to define our difference from our oppressors. If we do not, we will be defined by them—right-wing Christians, psychiatrists, academics, and so forth. Finding the myths and archetypes we identify with and then asking why is one of the most effective ways of discovering who we are that I know of.

As I worked on this collection, however, I began to understand why our attempts to explore and define our gayness so often get stuck. Many of us in gay politics and spirituality have been trying to understand gayness as if it were a single, unified thing. Understandably, we felt that a shared sense of identity would provide a source of political unity and shine light on our presence in the past. I tried, for example, to find ways of understanding contemporary gay s/m experience and drag balls as aspects of some common underlying gay trait. After all, both involve images of gender carried to an extreme that reveals the artificiality of gender altogether, and many gay men I know are adept at both. But this was really forcing the issue. As the myths and stories included here indicate, gay men follow not one but many different paths—just as the actual practices of same-sex love and identity found throughout the world take many forms. The fact is, our present way of labeling people on the basis of sexual preference lumps together men and women with very different emotional and psychological orientations, gender identities, and sexual role preferences (e.g., top/bottom, butch/femme, etc.).

The work of anthropologists and the emerging voices of lesbians and gay men from non-Western cultures have contributed immensely in recent years to our understanding of the various forms that homosexuality and gender difference can take. We are beginning to realize that, while the patterns are diverse, they are not infinite. Three of the most common are the following:

- a *gender-based* pattern, of which the North American third-gender or two-spirit role is the most well known;

- an *age-based* pattern, in which sexual relations between males of different age groups and at specific times of their lives are approved, of which classical Greek homosexuality is an example;

- an *egalitarian* pattern, characteristic of contemporary North American and European lesbian and gay lifestyles, in which individual erotic attraction, more than social traits, guides the choice of partner and relationships are based on reciprocity.

Some of these patterns are more common in certain parts of the world than in others; each has a definite history. More important, each pattern is associated with its own system of images, stories, heroes, and gods. Since they will show up throughout this collection, it might be helpful to talk about them a little more here.

The archetypal image associated with the gender-based pattern is the one I refer to as the Two-Spirit, borrowing the term used by contemporary Native Americans to describe the berdache or third-gender role of their traditional cultures. In contemporary gay slang, we might call such people *queens*, although this term conveys none of the spiritual meaning and social respect that two-spirits enjoyed. Other examples of social roles based on the two-spirit pattern are the *mahu* of Polynesia, the *hijra* of India, and the *galli* of ancient Rome. I use the term Two-Spirit to distinguish this archetype from the usual image of the Androgyne. The individuals who occupied two-spirit roles were not seen as men who had become women or as individuals who combined or merged male and female—although some examples of these are included here. Rather, they were seen as being outside male and female categories. One of the most ancient terms for this kind of role, *trhytīyām prakrhytim*, comes from Sanskrit and literally means "third nature."

Problems of translation arise, however, whenever these roles are made to fit into a dual gender system. In this system, if an individual does not fit into one category, then he has to be assigned to the other. Nonmasculine men are automatically assumed to be imitating women. What else is there? Because of these assumptions, two-spirits and others have been described as crossing genders when in fact they occupy a third gender. As the myths in this collection show, the power of these individuals derives from their paradoxical state of being *neither* male nor female.

The Androgyne, on the other hand, is usually thought of as half male and half female, not as something distinct from male and female. Such an image is most often a projection of a heterosexual longing for completion. For heterosexual men and women, sexuality and identity are based on distance and separation from their "opposite," but this separation is painful. The heterosexual Androgyne heals the wounds of gender, reuniting halves into a single, complete being. The Hindu deity Ardhanarisvara is the product of such a coupling between Shiva and Parvati, much as the Greek god Hermaphroditus is the result of his merger with the oversexed nymph Salmicis. The Chinese yin/yang design is the perfect symbol of this form of androgyny. These are Androgynes of union and resolution. They are typically depicted as sensuous and passive figures. They represent the release of tension between men and women and, more generally, harmony and balance.

The archetypal Two-Spirit, on the other hand, is the opposite of resolved and balanced. "She" is pure catalytic energy. The Navajo Indians recognize this in their term for two-spirits, *nádleehé*, which literally means "the one who continually changes." Two-spirit energy is chaotic and disruptive. Male and female are not united; rather, it is as if there were two entirely distinct, often incompatible people crammed into a single body. The archetypal counterpart of this is a two-fold Androgyne, a figure who is often frightening and monstrous. For those who can channel its chaotic energies, however, this archetype can be a source of immeasurable personal power. Two-spirits have a special energy, a way of attracting attention, a biting edge. Everyone knows when a two-spirit walks into the room. He/she is the center of attention. And if you want to organize anything, whether it's a party or a political organization, be sure to get a two-spirit on your side because no one knows better how to get people's attention and make things happen.

Whenever I describe this archetype, I think of Tede Matthews, now deceased, the radical queen who appeared in the film *Word Is Out*. For years, Tede played a key role in the progressive-left community in San Francisco, functioning as a bridge between the left and the gay communities and between communities of men and women. I'll never forget the time that Tede performed at a fund-raising event organized by the Sisters of Perpetual Indulgence, dressed as Emma Goldman and tap dancing to the "Internationale." Everything about Tede was intense, from his drag queen persona to his politics.

Age-based homosexuality involves a very different principle. In societies like ancient Greece, medieval Japan, and up to recent times Melanesia, youths, usually in their teens, have sex with adult men during a period of their initiation or education. The younger men (ideally) are receptive in either oral or anal intercourse, the older men taking the inserting role. Outside these boundaries, homosexuality was discouraged, even forbidden. This pattern is most closely associated with the archetype of Initiation. This is clearest in the case of New Guinea societies, where homosexual acts are considered a form of magic to be used specifically for the initiation of youths. The semen that youths receive from adult men is believed to help "grow" them into men; it is a symbolic substitute for their mother's milk and for her influence, from which they must be weaned. The most obvious manifestations of Initiation themes in gay culture today are centered around the figure of the leatherman and the exploration of sexual roles, such as top/bottom, master/slave, daddy/boy, and so forth.

The egalitarian pattern of homosexuality may be the most limited historically and geographically speaking, being predominant mostly in North America and northern Europe and only in modern times—both age- and gender-based forms prevailing earlier. Egalitarian relationships emerged as a conscious ideal in the nineteenth century with the poetry of Walt Whitman. But even Edward Carpenter, the gay English reformer at the turn of the century who helped popularize Whitman in Europe, preferred relationships with working-class men rather than men of his own middle-class background. Of course, there are plenty of examples of love between men of equal standing throughout history. But only with the emergence of gay liberation did an egalitarian pattern become an avowed ideal. "Gay" identities in other parts of the world—such as Latin America and Asia—are as much influenced by local traditions of age- and gender-based homosexuality as they are by the example of North American gays.

The egalitarian pattern is most closely linked to the archetypal figures of the Divine Twins, male couples who typically appear in myths as the slayers of monsters and the inventors of the arts, medicine, and social institutions. There are some striking examples of Divine Twins from around the world, such as the Iroquois Dekanawida and Hayonhwatha and the Old Norse figures Loki and Baldr, whose stories are included herein. The power of these male couples comes from a psychological process unique to same-sex bonding, which Mitch Walker has described as "magickal twinning": "The action of Magickal Twinning is a kind of duplication where the spirit-essence of one object is infused into another, making spirit twins, yet where the two duplicates are bound together through their common spirit-essence into a third object, an indivisible unity." This unity, however, is not in the nature of a mixed thing, like the half-male, half-female androgyne. The bonds of gay love result in something more like twin stars, two independent and whole bodies locked in permanent orbit around each other so that they function as a unit.

Let me try to explain these ideas a little more because they are important themes in this book. Heterosexuality (and some forms of homosexuality, too) is based on difference and opposition between partners. In the best relationship, each of these partners brings something that the other lacks. This is how Aristophanes accounts for heterosexuality in his speech in Plato's *Symposium*. Doubled beings who were originally a man and a woman united in a single body were divided in half by Zeus.

Since then, men and women forever seek each other, hoping to reunite with their lost halves.

But what's going on in the case of gay relationships in which the ideal is that of equality between partners? In this case, the power and mystique of bonding comes from the way in which partners of the same gender psychologically mirror and reinforce each other. They create a feedback loop that heightens self-awareness and enhances self-esteem, and this is usually an exhilarating experience. As my friend John Burnside likes to say, rather than *complementing* or completing each other as heterosexual men and women do, we gay people tend to *supplement* each other in our relationships. We structure them around an ideal that assumes that each partner is already a whole person. Our attraction for each other is not that of halves who hope to become whole again but that of two wholes who affirm, enable, and reveal the inner nature of each to the other—what Harry Hay means by subject-SUBJECT relating. In terms of sexuality, this translates into "enjoying each other's enjoyment," an ideal that I think can be applied in all our relationships, whatever archetype inspires them.

I still remember vividly the first time I found ideas like these expressed in writing. I was a sophomore in an American literature class at the University of Montana, and our reading included Walt Whitman's *Leaves of Grass*. Like so many other young gay men before me (although I thought I was the first), I was transfixed by Whitman's praise of comradeship, of its beauty and its social potential. Perhaps I had seen Whitman's poetry before, but at that point in my life it arrived just when I was ready and needed the words. What inhibited me most from coming out was that the only images of a gay lifestyle available at that time were stereotypical and degraded. Whitman showed me the beauty of love between men and its place in a democratic society. After that, I was ready to come out.

In the years since then, I've learned a lot more about the dynamics of difference in gay relationships, and I've discovered that other archetypes have shaped my sexuality and identity besides that of the Divine Twins. But the idea of the Twin has always remained the most powerful gay archetype for me. If only I could have met another gay boy like me when I was twelve or thirteen, instead of twenty!

In this book, I've tried to include material representative of all three archetypes of same-sex love. Coming to terms with age-based homosexuality, however, proved an interesting challenge for me. What makes it difficult to compare age-based patterns to contemporary gay lifestyles is that this form of homosexuality was often compulsory—just as compulsory as heterosexuality is today. In Melanesia, all youths were expected to participate in homosexual relations with older men and then, a few years later, switch their erotic interest to a wife and younger men. As a gay man interested in reciprocal relationships, there seems little for me to identify with in this pattern. Nor can I go along with those who suggest that societies like ancient Greece prove that all men are a "little homosexual." Certainly, it's true that everyone is capable of being flexible in their sexual responses over the course of a lifetime. But the incidental capacity of heterosexual men to respond homosexually cannot be compared to lifelong same-sex emotional orientation.

Working on this book, however, I have come to appreciate the historical and psychological connections between age-based patterns of homosexuality and the images of the Initiation archetype—images that Jungian therapist Robert Hopcke has found in the psyches of most gay men. Here is the true meaning of the powerful male figures that occupy our erotic fantasies, the fascination with top and bottom roles, the experimentation with s/m, the constant refinement of our sexual responses. We may be adult men of the same age and social status, but our fantasies and erotica are filled with leather daddies who have sex with their slave boys, uncles who screw nephews, coaches who do athletes, policemen who get off on prisoners, and so on, and so forth.

Now I can see the connection between figures like Batman and Robin and Zeus and Ganymede. Both relationships involve an age difference. This had no appeal to me when I was a boy, but as an adult I have found that the fantasy of being with a man who was older, taller, stronger, or richer (not necessarily all those things at once!) sometimes does appeal to me. So does the fantasy of imparting knowledge to someone younger. In all these fantasies, however, I see us treating each other as equals and seeking each other's well-being, just as Batman and Robin did. Even so, I can no longer pretend that the disturbing story of Zeus kidnapping Ganymede has nothing to do with my own psychic world.

This insight was both helpful and challenging. The appearance of age and status differences in our fantasies may reflect actual desires, but they have a deeper meaning as well. They reflect the yearning for an experience of initiation, a rite of passage that leads us from our ugly duckling childhood to swan-like adulthood as self-accepting gay men—a symbolic and ritual marking of the break with self-hatred. In the end, I think that we have to accept that the unconscious, which generates these images and is the source of erotic desire, is never politically correct. The fact that we have *fantasies* in which power symbols and relations appear is no reason to feel guilty or to punish ourselves. As Mark Thompson writes, "As we descend through the psyche's strata we discover violence: Dream images of strange drama and torture are not uncommon. The inner world is a place of blood and fire, tears and mud. . . . We cannot put a lid on our soul business and its disquieting work." The more conscious we are of our fantasies, and the more comfortable we are talking about them, the less likely we are to make the mistake of the fundamentalist—to read them literally instead of metaphorically or to act them out unconsciously. Working with our unsocialized impulses—whether on a purely psychic level, in creative media, or in the controlled setting of consensual sex play—does not free us of them, but it can lead to greater consciousness of them and more choice about their effect on our behavior.

It might not seem like there is any connecting thread between these patterns and their archetypes—except for a couple of things.

First, one type of homosexuality sometimes changes into another. In premodern Japan, for example, an age-based pattern of homosexuality involving samurai warriors and youths evolved into a gender-based pattern, in which the youths who were the partners of older men were viewed as "feminine" because of their receptive sexual role. In earlier times, as in classical Greece, youths who were lovers of older men were not "feminized" as long as they switched sexual roles when they grew older.

A second observation concerns the variety of sexual expression and lifestyles that we see in today's lesbian/gay communities. If you look closely, I think that you will find examples of all the patterns of homosexual expression found in the past and around the world being pursued today. One can find relationships between men who differ in age, class, and race; between men of similar age, race, and class; between men who differ in terms of relative masculinity and nonmasculinity; and between men whose preferences for "top" and "bottom" roles sometimes do and sometimes do not conform to stereotypes of their socioeconomic status.

Further, the boundaries between these patterns are not fixed. In fact, the life path of many gay men today seems to involve a sojourn in the psychic worlds of all three archetypes at some point in their lives. Although some gay men may find a strong identification with a single tradition or image, many of us seem to find ourselves identifying variously with the Two-Spirit, the figures of Initiation, and the Divine Twins. It's possible to imagine hybrid figures as well—severe Queens who supervise initiations, Twins who are sissies, leathered Two-Spirits.

It is fitting that contemporary lesbians and gay men throughout the world should be the inheritors of all these traditions. If our generation has gained unprecedented freedom to lead gay lives, what better use of that freedom than to reclaim and reconstitute the time-honored insights of these social patterns within our lives, to find the best and the worst of them, and to use their wisdom to make choices about how we live today? I'm not calling for some kind of blind imitation of native traditions from around the world, but for a knowledge of them to inform our actions in a society that has provided us with precious little by which to guide our growth. Myths are to be imagined, not imitated. Used in this way, they can lead to ethical choices attuned to the complex world we live in.

SOURCES Arthur Rimbaud, "Memories of the Simple-Minded Old Man," in *Rimbaud: Complete Works, Selected Letters*, trans. Wallace Fowlie (Chicago: University of Chicago Press, 1966), p. 163 (my translation); Claude Lévi-Strauss, *Anthropology and Myth* (Oxford: Blackwell, 1987), p. 201; Carl Jung in C. G. Jung and C. Kerényi, *Essays on a Science of Mythology* (Princeton, N.J.: Princeton University Press, 1963), p. 79; Mitch Walker, *Visionary Love: A Spirit Book of Gay Mythology* (San Francisco: Treeroots, 1980), p. 23; Robert H. Hopcke, *Jung, Jungians and Homosexuality* (Boston: Shambala, 1989); Mark Thompson, ed., *Leatherfolk: Radical Sex, People, Politics, and Practice* (Boston: Alyson, 1991), p. xviii.

Stories

for

Boys

Childhood is always a time of discovery and wonderment, when imagination and fantasy are allowed, even encouraged. And in the worlds we create in our play there's always a place for ourselves; we always belong; we couldn't imagine it otherwise. In fact, because the world of children is expected to be imaginative—a temporary, safe haven from the values of the male-dominated adult world and its harsh enforcement of conformity—it includes many stories and characters and games that gay children can identify with. Of course, these are never labeled as *gay*. But in our attraction to the queerer facets of children's culture we catch the first reflections of our difference.

The stories that follow invoke for me all these themes—the freedom of play and imagination, the discovery of stories and characters that speak to us, our first encounter with the boundaries of gender, the awakening of desire, the first boy we loved. These are fairy tales for gay adults, but someday in the future as I dream it parents will read them to their gay children.

Invocation

Littleboys. underground / river of / HOMOSEXUALITY
Sucking each other by matchlight/ in / Blackbowled caverns
        Littleboys in denims
        Baseball
           caps . . .
        Balling
           one another behind broken
        Backstops
Littleboys. naked / Rolling in th stickers . . .
Littleboys courting th most ENORMOUS/ of / Bigboys' thornes
        Littleboys. clothed.
           their little
        Penises, wobbling
           up out of their
        Juvenile flies . . .
        Delinquents in behalf of LOVE

Breaking th law in innocence / Believing in sex:
Writing it on walls . . .
LITTLEBOYS COME!

Quivering with pleasure. / Hiding it in toilets:
Sucking th OLDMEN . . .
LITTLEBOYS COME!

Q U E E R

Yelling from treehouse / to / Treehouse. then sucking
    each others'
Boyhood tasting manhood . . .
LITTLEBOYS COME!

COME IN TH TREEHOUSE!
        (Yelling into th sky)
COME IN TH CAVERN!
        (Burning into th damp)

              out of th
           Ground like artesian water
              out of th
          Forest
        under
     Snow.

            LITTLEBOYS COME!

Come in each other / Rivers that mingle . . .
    like artesian
Springs
    their little
PENISES
COME!

LITTLEBOYS. those underground rivers / of /
                HOMOSEXUALITY. COME!

                Jim Eggeling (J.L.S.E.)

S P I R I T S

The

Golden

Key

Our sense of being different is the "golden key" that opens the door to the full realization of our individual potentials. If we use that key, if we open the treasure chest, a rich, rewarding, challenging life awaits us, one of continual growth and discovery. As my friend John Burnside likes to point out, gay people are always working on themselves. It does seem to be true for many of us that we are always trying to improve ourselves, trying to understand ourselves better, trying to find where we belong in the world. We keep changing long past the time that our heterosexual peers settle down to adult conformity.

Difference is always a question mark. Of course, everyone is different from everyone else, but for gay people the sense of being different is acute, something we are constantly aware of and reminded of. Being the same is logical, understandable, predictable. Being different requires explanation. And, in this sense, it is a great blessing, a golden key, because it calls us to examine ourselves and to find our talents, to find the reason and justification for our difference.

This story, originally collected by the Grimm brothers and retold here by storyteller Peter Cashorali, captures the magic of that moment when, away from our heterosexual peers and family, deep in the green forest of our imagination, we discover that we hold a golden key, something that makes us special. Of course, as boys, we can only imagine what it will open up, where it will lead us. And so the story ends with the turning of the key and a boy on the edge of the future. It seems an appropriate opening for this collection.

➤ ➤ ➤

Once, on the other side of the mountains, on the edge of the Endless Forest, a boy lived in a cottage with his mother and father, his brothers and sisters. It was winter, the coldest winter the boy had ever experienced, the coldest winter anyone could remember in a land memorable for the coldness of its winters, and there was no firewood in the cottage for the boy. There was firewood for his brothers, who would grow up to be just like their father, and firewood for his sisters, who would grow up to be just like their mother. But for the boy, who would grow up to be like himself and no other, there was none.

One morning the boy woke up before sunrise. The night had been the coldest one yet, and the frost was heavy on his blankets. The boy determined that, rather than spend another such night, he'd go into the forest and get firewood for himself. He dressed and left the cottage while everyone slept, dragging his sled behind him over the snowy fields and under the eaves of the forest. Here everything was frozen and silent, and because the winter had been so hard there wasn't much wood to be found. The boy ventured deeper into the forest, finding a few twigs here, a pine cone there, a fallen branch further on, and gradually he loaded his sled.

By the time he had enough wood, he was so cold and had wandered so far that he decided to build a fire for himself right where he was. He was brushing the snow away when suddenly the sun, which had risen while he searched, gleamed on something at his feet. The boy saw it was a key, a golden key, and picked it up eagerly. "It's mine," he laughed, tossing it into the air and catching it, and the key sparkled and glittered in the sunlight as if it were laughing with him.

After a while it occurred to him that where there was a key, there must be a lock that opened to it. He swept the snow away all around him but, finding nothing, began digging into the ground. Oh, the ground was hard, harder than stone, harder than steel, and the boy had no tools to work with but his hands. It was a long while that he dug, but whenever he got tired or discouraged he pulled the golden key out of his pocket, and let his eyes rest on its promise, and went back to his labor refreshed.

At last he uncovered a small iron chest and pried it away from the grip of the frozen earth. He turned it in his hands, searching for a lock, and at first it seemed there was none. The boy was patient, though, and finally he found one, so small he'd missed it. He fit the key into the lock and began to turn it. And now we must wait for him to unlock his chest completely, and lift its lid, before we learn what its wonderful contents are, and how they changed his life in ways no one could have imagined. . . .

Peter Cashorali

Two

Pretty

Men

Nursery rhymes bubble over with play and wonder. Images and characters from everyday life are singled out for their quirks or foibles. None are too high, and no subject too low, for the irreverent treatment of the nursery rhyme. Many of the Mother Goose rhymes originated as satires of historical figures. Others are frankly obscene. Victorian compilers had a field day cleaning them up.

In the nursery rhyme, everything is familiar, but also somehow strange and larger than life—the keyhole view of the child. Of all the forms of so-called children's literature, rhymes are one of the only ones that children actually tell each other. There is also a ritualistic quality to nursery rhymes, in their simple rhythms and repetitious language. Sometimes the words are nonsense, and the rhyme becomes a chant. Others delight in the play of sounds and images. This kind of language has a way of sticking in one's mind, repeating itself over and over, insinuating itself deep into our memories.

The following are three examples of nursery rhymes that I enjoyed as a child. "Little Boy Blue" was always one of my favorites. To me, Boy Blue wasn't being lazy—he simply preferred to dream dreams rather than tend silly cows and sheep. I can still hear my parents' voices, reciting it to me. I was exactly that kind of distracted, daydreaming boy it describes.

➤　➤　➤

Q U E E R

Little Boy Blue, come blow your horn,
The cow's in the meadow, the sheep in the
    corn:
But where is the little boy tending the sheep?
He's under the hay-cock fast asleep.
Will you wake him? No, not I,
For if I do, he's sure to cry.

➤ ➤ ➤

Jack Dandy was another interesting nursery rhyme figure. He was also
called "Handy spandy, Jack-a-Dandy" and "Namby-pamby, Jack-a-
Dandy." "Namby Pamby" was a nickname given to Ambrose Phillips by
the homophobe Henry Carey (d. 1743) in his satire of Phillips's writing
style. As Carey characterized Phillips, "Namby-Pamby's doubly mild, /
Once a man, and twice a child."

➤ ➤ ➤

Nauty Pauty,
Jack Dandy,
Stole a piece of
Sugar Candy,
From the Grocer's
Shoppe Shop,
And away did
Hoppe Hop.

➤ ➤ ➤

S P I R I T S

And what's a boy to make of Robin and Richard, two "pretty Men" buried under their covers, hiding from the sun father's glaring eye? The phrase "pretty Men" is particularly rich in meaning. I've never forgotten the time that one of my first boyfriends told me I was a "pretty man." I had never heard someone describe a man that way before—let alone me. Of course, gay men often are pretty, in the best sense of the word. So it's not surprising to learn from the *Oxford English Dictionary* that, in addition to "attractive," the definition of *pretty* includes "cunning, crafty, wily, artful, astute," while a "pretty fellow" was "a fine fellow, a 'swell,' a fop." This last meaning was current in the 1700s, when the following rhyme was first collected.

➤ ➤ ➤

Robin and Richard
Were two pretty Men.
They lay in Bed
   'Till the Clock struck Ten:
Then up starts Robin
   And looks at the sky,
Oh! Brother Richard,
   The Sun's very high
You go before
   With the Bottle and Bag,
And I will come after
   On little Jack Nag.

TEXTS *Tommy Thumb's Pretty Song Book*, ca. 1744; John Newbery, *Mother Goose's Melody; or, Sonnets for the Cradle*, ca. 1760.

S P I R I T S

The Basket

and the

Bow

For many of us, our sense of being different first emerges in the games and toys we like as children. When I was in the first grade, I decided to bring a jump rope to school to use at recess because that was the activity that looked like the most fun to me. Only later did I discover that jumping rope was a "girl thing." Until then it had never occurred to me that there were limits to the games I could play because of my sex. I had chosen the activity that felt right for me, that appeared most enjoyable and rewarding.

If I had been lucky enough to be born into a traditional Native American family, my choice of a girl's toy would not have been greeted with horror and punishment. Such an inclination would be taken as a sign of my true nature, of the life path I was going to follow, and of the kind of training and guidance I would need. Among Plains Indians, such an inclination was often confirmed by a dream or vision. It was not for humans to second-guess matters of the spirit.

While some tribes simply observed children to see what their gender and sexual orientation might be, others performed a specific rite to determine whether a boy was a two-spirit. This passage describes a procedure common among Southwest and Great Basin tribes. The results of the test were considered final. It revealed the boy's true nature not only to his family but to the whole community. Today, contemporary lesbian and gay Indians have proudly reclaimed the tradition of "the basket and the bow." One of the first conferences for gay Indians in North America was called "The Basket and the Bow: A Gathering of Lesbian and Gay Native Americans."

The following passage, written by anthropologist Ruth Underhill in the 1930s, describes this rite among the Papago Indians of southern Arizona. Underhill goes on to quote her informant's account of a particular two-spirit named Shining Evening.

➤ ➤ ➤

The berdache was said to have been discovered in early childhood. If the parents found that a boy liked female pursuits they tested him. The regular pattern, mentioned by many informants, was to build a small enclosure and place in it bow and arrows and basketry materials. The child was told to go in and play and then the parents set fire to the enclosure. They watched what he took with him as he ran out and if it was the basketry materials, they reconciled themselves to his being a berdache.

The berdache performed women's work. He [was] made one of the group of women on food gathering expeditions and was treated as one of themselves. He was often a clever potter and basket maker and an asset on food gathering expeditions, because he "didn't get tired as we did." He also played an important role in the village.

When the Apache trophy was hung up, if there was a berdache in the village, he might dance around it with a bow taunting it: "See what you are reduced to! The men will not look at you, but I, even I, can shoot you."

The berdache might marry, but often, since he was entirely able to work and support himself, he lived alone and was visited by the men. To each visitor he gave an obscene nickname and the men were very proud of these, since they were often bolder than those bestowed by women. No scorn was felt for the berdache. He was respected and liked by the women and his sex life with the men was a community institution.

One informant thus described her berdache brother-in-law:

"We girls used to spend all day with that man-woman, Shining Evening. She went off with us to gather plants and she could carry more than any of us and dig longer. She ground corn with us, all taking turns at my mother-in-law's grinding slab. Our husbands used to tease us girls. 'How do we know these children running around the house belong to us? We are away in the mountains all the time and in the fields. It is Shining Evening who is with the women.' Then they would laugh and say to the babies, 'Run along. Over there is your daddy. . . .'

"When we learned from the Whites to make skirts with drawstrings, Shining Evening was the first to have one. A man pulled the string and said, 'What's that?' and she said squealing, 'Skirt string!' So after that the man was always called skirt string.

"There was a berdache in the next village and that one had a husband. She came with him to the drinking ceremony and I saw her cooking for him on the fireplace of some of her relatives. They seemed happy."

TEXT Ruth M. Underhill, *Social Organization of the Papago Indians*, Columbia University Contributions to Anthropology 30 (New York: Columbia University Press, 1939), pp. 186–87.

A Temple
of the Holy
Ghost

As a child, I can remember thinking that, since dogs chased cats, all dogs must be boys and all cats were girls. I was just beginning to become aware that the world was divided into male and female, and I obviously had a few more lessons to learn!

The discovery of gender, of the difference between male and female bodies and of male and female symbols, is a great shock and mystery to most children. Quickly we scramble to master its fine points. We practice enforcing gender distinctions on other children. But what happens when a gay child plays "family" with his friends? I've often asked this question of my gay friends and found that many of us insisted, even as children, on altering the rules of the game to make room for our innate sense of being different. Some of us took the female roles quite gleefully. Others of us were "daddies" and "husbands," but of a different sort (I refused to go to work or to punish the "children").

The following excerpt from Flannery O'Connor's short story describes one child's first glimpse into the mysteries of gender as embodied in the strange, hypnotic figure of the Androgyne.

The half-and-half, or hermaphrodite, "act" was once a common feature of the freak shows and carnivals that visited small American towns in the nineteenth and early twentieth centuries. I learned about this sideline of American gender history from David Spencer, a former clown, who generously shared his knowledge of circus history with me, before his untimely death. The half-and-half act consisted of a simple dance by the performer, perhaps a striptease, leading up to a

display of the half-and-half's double-sexed body—how much you saw
depended on what you were willing to pay. In practice, the act could
be done two ways. David knew a famous clown who, in his early days,
did the act by cleverly hiding his very small penis. Voilà! instant hermaphrodite. Another way to do the act was to make one side of the
body as masculine as possible, by developing the muscles, tanning,
and so forth, and keeping the other side pale, thin, and feminine.
The half-and-half encountered by the child of O'Connor's story
appears to have been along the lines of the first example.

➤   ➤   ➤

The child didn't move. "One time," she said, her voice
hollow-sounding in the dark, "I saw this rabbit have
rabbits."

There was a silence. Then Susan said, "How?" in an indifferent tone and she knew that she had them. She said she
wouldn't tell until they told about the you-know-what. Actually she had never seen a rabbit have rabbits but she soon
forgot this as they began to tell what they had seen in the
tent.

It had been a freak with a particular name but they
couldn't remember the name. The tent where it was had
been divided into two parts by a black curtain, one side for
men and one for women. The freak went from one side to the
other, talking first to the men and then to the women, but
everyone could hear. The stage ran all the way across the
front. The girls heard the freak say to the men, "I'm going
to show you this and if you laugh, God may strike you the
same way." The freak had a country voice, slow and nasal

and neither high nor low, just flat. "God made me thisaway and if you laugh He may strike you the same way. This is the way He wanted me to be and I ain't disputing His way. I'm showing you because I got to make the best of it. I expect you to act like ladies and gentlemen. I never done it to myself nor had a thing to do with it but I'm making the best of it. I don't dispute hit." Then there was a long silence on the other side of the tent and finally the freak left the men and came over onto the women's side and said the same thing.

The child felt every muscle strained as if she were hearing the answer to a riddle that was more puzzling than the riddle itself. "You mean it had two heads?" she said.

"No," Susan said, "it was a man and woman both. It pulled up its dress and showed us. It had on a blue dress."

The child wanted to ask how it could be a man and woman both without two heads but she did not. She wanted to get back into her own bed and think it out and she began to climb down off the footboard.

"What about the rabbit?" Joanne asked.

The child stopped and only her face appeared over the footboard, abstracted, absent. "It spit them out of its mouth," she said, "six of them."

She lay in bed trying to picture the tent with the freak walking from side to side but she was too sleepy to figure it out. She was better able to see the faces of the country people watching, the men more solemn than they were in church, and the women stern and polite, with painted-looking eyes, standing as if they were waiting for the first note of the piano to begin the hymn. She could hear the freak saying, "God made me thisaway and I don't dispute hit." And the people saying, "Amen. Amen."

"God done this to me and I praise Him."

"Amen. Amen."

"But he has not."

"Amen."

"Raise yourself up. A temple of the Holy Ghost. You! You are God's temple, don't you know? Don't you know? God's Spirit had a dwelling in you, don't you know?"

"Amen. Amen."

"If anybody desecrates the temple of God, God will bring him to ruin and if you laugh, He may strike you thisaway. A temple of God is a holy thing. Amen. Amen."

"I am a temple of the Holy Ghost."

"Amen."

The people began to slap their hands without making a loud noise and with a regular beat between the Amens, more and more softly, as if they knew there was a child near, half asleep.

TEXT Flannery O'Connor, "A Temple of the Holy Ghost," in *The Complete Stories* (New York: Farrar Straus Giroux, 1971), pp. 245–46.

S P I R I T S

Behind

the

Hill

As we become aware of gender and our relationship to it, we also become aware of our sexual desires—although at first they may amount to little more than the desire to roll around in the grass with our best friend. Even so, discovery of our desire for other boys often comes in memorable moments.

In the following story, by Samuel M. Steward, a boy suddenly discovers the possibility of gay love and—in the kind of twist typical of Sam—from his own father. The story was first published in 1930, and its innuendos were quite bold for the time. A prolific writer, Sam's work is a unique contribution to contemporary gay mythology. He agreed to let me include this story shortly before he died in December 1993.

In the original Greek tale, Endymion was the beautiful son of Zeus. He was kissed by the moon goddess Selene while he lay sleeping in a cave—that is, within the Earth Mother—and fell thereafter into a permanent, ageless sleep. There's not much more to his story than this. Sam's rendition reveals how the gay imagination works—finding small clues in the culture around us that we can use to open the door to gay possibilities.

➤ ➤ ➤

The lad Arythra walked behind his father. It was night and they were going out to watch over their sheep and keep them safe from harm. Arythra liked to sit on the warm sheep-skin his father always brought for him and watch the slow march of the silver moon across the dark sky while his father guarded the flock. Once his mother had said the sky was like the purple nap of a butterfly's wing. It was nice, too, to see the mists gather in the valleys, like little lakes, and to watch the dew sparkle when the moon looked at it.

Arythra carried a shepherd's crook of cedar wood just like his father's, only much smaller. As they strolled slowly up the gentle rise at the foot of Mount Latmos the moon was beginning to hide behind the silver peak of the mountain; it always stayed behind so long.

"Daddy," said Arythra, "why does the moon hide behind Mount Latmos for such a long time?"

His father looked up at the peak, and at the clouds which showed where the moon was.

"Arythra," he said, "I will tell you the story tonight, when we get to our sheep. They are not far; do you see them over there?"

Arythra nodded. The sheep moved slowly along, nibbling at the silver grass. Like a thousand clumps of cotton they were, whitened on their backs by the reflection of the moon from behind the hill and shadowed on the rest of their bodies.

When they came to the sheep, Arythra's father spread out the sheep-skin and Arythra sat down on it. His father leaned on his crook and looked at the sky and started to speak. And this was his story.

"Once there was a shepherd who tended his sheep on the other side of Mount Latmos, this very same mountain.

Every night he would sit and watch the moon, just as we are doing now, and sometimes he would get so lonely he wished he were dead. But he was lonesome only at night, for in the daytime he danced and frolicked in the wind with his sheep, or he picked the white mountain argith-flowers and wove them into wreaths. When he was tired he would sit on a rock and play upon his queer harp that he had made for himself from a turtle shell and had strung with dried ivy vines so that the sound it gave was like the sibilant sigh of the winds through the long grasses.

"And oh, but he was beautiful! More beautiful than the loveliest woman, Arythra, and he was named Endymion. All the nymphs and oreads who dwelt in the caves and the trees fell in love with the beautiful Endymion and the way his hair curled on his head and the way his lips looked in the moonlight."

"As nice as mother's, daddy?" Arythra's little face was a question mark in the gloom.

"Oh, yes. . . . Now, one night Endymion was so sleepy that he couldn't stay awake, and so he stretched out on his sheep-skin, turned his face towards the sky and went to sleep with a prayer to Diana to guard his flock. And as he slept Diana drove her moon-chariot in its silver arc across the blue heaven. As she passed over the tip-top of the peak up there, she chanced to look down and saw the lovely Endymion asleep on his yellow sheep-skin, and straightway she loved him.

"So that she might see him more plainly, she shot some of her silver arrows down around him, and when they had illumined him she saw his beauty and climbed over the side of her silver chariot, which became dark the moment she left it. She slid down the moonbeams and sat and watched over him, kissing his lips again and again.

"Diana was so in love with Endymion that she neglected her work as moon-goddess and drove back to Olympus sometimes as much as eight hours late. Of course her father Jupiter could not but notice her irregular hours, and the good people on earth were surprised to see her drive across the heavens at noon, so pale and forlorn in the light of the sun. Jupiter, too, noticed her pallor and weariness. These long vigils of watching over Endymion robbed Diana of her sleep, for now Endymion slept every night.

"Finally, Arythra, one of the jealous oreads saw Diana at the side of Endymion and ran and whispered her news in Jupiter's ear. Jupiter was very angry and called the shepherd up to Olympus. Endymion was frightened when he came into the temple of the gods, the temple of marble and emerald and gold, and heard the thunders chasing through the halls and saw the blinding light that hid the Deity on his throne of a metal peacock, with Diana standing morosely at its side.

"'Endymion,' came a thunderous voice from the heart of the light, a voice like one from a deep well, a voice that made the poor shepherd's chest vibrate and quiver, 'you have been honored by receiving the love of my daughter, but she has told me that you know nothing of it. Had you caressed her, you would be dead by now. As it is, I will give you a choice between death by the hemlock or by the knife, and perpetual youth united with perpetual sleep. It is said, Endymion, that no mortal may love a goddess without punishment. Choose.'

"Warily Diana motioned to Endymion to choose the latter, and so he did with a great tear in his eye, for none loved better than he the way the wind sang through the grass or the way the sky looked on a summer day.

"So, Arythra, he sleeps eternally on Mount Latmos, high in a cave. Often people have looked for him but none can find him. That is why the moon takes so long behind Mount Latmos; she bends over Endymion who sleeps in one of the cool caves."

The moon showed her rim on the other side of the peak; the little white clouds marshalled themselves around her and all traveled east. Arythra thought she looked especially happy.

"That is why," said his father, "that you see those little white clouds in the sky. Diana promised to guard his sheep and tend their increase, so she took them into the sky with her."

"But daddy," asked Arythra, "why is that big tear in your eye?"

"I have seen strange things which no mortal should see. I have climbed Mount Latmos and followed the moon into a dark cave. I have seen Endymion. . . ."

TEXT Samuel M. Steward, "Behind the Hill," in *Pan and the Fire-Bird* (New York: Harrison, 1930), pp. 28–31.

S   P   I   R   I   T   S

First

Contacts

Sometimes the discovery of our sexuality comes in a joyful rush when we first touch another boy. Sometimes it comes as a revelation that leaves us impressed with a lifelong erotic image. I can still remember the first adult penises I saw in the shower at the neighborhood swimming pool when I was nine years old and the elaborate games I invented with my male friends that always ended up with us naked.

The following passages describe similar experiences of two gay boys. The first comes from the underground classic *The White Paper*, Jean Cocteau's confession of same-sex love, published anonymously in the 1920s. The second comes from a story by Native American author Clyde Hall (M. Owlfeather), first published in 1988 in *Living the Spirit*.

➤ ➤ ➤

The second time it was the following year. My father had allowed some gypsies to camp at the end of his park where I had lost consciousness. I was walking with my maid. Suddenly, crying out, she dragged me away, forbidding me to look backward. There was a dazzling heat. Two young gypsies were naked and clambering in the trees. A sight that shocked my maid and framed my disobedience in an unforgettable way. If I live a hundred years, thanks to that cry and that flight, I will always revere a gypsy wagon, a woman cradling a newborn infant, a smoking fire, a white horse eating grass, and, clambering in trees, two bodies of bronze three times spotted with black.

TEXT Anonymous [Jean Cocteau], *Le Livre Blanc* (Paris: Persona, 1981) (my translation).

➤ ➤ ➤

It was during a hot, dry and dusty Idaho summer, when I was eleven, that I had my first real contact with another male. I had more freedom then. I had both a pony and a red bicycle. With those possessions my circle of friends widened. I met a boy who lived a few blocks down from my grandmother's cabin. He was a local white boy some years older than myself. I admired his independent and cocksure ways. He seemed to be everything that I was not; good in sports and, above all, sure of himself in every situation. He had tousled brown curly hair and was somewhat stocky. He became my hero in the eye of my budding desire.

The local boys our age frequented several well-known swimming holes on the reservation. We always picked one that was well-secluded with overhanging trees and green grass on the banks. One day towards the end of summer— on the kind of day when the light is hazy and diffused and the air is barely moving and heavy to breathe—my friend and I decided to have an impromptu swim before returning home. The water was cool and clear as we dove in. I came up from under the water first. He came up right behind me and reached around and into my shorts (we always swam in our undershorts). I noticed that he was hard, as he rubbed against my backside. As his hands reached around me . . . I became aroused and hard too. It felt good and right, like something that was supposed to be. I knew then that this is what I had been waiting for and I have never looked back since.

TEXT M. Owlfeather, "Children of Grandmother Moon," in *Living the Spirit: A Gay American Indian Anthology*, ed. Will Roscoe (New York: St. Martin's, 1988), p. 102.

SPIRITS

We Two Boys
Together
Clinging

We two boys together clinging,
One the other never leaving,
Up and down the roads going, North and South
    excursions making,
Power enjoying, elbows stretching, fingers clutching,
Arm'd and fearless, eating, drinking, sleeping, loving,
No law less than ourselves owning, sailing, soldiering,
    thieving, threatening,
Misers, menials, priests alarming, air breathing, water
    drinking, on the turf or the sea-beach dancing,
Cities wrenching, ease scorning, statues mocking,
    feebleness chasing,
Fulfilling our foray.

TEXT Walt Whitman, "We Two Boys Together Clinging," *Calamus*.

Rites

of

Passage

Childhood, for gay children, often has a sinister side. Other children and even our own families can sense our difference, sometimes even before we do. Like rats sniffing out an alien in their midst, they rudely toss us out of the nest. Suddenly we find ourselves on the other side of the chain-link fence that circles the playground, outsiders looking in on the heterosexual world.

Often, without ever being able to put it into words, we sense the terrible contingency of our place in our families and in the world. We begin to discover the countless boundaries of behavior and attitude that must not be stepped over—always by stepping over them. We learn that unconditional love has conditions. Difference, imagination, spontaneity, and affection—all go underground, forgotten or carefully tucked away in protected spaces deep within us, places we visit only in secret and alone. I can still remember vividly my childhood nightmares—gigantic monsters stalking across the land, coming to my town, coming to my house, coming to my room. Why did they always know where to find me, no matter where I tried to hide?

Childhood can be an all too brief moment of innocence for us. The years that follow are often filled with profound self-doubt and alienation, when we lose the child-like ability to imagine a world and see ourselves in it. Our parents and families, often with the deepest sense of love and care, assume that we are heterosexual and raise us as such. But this socialization goes deeply against our nature. *Indeed, raising children to be something that they are not and cannot be is a form of child abuse.* As adult lesbians and gay men, we are all survivors of this abuse, and I think this shows up in the many destructive behaviors we see in our community.

We seem much more ready to attack each other, to engage in trashing and flame wars and politically correct one-upmanship, than to vent our anger on those heterosexual males who are our real oppressors. But this is what you learn to do in an abusive family. You hurt the ones you love because loving and hurting have become hopelessly, perversely confused.

Whether our childhoods are innocent or not, the teenage years for gay men seem to be universally bleak. Our behavior becomes the subject of the most intense surveillance. In the glaring light of peer pressure, we are rarely allowed to go our own way. We must stand up and be counted as heterosexuals. So we twist and distort our true natures, we lie about who we are, we pretend feelings and emotions we don't have—or we accept abstinence and stifle our emotions altogether. We begin to live like spies in a heterosexual dictatorship. The exploration of sexuality, the experimentation with intimacy through dating, all this is postponed for young gay men until their twenties—and for many men, even today, until their thirties or forties, following valiant but unsuccessful attempts to be "normal."

All this makes coming out the single most profound act in the lives of most gay people. Nothing else we do has as great an impact on our futures, our self-esteem, and our personal growth as coming out, by which I mean the process of telling significant others that we are gay. But even if this weren't the case, even if we lived in societies (and some of us do, even today) where we did not have to repress our same-sex desires, the process of entering into adult sexuality and adult relationships is still an important rite of passage.

The irony, of course, is that there is no final, definitive "coming out." We must come out again and again, as long as there are heterosexuals who assume that everyone else is heterosexual. And we must repeatedly come out within, to face ourselves, as long as we continue to internalize the judgments of others and allow our fears to keep us from following our inner voice.

What One

Dreams,

That Will Be

In societies with recognized roles like the Native American two-spirit, "coming out" was a public rather than a private event. Entry into two-spirit identity was formally acknowledged by family and community alike. Among the Mohave Indians of the Colorado River area, this took the form of a ceremony usually held before the two-spirit, or *alyha·*, was a teenager. The following account was told by a Mohave man named Nyavarup and transcribed by the anthropologist A. L. Kroeber in 1902.

The procedures described fall into a typical pattern for initiation rites. At first, the initiate is separated and isolated, dramatizing a ritual death. At the end of this period, he is reborn into his new identity. He is given new clothes, and he is led outdoors for a public bathing. After a four-day period, two women paint his face, and he is reincorporated into the community in his new social role. The design, as described by the narrator, is a *male* face-painting design, underscoring the way in which two-spirit identity involves a bridging and combining, rather than a crossing, of gender.

Mastamho is the Mohave creator god, responsible for instituting the two-spirit role at the beginning of Mohave history.

➤   ➤   ➤

An alyha sends for me. Four [of us] doctors come and stay the night. The boy, or young man, has dreamed he will be an alyha; he has seen it so with Mastamho: then he will be one, he cannot help himself, because what one dreams, that will be.

Now he lies in the middle of the house, covered up; and the doctors, all night long, sing, and tell what Mastamho did and said, and how it was all instituted in the beginning. Three of them work on the woman's dress of willow inner bark. One of them shreds and folds and trims the bark; one spins cord on his thigh; the third binds it into the (bunches of shredded) bark. The fourth one—that is I—holds the finished dress on his right arm and sings with it. As each one works, there is a song for it. Thus, spinning the cord, one sings, with each motion: "That-nye-vuthi, ihat-nya-va'ema," "Roll it this way, roll it that way." This is how the doctors heard and saw Mastamho doing in the beginning with the first alyha.

In the morning, the young man is waked. A woman is sitting at each side of him. The one to the east gives him the hip skirt part of his new dress, the one to the west the front apron part. Then they help him to rise, the one on the east taking his left arm, the west one his right. Then one of the doctors—myself—puts an (old) woman's dress on himself and sings and dances; the alyha follows and imitates him, with his hands on the doctor's shoulders. All the people present dance too.

Then they move to the river, dancing and stopping four times on the way; the fourth time they reach the bank. The doctor lets fall the dress he is wearing, enters the water, and bathes; and all follow him. When they come out, the alyha stands like a woman, covering his privates and rectum.

S   P   I   R   I   T   S

Then two women hand him the newly made clean dress to put on. Then they bite off and chew white paint and spit it over his face. Then they go home.

The new alyha is still ashamed. So after four days, the two women again paint him white. They paint a vertical stripe down from each eye and another down the nose to the mouth. Then he is known as an alyha and is not ashamed any longer.

Now he always wins at gambling. Sometimes a man will give him beads to go off with him somewhere and then many come and have intercourse with him in *ano*. And he dies young: that kind does not live long. At gatherings, they speak and laugh and dance like women.

TEXT Alfred L. Kroeber, *More Mohave Myths*, Anthropological Records, vol. 27 (Berkeley: University of California Press, 1972), p. 20.
OTHER SOURCES Alfred L. Kroeber, *Handbook of the Indians of California* (New York: Dover, 1976), pp. 748–49.

The

Ugly

Duckling

When I asked friends to name fairy tales and stories to which they were especially drawn as children, most of the examples that came up were by Hans Christian Andersen. One friend cited "The Princess and the Pea" as an example of the hypersensitivity of queens. Another pointed to "The Emperor's New Clothes," in which a little boy is the only one not afraid to tell the king that he is naked—as gay people we, too, see through the pretenses of heterosexual society. But, of all Andersen's stories, "The Ugly Duckling" seems quintessentially gay, telling the story of a young swan mistaken for a duck who discovers his true beauty only after a series of harsh trials. Every element corresponds to the gay experience of coming out.

I was certainly an "ugly duckling" myself. Like many gay men, nothing would be more embarrassing than to have a picture of the way I look now juxtaposed to how I looked at sixteen. With coke-bottle glasses, unmanageable curly hair, bell-bottom pants not long enough to hide my bony ankles, and tottering on top of blue and white platform shoes, I was as self-conscious as a teenager could be. It took contact lenses, the advent of the "clone" look (short hair, tight jeans), and the invention of weight-lifting machines (no coordination required) to change my self-image. But, even more so, it took coming out and the discovery of sexuality to teach me to love my body and to put an end to my ugly duckling days. This was a total transformation of both body and soul—what was ugly became beautiful; what was sinful became holy. That last phrase probably reveals my Roman Catholic background, but I've heard gay men from many religions and cultures describe their coming out in similarly moving terms.

Hans Christian Andersen was himself a repressed homosexual who may never have fully realized his emotional and sexual longings with another man—he had the bad habit of falling in love with heterosexual men unable to reciprocate his feelings. Andersen lived through his stories instead, and as a result he has left us with a wonderful legacy of tales rich in gay imagination.

➤   ➤   ➤

It was lovely summer weather in the country, and the golden corn, the green oats, and the haystacks piled up in the meadows looked beautiful. The stork walking about on his long red legs chattered in the Egyptian language, which he had learnt from his mother. The corn-fields and meadows were surrounded by large forests, in the midst of which were deep pools. It was, indeed, delightful to walk about in the country. In a sunny spot stood a pleasant old farm-house close by a deep river, and from the house down to the water side grew great burdock leaves, so high, that under the tallest of them a little child could stand upright. The spot was as wild as the center of a thick wood.

In this snug retreat sat a duck in her nest, watching for her young brood to hatch; she was beginning to get tired of her task, for the little ones were a long time coming out of their shells, and she seldom had any visitors. The other ducks liked much better to swim about in the river than to climb the slippery banks, and sit under a burdock leaf, to have a gossip with her.

At length one shell cracked, and then another, and from each egg came a living creature that lifted its head and cried, "Peep, peep."

"Quack, quack," said the mother, and then they all quacked as well as they could, and looked about them on every side at the large green leaves. Their mother allowed them to look as much as they liked, because green is good for the eyes.

"How large the world is," said the young ducks, when they found how much more room they now had than while they were inside the egg-shell.

"Do you imagine this is the whole world?" asked the mother. "Wait till you have seen the garden; it stretches far beyond that to the parson's field, but I have never ventured to such a distance. Are you all out?" she continued, rising. "No; I declare, the largest egg lies there still. I wonder how long this is to last. I am quite tired of it"; and she seated herself again on the nest.

"Well, how are you getting on?" asked an old duck, who paid her a visit.

"One egg is not hatched yet," said the duck. "it will not break. But just look at all the others, are they not the prettiest little ducklings you ever saw? They are the image of their father, who is so unkind, he never comes to see me."

"Let me see the egg that will not break," said the duck; "I have no doubt it is a turkey's egg. I was persuaded to hatch some once, and after all my care and trouble with the young ones, they were afraid of the water. I quacked and clucked, but all to no purpose. I could not get them to venture in. Let me look at the egg. Yes, that is a turkey's egg; take my advice, leave it where it is and teach the other children to swim."

"I think I will sit on it a little while longer," said the duck; "as I have sat so long already, a few days will be nothing."

"Please yourself," said the old duck, and she went away.

At last the large egg broke, and a young one crept forth crying, "Peep, peep." It was very large and ugly.

The duck stared at it and exclaimed, "It is very large and not at all like the others. I wonder if it really is a turkey. We shall soon find it out, however, when we go to the water. It must go in, if I have to push it myself."

On the next day the weather was delightful, and the sun shone brightly on the green burdock leaves, so the mother duck took her young brood down to the water, and jumped in with a splash.

"Quack, quack," cried she, and one after another the little ducklings jumped in. The water closed over their heads, but they came up again in an instant, and swam about quite prettily with their legs paddling under them as easily as possible, and the ugly duckling was also in the water swimming with them.

"Oh," said the mother, "that is not a turkey; how well he uses his legs, and how upright he holds himself. He is my own child, and he is not so very ugly after all if you look at him properly. Quack, quack! come with me now, I will take you into grand society, and introduce you to the farmyard, but you must keep close to me or you may be trodden upon; and, above all, beware of the cat."

When they reached the farmyard, there was a great disturbance, two families were fighting for an eel's head, which, after all, was carried off by the cat.

"See, children, that is the way of the world," said the mother duck, whetting her beak, for she would have liked the eel's head herself. "Come, now, use your legs, and let me see how well you can behave. You must bow your heads prettily to that old duck yonder; she is the highest born of them all, and has Spanish blood, therefore, she is well off. Don't you see she has a red flag tied to her leg, which is something very grand, and a great honor for a duck; it shows that every one is anxious not to lose her, as she can be recognized both by man and beast. Come, now, don't turn your toes, a well-bred duckling spreads his feet wide apart, just like his father and mother, in this way; now bend your neck, and say 'quack.'"

The ducklings did as they were bid, but the other ducks stared, and said, "Look, here comes another brood, as if there were not enough of us already! and what a queer looking object one of them is: we don't want him here," and then one flew out and bit him in the neck.

"Let him alone," said the mother; "he is not doing any harm."

"Yes, but he is so big and ugly," said the spiteful duck, "and therefore he must be turned out."

"The others are very pretty children," said the old duck, with the rag on her leg, "all but that one; I wish his mother could improve him a little."

"That is impossible, your grace," replied the mother; "he is not pretty; but he has a very good disposition, and swims as well or even better than the others. I think he will grow up pretty, and perhaps be smaller; he has remained too long in the egg, and therefore his figure is not properly formed;" and then she stroked his neck and smoothed the feathers,

saying, "It is a drake, and therefore not of so much consequence. I think he will grow up strong, and able to take care
of himself."

"The other ducklings are graceful enough," said the old
duck. "Now make yourself at home, and if you can find an
eel's head, you can bring it to me."

And so they made themselves comfortable; but the poor
duckling, who had crept out of his shell last of all, and
looked so ugly, was bitten and pushed and made fun of, not
only by the ducks, but by all the poultry.

"He is too big," they all said, and the turkey cock, who had
been born into the world with spurs, and fancied himself
really an emperor, puffed himself out like a vessel in full sail,
and flew at the duckling, and became quite red in the head
with passion, so that the poor little thing did not know
where to go, and was quite miserable because he was so ugly
and laughed at by the whole farmyard.

So it went on from day to day till it got worse and worse.
The poor duckling was driven about by every one; even his
brothers and sisters were unkind to him, and would say,
"Ah, you ugly creature, I wish the cat would get you," and
his mother said she wished he had never been born. The
ducks pecked him, the chickens beat him, and the girl who
fed the poultry kicked him with her feet. So at last he ran
away, frightening the little birds in the hedge as he flew over
the palings.

➤   ➤   ➤

What follows is a series of trials and tribulations for the little duckling.
Living on the moor, he befriends two geese, only to see them shot dead

by hunters. In a panic, he runs away until he comes on a cottage, where a woman, a tomcat, and a hen live. They let him stay with them but constantly put him down—he can't lay eggs, and he can't purr like a cat. He has nothing to contribute. Finally, he decides to strike out on his own again, and he finds some water where he can swim and dive to his heart's content. But then winter comes, and soon the duckling is very cold and alone again.

➤ ➤ ➤

One evening, just as the sun set amid radiant clouds, there came a large flock of beautiful birds out of the bushes. The duckling had never seen any like them before. They were swans, and they curved their graceful necks, while their soft plumage shone with dazzling whiteness. They uttered a singular cry, as they spread their glorious wings and flew away from those cold regions to warmer countries across the sea. As they mounted higher and higher in the air, the ugly little duckling felt quite a strange sensation as he watched them. He whirled himself in the water like a wheel, stretched out his neck towards them, and uttered a cry so strange that it frightened himself.

Could he ever forget those beautiful, happy birds; and when at last they were out of his sight, he dived under the water, and rose again almost beside himself with excitement. He knew not the names of these birds, nor where they had flown, but he felt towards them as he had never felt for any other bird in the world. He was not envious of these beautiful creatures, but wished to be as lovely as they. Poor ugly creature, how gladly he would have lived even with the ducks had they only given him encouragement.

S P I R I T S

The winter grew colder and colder; he was obliged to swim about on the water to keep from freezing, but every night the space on which he swam became smaller and smaller. At length it froze so hard that the ice in the water crackled as he moved, and the duckling had to paddle with his legs as well as he could, to keep the space from closing up. He became exhausted at last, and lay still and helpless, frozen fast in the ice.

Early in the morning, a peasant, who was passing by, saw what had happened. He broke the ice in pieces with his wooden shoe, and carried the duckling home to his wife.

The warmth revived the poor little creature; but when the children wanted to play with him, the duckling thought they would do him some harm; so he started up in terror, fluttered into the milk-pan, and splashed the milk about the room. Then the woman clapped her hands, which frightened him still more. He flew first into the butter-cask, then into the meal-tub, and out again. What a condition he was in! The woman screamed, and struck at him with the tongs; the children laughed and screamed, and tumbled over each other, in their efforts to catch him; but luckily he escaped. The door stood open; the poor creature could just manage to slip out among the bushes, and lie down quite exhausted in the newly fallen snow.

It would be very sad, were I to relate all the misery and privations which the poor little duckling endured during the hard winter; but when it had passed, he found himself lying one morning in a moor, amongst the rushes. He felt the warm sun shining, and heard the lark singing, and saw that all around was beautiful spring. Then the young bird felt that his wings were strong, as he flapped them against his sides, and rose high into the air. They bore him onwards, until he found himself in a large garden, before he well knew how it had happened. The apple-trees were in full blossom, and the fragrant elders bent their long green branches down to the stream which wound round a smooth lawn. Everything looked beautiful, in the freshness of early spring. From a thicket close by came three beautiful white swans, rustling their feathers, and swimming lightly over the smooth water. The duckling remembered the lovely birds, and felt more strangely unhappy than ever.

"I will fly to those royal birds," he exclaimed, "and they will kill me, because I am so ugly, and dare to approach them; but it does not matter: better be killed by them than pecked by the ducks, beaten by the hens, pushed about by the maiden who feeds the poultry, or starved with hunger in the winter."

Then he flew to the water, and swam towards the beautiful swans. The moment they espied the stranger, they rushed to meet him with outstretched wings.

"Kill me," said the poor bird; and he bent his head down to the surface of the water, and awaited death.

But what did he see in the clear stream below? His own image; no longer a dark, gray bird, ugly and disagreeable to look at, but a graceful and beautiful swan. To be born in a duck's nest, in a farmyard, is of no consequence to a bird, if it is hatched from a swan's egg. He now felt glad at having suffered sorrow and trouble, because it enabled him to enjoy so much better all the pleasure and happiness around him; for the great swans swam round the newcomer, and stroked his neck with their beaks, as a welcome.

Into the garden presently came some little children, and they threw bread and cake into the water.

"See," cried the youngest, "there is a new one," and the rest were delighted and ran to their father and mother, dancing and clapping their hands, and shouting joyously, "There is another swan come; a new one has arrived."

Then they threw more bread and cake into the water, and said, "The new one is the most beautiful of all; he is so young and pretty." And the old swans bowed their heads before him.

Then he felt quite ashamed, and hid his head under his wing; for he did not know what to do, he was so happy, and yet not at all proud. He had been persecuted and despised for his ugliness, and now he heard them say he was the most beautiful of all the birds. Even the elder-tree bent down its bows into the water before him, and the sun shone warm and bright. Then he rustled his feathers, curved his slender neck, and cried joyfully, from the depths of his heart, "I never dreamed of such happiness as this, while I was an ugly duckling."

TEXT Hans Christian Andersen, *Hans Andersen's Fairy Tales*, trans. Mrs. H. B. Paull (London and New York: F. Warne, [1882]).

OTHER SOURCES Wolfgang Lederer, *The Kiss of the Snow Queen: Hans Christian Andersen and Man's Redemption by Woman* (Berkeley and Los Angeles: University of California Press, 1986).

I

Am

Holy

The following passage is one of my favorite stories about a Native American two-spirit. It was related by a Hidatsa Indian in the 1930s; the events described took place in the mid-nineteenth century. The two-spirit in this story triumphs, not by force or superior weapons, but by his courage and strength of will. He calls the attackers' bluff. Can they be sure he doesn't have the powers that he claims? The image of this two-spirit putting the brave Hidatsa warriors to flight by waving his digging stick has always stuck in my mind.

➤ ➤ ➤

One day the Hidatsa war party found two women and a ber-dache digging wild turnips on the prairie. Until they were near they thought they were women, for all three Sioux were dressed alike. Before making the attack, Four Bears told his party that they would strike coups on the women but spare their lives. Four Bears got ahead of the others and struck both but the berdache was brave, saying, "You can't kill me for I am holy. I will strike coups on you with my dig-ging stick."

Then the berdache sang a sacred song and chased them. Four Bears shot an arrow at the berdache but it would not penetrate the robe. Then he knew that the berdache had great supernatural powers. Since he had been successful on all other military expeditions and did not want to spoil his luck, he called his party back. The expedition was successful, for they got the horse. Four Bears used good judgment, for it was hard to kill a berdache since they were holy.

TEXT Alfred Bowers, "Hidatsa Social and Ceremonial Organization," *Bureau of American Ethnology Bulletin* 194 (1965): 256.

Soft

Man

Mircea Eliade defines *shamanism* as a "technique of ecstasy," its most
characteristic feature being the "magical flight" or trance journey, in
which the shaman's soul leaves his or her body. During this journey,
the shaman encounters spirit beings and learns to control or derive
power from them. How shamans used their powers—whether to heal
others by locating and sucking out objects that have been "shot" into
their bodies or to advance their own fortunes or attack enemies—
varies greatly.

Although shamans are found worldwide, their practices appear to
be the most elaborate in Central Asia and Siberia. Among the Siberian
Chukchi, a special class of shamans, whose sex had been transformed
as a result of contact with female spirits, was called *soft men*. Soft men
took up women's work (but not necessarily their clothes) and married
other men. They are described in the reports of the Russian Vladimir
Bogoraz (also spelled Waldemar Bogoras), who had been exiled to Siberia in the 1880s and 1890s and later returned on scientific expeditions.
Eliade and others have frequently cited Bogoraz's accounts of the
Chukchi as a classic illustration of shamanism.

In this story recorded by Bogoraz, a soft man triumphs over his
detractors through a dramatic display of his supernatural powers.

➤   ➤   ➤

The branch of shamanism of which I am about to speak is
of a more special character, and refers to that shamanistic

transformation of men and women in which they undergo a change of sex in part, or even completely. This is called "soft man being" (*yirka'-la'ul-va'irgin*): "soft man" meaning a man transformed into a being of a softer sex. . . .

A young man who is undergoing it leaves off all pursuits and manners of his sex, and takes up those of a woman. He throws away the rifle and the lance, the lasso of the reindeer herdsman, and the harpoon of the seal-hunter, and takes to the needle and the skin-scraper. He learns the use of these quickly, because the "spirits" are helping him all the time. . . . The "soft man" begins to feel like a woman. He seeks to win the good graces of men, and succeeds easily with the aid of "spirits." Thus he has all the young men he could wish for striving to obtain his favor. From these he chooses his lover, and after a time takes a husband. The marriage is performed with the usual rites, and I must say that it forms a quite solid union, which often lasts till the death of one of the parties. . . .

In a tale widely circulated among the Chukchee, a "soft man," clad in a woman's dress, takes part, with other members of the family, in corralling the reindeer-herd. The wife of his brother taunts him, saying, "This one with the woman's breeches does not seem to give much help." The "soft man" takes offence, and leaves the family camp. He goes away to the border-land of the Koryak, who assault him in his travelling-tent. He, however, snatches his fire-board implement, and with its small bow of antler, shoots the wooden drill at his adversaries. Immediately it turns into a fiery shaft and destroys all of them one by one. He then takes their herds, and, coming back to his home, shows his newly acquired wealth to his relatives, saying, "See now what that of woman's breeches was able to procure for you. . . ."

"Soft men," of course, are supposed to excel in all branches of shamanism, including the ventriloquistic art, notwithstanding the fact that they are supposed to be women. Because of their supernatural protectors, they are dreaded even by untransformed shamans, who avoid having any contests with them. . . .

TEXT Waldemar G. Bogoras, "The Chukchee," *Memoirs of the American Museum of Natural History* 11, no. 2 (1907): 449–53.

OTHER SOURCES Mircea Eliade, *Shamanism: Archaic Techniques of Ecstasy* (Princeton, N.J.: Princeton University Press, 1964).

S P I R I T S

The Gallus

and the

Lion

Imagine yourself walking down the street, when suddenly you hear
the din of drums, flutes, and tambourines. Before you know it, you're
surrounded by a troop of gender-bending cultists. They're wearing
long parti-colored robes and bright yellow slippers. Their hair,
bleached and curled, streams wildly as they dance around you. Their
faces are painted white, their fingers are thick with rings, their necks
are hung heavy with religious trinkets, and some of them are waving
knives. Suddenly a voice shrieks, "Spare a quarter for the Goddess?"
You'd do well to empty your pocket, for a fearful curse awaits you if
you don't.

No, you're not lost on the streets of San Francisco, suddenly surrounded by the Sisters of Perpetual Indulgence. You're in Rome—or
any number of other cities small and large throughout the Roman
Empire—and you've just encountered the *galli*, priests of the gods
Cybele and Attis. Originally temple servants in ancient Phrygia (modern Turkey), *galli* began to appear throughout the Greek world as wandering devotees in the wake of Alexander's conquests. In Roman
times, they lived in collectives and were loosely attached to local
temples. They survived by begging for alms while they performed
their spectacular rites, including ecstatic dancing, prophecy,
self-flagellation, and bloodletting.

The *galli* also practiced self-castration, in imitation of their patron
god, Attis—although, as is the case with the contemporary *hijra* of

northern India, men who also devote themselves to a goddess, this practice may not have been universal. In any case, the *galli* occupied an ambiguous status as far as the Greeks and the Romans were concerned. "Neither is he changed into a woman, nor does he remain a man," wrote the early Christian father Augustine. Prudentius referred to *galli* as a *medium genus*, or "third kind." They were the gender radicals of their time, renouncing all male privileges in honor of their goddess. In fact, when I read the denunciations of the *galli* written by early Christians, I have a hard time distinguishing them from the invective of today's Christians denouncing Castro Street or Greenwich Village. For them, the battle against paganism has never ended.

Some of the earliest literary references to the *galli*, in the form of dedications and brief tales, appear in the *Greek Anthology*, a collection of poetry dating back to the second century B.C.E. In the dedications, written in the first person, *galli* devote the instruments of their priesthood to the Goddess on retiring. If we accept these texts at face value, then we have rare, almost unique examples of the voices of *galli* themselves, offering a glimpse into how they saw themselves and what their religion meant to them. Here is a typical dedication.

> To thee, my mother Rhea, nurse of Phrygian lions, whose devotees tread the heights of Dindymus, did feminine Alexis, ceasing from furious clashing of the brass, dedicate these stimulants of his madness—his shrill-toned cymbals, the noise of his deep-voiced flute, to which the crooked horn of a young steer gave a curved form, his echoing tambourines, his knives reddened with blood, and the yellow hair which once tossed on his shoulders. Be

kind, O Queen, and give rest in his old age from his former
wildness to him who went mad in his youth.

The following story, attributed to Antipater of Sidon, who lived in
the middle of the second century B.C.E., also comes from the *Greek
Anthology*. The *gallus* (Antipater uses a term that literally means
"long-haired male") escapes a dangerous situation by his wits alone.
Actually, the tale is filled with ancient symbols. We might begin by
noting that the *gallus* is somewhere out in the natural world, presum-
ably traveling from one place to another, perhaps on an important missionary journey. Hounded by the Goddess and chased by the snows of
the father god, Zeus, he seeks refuge in a cave—a womb-like space
within the Earth Mother. But retreat to the maternal world is not an
option. A lion, the ancient emissary of Cybele, who was frequently
shown riding a chariot drawn by lions, rushes in after the *gallus*. The
lion is described as a slayer of bulls, the other animal historically associated with Cybele. The *gallus* musters his courage, and, using the
instruments of his priesthood—the tambourine and his characteristic
cry—he saves the day.

The tambourine is made of bull's hide, so the whole scene suggests a
confrontation between the two spirit animals of Cybele, the bull and
the lion, with the *gallus* on the side of the bull. Although both are
powerful animals, the bull is a domesticated beast whose flesh is a
source of food. The lion, however, is more likely to eat people than be
eaten by them. In the Roman worship of Cybele, the sacrifice of a bull
became an important part of her religion. Its blood was allowed to
drain onto the high priest, the *archigallus*. Here, in this story, it seems
that the *gallus* finds a safe haven from both the father god and the
mother goddess by identifying with a symbolic animal who bridges

both worlds. This is often what we must do in our own lives in the process of coming out.

➤ ➤ ➤

Goaded by the fury of the dreadful goddess, tossing his locks while spinning around in a wild frenzy, in women's dress, adorned with twisted hair and crowned with a pretty knotted hair-net, a long-haired man once took shelter in a mountain cavern, driven by the numbing snow of Zeus. But behind him rushed in unshivering a lion, slayer of bulls, returning to his den in the evening, who looking on the man, snuffing in his shapely nostrils the smell of human flesh, stood still on his sturdy feet, but rolling his eyes roared loudly from his greedy jaws. The cave, his den, thunders around him and the wooded peak that mounts nigh to the clouds echoes loud. But the priest, startled by the deep voice, felt all his stirred spirit broken in his breast. Yet he uttered from his lips the piercing shriek they use, and tossed his whirling locks, and holding up his great tambour, the revolving instrument of Olympian Rhea, he beat it, and it was the saviour of his life; for the lion hearing the unaccustomed hollow boom of the bull's hide was afraid and took to flight. See how all-wise necessity taught a means of escape from death!

TEXT *Greek Anthology*, vol. 1, trans. W. R. Paton, Loeb Classical Library (Cambridge, Mass.: Harvard University Press, 1916), 6.51, 6.219.
OTHER SOURCES A. S. F. Gow, "The Gallus and the Lion," *Journal of Hellenic Studies* 80 (1960): 88–93.

S   P   I   R   I   T   S

Gay Ways

The Path

of the

Two-Spirit

In 1975, at the age of twenty, I came out in my hometown of Missoula, Montana. Although the nearest gay bar was hundreds of miles away, I was surprised to find that Missoula hosted not one but two networks of gay men. One was centered around two older gentlemen, who owned and operated a local movie theater. They had a long-standing policy of employing every good-looking young man, gay or straight, who applied for a job. Actually, most turned out to be gay, and, if they were favored, they were invited to cocktails after closing hours in the well-appointed apartments of their employers, several stories above the theater, in a building that, since the 1930s, had been the closest to a high-rise that Missoula had. On the one occasion on which I was invited for cocktails, I couldn't stop staring out the windows with their sweeping views of my little city nestled among the mountains. This must be what it's like to live in Manhattan, I thought—minus the mountains, of course.

When I was elected president of the local gay student group (actually the first gay organization in the state), I became much too visible for this crowd. There would be no more cocktail parties with clean-cut ushers and private screenings of super-8 porno movies for me. I fell in instead with a younger gay network. Their center was Missoula's only vegetarian restaurant, the High Mountain Cafe, owned by a large ex-hippy named Debbie, a tough-on-the-outside, soft-on-the-inside fag-hag who hired every long-haired gay man who walked into her restaurant. Debbie and her gay friends all lived together in a rambling house on the north side of town. If the outlook of Missoula's upscale gays could be characterized by the film *Boys in the Band* and the worship of Judy Garland, the cultural wellsprings of Debbie's circle were closer to John Waters's *Pink Flamingos* and Janis Joplin.

It was in Debbie's house that I had my first overnight "trick" (what gay men today call a "date") with a man named Greg (nicknamed "Greta Garbage" on the basis of an unforgettable drag appearance). I can still remember the wonderful feeling of holding him in the morning while the various occupants of the house began the day bantering with each other from their respective bedrooms. I suddenly thought, "This is what family is like," a sensation I had never really had before. To be not only with a lover but in a community, too. That morning, in Greg's arms, I felt embraced by an entire household, a house/hold in the true sense. (In fact, houses have always been important symbols for me. In my dreams, I'm frequently returning to the houses of my childhood, rummaging around in the basement—a good symbol for the unconscious.)

There are so many things to learn on coming out of the closet, and I decided to learn them all. In those years, before Anita Bryant campaigned against us and before AIDS, there was the sense that nothing could hold us back, that being gay—and being fully, outrageously, visibly gay—was no longer an obstacle in life. In fact, it was the most important thing we could do. We were exploring uncharted worlds of gender and sexuality, and it was all so much *fun*.

And so, with the help of my newly found girlfriends (most of whom were also boyfriends at one point or another), I began learning the language, the style, the fashion, the sexual techniques of being a thoroughly modern gay man. I can still remember the disconcerting sensation the first time I heard gay men referred to as *she*, and the painstaking explanation of one friend concerning the meaning of the terms *gay aunt* and *gay mother*—those older gay men who served as mentors for newcomers like me. Yet another friend undertook to teach me how to dance, to loosen up enough to do the Bump without causing bodily harm. I finally knew that I had graduated when two friends showed up one Saturday afternoon with a black corset and high heels they had found at a yard sale, insisting that I wear them that night to a party at Bill's, whom we called Prissy. I had never done drag before, and this would require driving across town wearing a corset and a wig, parking in front of the Safeway on the main road through town, and walking down the street to Prissy's apartment. My friends insisted.

When Prissy saw me tottering up the stairs, he started screeching, "It's *Kitty*! It's Kitty Litter!" And so I received my "drag name." In our group, it was a significant rite of passage. Only recognized members of the group had them, and they had to be bestowed by someone who was already a member. The best names originated like mine—spontaneously, in connection with a memorable episode in which one's "real" nature as a queen was revealed. Just a few months earlier, I had "come out" in a gay studies class in college; now I had "arrived," a full-fledged member of my new community.

Prissy was one of the most influential members of our group. He was only a couple of years older than I was, but he had come out sooner and had spent a much longer time acquiring the skills that made him the epitome of what I thought a modern gay man should be. Prissy could do everything. On the salary of a waiter, he turned his three-room apartment into a den of exotic comforts, overflowing with vibrant pink and purple coleus plants. With his tiny sewing machine, he not only produced fabulous drag outfits but also knew how to take up the crotch in men's pants to make them tighter in the ass, another gay fashion we were all trying to follow.

But that was not all. Prissy could take the change out of our pockets, run over to the Safeway, and, before we knew it, have a delicious meal of chicken cacciatore bubbling away on the stove. Prissy was a great dancer and not a bad singer. And he was spiritual. He had listened to every album by the group Yes and memorized the words. One night, when we took some acid together, he made me admit that I too was drawn to spirituality, despite my cynical attitude toward his new age pronouncements. I had been secretly hoarding books on astrology and the occult since I was twelve. Early that morning, I left with a clipping from his favorite coleus.

When Prissy's truck broke down, she got out and fixed it herself. I still remember the day he left for San Francisco, the old pickup stacked high with the antique furniture he had rescued from yard sales and refurbished and all his suitcases of clothes and drag.

As far as I was concerned, Prissy was where it was at. He could do *everything*, boy things, girl things, gay things. Being able to fix your truck so that you can get to the party in time to make an hysterical entrance in full drag was my idea of liberation from sex roles. I guess that, because of the negative stereotypes I had grown up with, I had assumed that being gay meant one could *only* be campy and that committing oneself to gay identity meant being cut off from a large slice of human experience. I certainly felt limited by the male role I had been assigned—so many of the interesting things to do turned out to be "girl things." I also thought that the gay role would be limiting, as well. Through my friendship with Prissy, however, I discovered that the real meaning of being gay is liberation from *all* roles and *all* predetermined gender assignments. It meant freedom. I could be an excellent cook and change my oil. I could enjoy costumes and the maleness of my body. I could walk into every corner of life, male or female, well to do (like the high-rise queens) or hand to mouth (like Prissy). I could be a full human being.

To some degree or other, socialization into a gay community usually follows coming out for most gay men. This is always a very special time in which we are particularly impressionable and receptive to new ideas and new ways of doing things. There are so many things to learn about this world and about sex and relationships. Few of us get it right the first time! Today, the gay community in any number of cities is much more diverse than the little network that nurtured me years ago. Young men who come out with the determination to master the arts of being gay have many more paths to choose from. So far this book has followed a single route through the experiences most common to us in the years before we come out. *But now the path divides*, and there is really no limit to the variations in the course that our lives can take.

Of course, we are most interested in the inner life of gay men, as revealed in myths and tales. Here, the broad themes and their archetypes that I identified in the introduction come into play—the path of the Two-Spirit, the Divine Twins, and the Way of Initiation. These certainly don't exhaust the list of archetypes that are important in our lives. But, in my own study and exploration, I have found that these three, each based on a distinct historical pattern of same-sex love, offer the most concentrated form of the images and themes relevant to gay men. Both the social patterns and their images come up again and again in various world cultures, and they come up repeatedly in the dreams and fantasies of contemporary gay men. As we pursue a gay lifestyle, we are likely to find ourselves and others involved with one or more of these archetypes at various points in our lives. By *involved*, I mean attracted to and unconsciously patterning ourselves—our behavior, our relationships, and even our appearance—after the images associated with these archetypes.

In the next three sections, beginning with this one, I have organized selections to illustrate these gay ways. I do not mean to suggest anything by the sequence in which I've chosen to place them—we might find ourselves exploring any one of these paths at any point in our lives, or sometimes all at once.

As I came to understand in a roundabout way, my friend Prissy perfectly embodied the archetype of the Two-Spirit or radical queen. I would meet another Prissy many years later in my research on Native American traditions, dressed like a Pueblo Indian and named We'wha. We'wha was a famous berdache or two-spirit of the Zuni tribe who died in 1896. Like Prissy, We'wha could do everything. In fact, "she" insisted on it. Accomplished in the female crafts of pottery and weaving, she also participated in the religious societies of the men and worked in the fields as they did. The fact that she wore the clothes of a woman was no limitation on her freedom of movement or physical prowess. We'wha regularly climbed nearby mesas to retrieve heavy loads of clay. In the photographs taken during "her" 1886 visit to Washington, D.C., the strength of "his" arms and biceps is apparent. Six years later, when American soldiers tried to arrest a member of his family, We'wha slugged one of them and slammed the door in their faces—a story I relate at length in *The Zuni Man-Woman*.

In my research, I found that many tribes had two-spirits like We'wha—energetic and confident, accomplished in both male and female pursuits, respected by their communities. More recently, I've been learning that roles like these existed, and still exist, in many other parts of the world as well. The Polynesian *mahu*, the *hijra* of India, the *galli* of ancient Rome, and the *kalû*, *kurgarrû*, and *assinnu* of Mesopotamia are all examples of alternative genders defined as neither male nor female. As the following myths reveal, the ability to engage in, and often excel at, both male and female activities was viewed as a kind of virtuosity and associated with distinct powers—the ability to mediate, to bridge opposites, to arrange affairs between men and women, to heal, to foretell the future, to utter both blessings and curses, to lead dances, to produce art. The recurrence of these themes in far-flung parts of the world is reason to take our own arts of camp and our skills in unleashing gender more seriously. In other times and places, these skills would make us respected figures in our communities.

A question that often comes up is whether we should think of two-spirits as shamans. In some cases, we can. The "soft men" of the Chukchi were a special class of shamans whose sex had been transformed by their contact with the spirit world. But not all Chukchi shamans were two-spirits. In North America, the roles of shaman and two-spirit were usually distinct, many tribes having both. In general, the shaman was a heterosexual man or woman who specialized in mediating the opposition between the social world and the spirit world, an often lonely, dangerous, heroic mission—and this is perhaps why the image of the shaman has captured the imagination of so many today, coming from the individualistic culture of Western societies. The Native American two-spirit, on the other hand, specializes in bridging oppositions *within* the community, the social differences between men and women, old and young, and so forth. The involvement of two-spirits, in arts and crafts, as both the conservators and the innovators of tribal traditions, also distinguishes them from shamans. All this is to say that we overlook an important spiritual tradition in the two-spirit role when we focus exclusively on the more spectacular techniques of shamans.

Of the worldwide two-spirit roles, those of native North America are the best documented. I've grouped these selections first and followed them with accounts of similar roles from other places and times. They all share the theme of "powers," the traits and abilities that await those who venture down the Path of the Two-Spirit.

SOURCE Will Roscoe, *The Zuni Man-Woman* (Albuquerque: University of New Mexico Press, 1991).

They Have
Been Given
Certain Powers

In his 1972 autobiography, as related to Richard Erdoes, the Sioux medicine man Lame Deer gives a memorable account of the *winkte*, or two-spirit, in his tribe. Unlike so many anthropologists who have commented on two-spirits, Lame Deer actually spoke with one, and this makes his words especially valuable.

➤　➤　➤

> We think that if a woman has two little ones growing inside her, if she is going to have twins, sometimes instead of giving birth to two babies they have formed up in her womb into just one, into a half man–half woman kind of being. We call such a person a *winkte*. He could be a hermaphrodite with male and female parts. In the old days a *winkte* dressed like a woman, cooked and did beadwork. He behaved like a squaw and did not go to war. To us a man is what nature, or his dreams, make him. We accept him for what he wants to be. That's up to him. Still, fathers did not like to see their boys hanging around a *winkte*'s place and told them to stay away.
>
> There are good men among the *winktes* and they have been given certain powers. As far as I know no white man has ever interviewed a *winkte*. That's why we went to this bar where I knew I could find one. I guess you weren't even sure of whether I was talking to a man or to a woman.

Well, the first thing this *winkte* asked me was, "Do you have some wine?" I told him he could have all he wanted if he told me the truth about *winktes*. He told me that if nature puts a burden on a man by making him different, it also gives him a power. He told me that a *winkte* has a gift of prophecy and that he himself could predict the weather. In our tribe we go to a *winkte* to give a newborn child a secret name. Most often this is done for boys, but sometimes he could give such a name to a girl. Ida, for instance, got one. A name given by a *winkte* is supposed to bring its bearer luck and long life. In the old days it was worth a fine horse—at the least. The *winkte* told me that these names are very sexy, even funny, very outspoken names. You don't let a stranger know them; he would kid you about it. Having a *winkte* name could make a man famous. Sitting Bull, Black Elk, even Crazy Horse had secret *winkte* names which only a few people know. The *winkte* in the bar does a little prophesying. He told a woman she would live to be eighty years old, and she gave him a fine pair of moccasins for that. He also does certain cures and uses herbs known to *winktes*. Well, this man-woman told me that in the old days the *winktes* used to call each other sisters and had a special hill where they were buried. I asked him when he died, when he went south, what he would be in the spirit land, a man or a woman. He told me he would be both. It was a long interview, lasting through two bottles of wine.

TEXT John Fire (Lame Deer) and Richard Erdoes, *Lame Deer: Seeker of Visions* (New York: Simon & Schuster, 1972), pp. 149–50.

A Very

Great

Doctor

Many two-spirits were powerful healers. In this account, related by a Plains Cree elder named Fine Day and recorded by anthropologist David Mandelbaum in the 1930s, a traditional two-spirit gains respect and prestige for his powers to "doctor" and his willingness to help others. He uses the shamanic technique of "sucking" to draw out the sources of injuries and illnesses. It is also interesting to note how the theme of gambling turns up again—the Mohave account in the last chapter credited two-spirits with special luck at gambling.

➤ ➤ ➤

They were called *a:yahkwew*. It happened very seldom. But one of them was my own relative. He was a very great doctor. When he talked his voice was like a man's and he looked like a man. But he always stayed among the women and dressed like them. He was a great gambler and when he lost all his clothes he made others for himself. He was a good worker and would go digging wild turnips with the women.

His father got sick and died. He cried a lot and said, "Although I knew I could save a life, I was ashamed to doctor my father." Some time later his little brother got sick. He got someone to make two drums for him. He made his own rattle. Before it dried he put marks on it and then hung it up. He put nothing inside but four nights later it rattled in the wind. He took it down.

His brother was pretty weak and had lost consciousness. He got someone to call the old men together to sing with him. They had a big tipi where there was a lot of wood along the river. Pretty soon you could smell the sweetgrass. You saw a big fire, the sound of the rattle, and then you could hear his voice sounding very loud as he prayed. The drums beat at the same time.

I was not inside the tipi, but we could hear him stand up. He stood on the fire. Then he started to blow on his sick brother. His blowing made a loud whistling noise. The young fellow began to feel better. Then he sang and blew on him again. Then he sucked at him where he was sore. "This is what has been hurting you. You will be all right now." When he was finished he said, "I will have another name now. They will call me *piecuwiskwew*, Thunder-woman. My brother's name will be Thunder-child." He doctored the boy for four nights and saved him.

We called the boy Thunder-child from then on, but we called him *a:yahkwew* still for that's what he was. He had another name, Clawed-woman. He wanted to be called *piecuwiskwew*, because Thunder is a name for a man and *iskwew* is a woman's name; half and half just like he was.

He never took a wife, nor did he bother the women or the men. We never teased him or made fun of him. We were afraid to, because he was a great doctor.

Once an old man brought him some clothes and a horse to doctor a boy who had fallen from a horse. He took them right away. He called for my father to sing with him. Again he made a big fire. He took his dress off, just wore a breechclout. I heard the sound from the outside as he stood on the fire. He blew at the side of the boy and called for a wooden bowl. "He has got matter inside of him, but not in his lungs." He sang again, he held his hands over the sweetgrass and tapped one hand over the other. Suddenly, you could see bearclaws sticking from his palm. He stuck the bearclaw in the boy's back. Then he sucked out a lot of matter and spit it into the bowl. He rubbed his hands over the wound and though it was daylight we couldn't see any marks on the boy where he had been stuck. "I've got pretty nearly all the matter out. But there is some left. I don't want to take it all for fear that I'll hurt the boy. I'll take the rest out this evening." In the evening he went back and took more out. He saved that sick boy.

He saved a lot of people. Sometimes he would doctor them only once and they would be well. He got lots of horses that way. Even those who had only one horse would give it to him so that he would doctor.

TEXT David G. Mandelbaum, "The Plains Cree," *Anthropological Papers of the American Museum of Natural History* 37, no. 2 (1940): 256–57.

I Alone
Keep Up
Life

One of the most common powers associated with the two-spirit role is that of mediation, the ability to travel between and to bring together opposites. The actual application of this principle varied from tribe to tribe. Among the Navajo Indians of the Southwest, two-spirits, or *nádleehé*, were often go-betweens in arranging affairs between men and women and experts in both male and female activities. The famous *nádleehé* Hastííń Klah (1867–1937) combined his skills in the female art of weaving with his knowledge as a medicine man, a male domain, to produce striking tapestries based on religious designs. In Navajo mythology, supernatural two-spirits bridge the opposites of male and female, hunting and farming, and old and young.

Respect for the *nádleehé* role in Navajo society can be traced to a particular episode of the Navajo origin myth. This episode begins with a quarrel between First Man and his wife, who is caught committing adultery. She accuses First Man of being both economically and sexually superfluous. "I am master of all things, I am responsible for them all," she boasts. "I myself, by myself, make myself live! . . . What, now, do you think of yourself?" First Man repeats her words at a council of the men and says, "Now think it over, because of us, who are men, it was spoken in a manner as though we are unnecessary in life." The men decide to live without the women, on the opposite side of a river. Before finalizing their decision, however, they call in *Nádleeh* (i.e., *nádleehé*) for advice.

The role of *Nádleeh* in the myth is pivotal and complex. At first he/

she approves of the separation. Then, by joining the men and contributing his skills, he tips the balance in their favor. When reconciliation is proposed, his approval is again required. In other words, he is crucial in both the separation and its resolution. He represents the very principle of boundaries, both defining and erasing them.

The following account was narrated by a Navajo named Curly and recorded by Father Berard Haile, a Franciscan missionary, in 1932. Haile, who was fluent in the Navajo language, translated the story in a way that retains much of the original quality of oral narration, in particular the use of repetitive and formulaic phrases, which lend the narration rhythm and punctuation. To get a feel for this you might try reading a few lines aloud.

The passage opens at the council of the men called by First Man.

➤   ➤   ➤

Thereupon a discussion was held about it. "It is not for us to say it shall be (done) in this particular way, no! You yourself say the word! Who is there that could decide upon it as your equal!" they said to him. "Well, four days ago I began to think about it, and now I have made up my mind about it," he said. "I think we should go across to the other side. Everyone of us men will cross over, without exception, since we are unnecessary in life. On that side we will make our homes. Let them! Let the women live alone on this side."

But it happened that the *nádleeh* had not entered with the rest. So now a messenger was sent out after him. And when he was told to come, he (left) his home and entered here. The causes for it which had been told here about himself were repeated in every detail. Also, that they had decided upon this crossing to the other side. " 'Now so it shall be,' we have said," he was told. "Now think this over, you see, so it is now," he was told.

"All right, so I see we are unnecessary in life!" he said. "You who are First Man, do you really and truly think it shall now be this way?" he asked him. "It certainly shall be so, that is exactly the way I think. I already said that," he said. "But what are you able to do, my Grandfather, my Grandmother?" he asked him.

"I myself (can) plant, I myself make millstones, that's settled," he said. "I myself make baking stones. I make pots myself and earthen bowls; gourds I plant myself. I (can) make water jugs," he said, "and stirring sticks and brooms," he said. He was counting up, it seems, the things women usually do. "Liquid corn mush," he mentioned, "stiff corn mush, and baked on stone (paper bread), and dumplings I can make," he said, "three-eared (gruel in cornhusks) I make, and many breads (biscuits baked in ashes), and baked in the trench and sweet (corn) cake, and one-day corncake." "Whirling-around-ones I make," he said. "Lizard-tail-like (-ones) I make," he said. "Boiled dough balls I make," he said. "No cedar gruel I make. Water-is-put-in I make," he said. You see, up to this (point) he had counted up all in the line of women's work, without omitting one. "What she said [First Man's wife, during their quarrel], 'I alone keep up life,' I can also say," he said.

"So it is, I see, you can make everything, you can do anything, I see, my Grandfather, my Grandmother! Nothing is lacking, I see. This thing in particular, which I have just mentioned, just so it will be done," he told him. "But, since

I took my last swallow four days ago. What shall I eat?" he asked him. "There is something! You shall eat indeed! What I myself make, not what (a) woman makes, my Grandchild," he told him. And having left there he brought him a dish of paper bread. He ate, he drank. "Thanks, my Granduncle, my Grandmother, I have my fill," he said to him. "What I just said to ye in particular, exactly so it shall be done now," he said. "It will be known, soon we shall see what comes of it," he said. . . .

At length it was said: "Assemble, come now from there to this place!" From those twelve days till now, whatever their Granduncle-Grandmother, the *nádleeh*, could make in the way of food, that alone served them for food while (this float) was being prepared. And, what the women usually make they did not eat. And so, it seems, finally the meeting was held for it. And when they were leaving those with whom they had been living, they wept. Without feeling backward about it they wept, some did, (of those who) had great love for one another. And so, simply folding their arms they left the women, taking merely working tools with them—and of these only their own, as well as their arrows and their flints. All the belongings of that *nádleeh*, his foods and cooking utensils all told, were first to be put on that float. . . .

When all had gone across from them she certainly was not quiet, orders being issued (by Woman Chief) could be heard. Nevertheless, right among them (also) wailing was heard in places. It turned out that these were such (who had parted from men) whose love for them was mutual. These were wailing, these were crying for them, it seems.

But Woman Chief meanwhile spoke: "What is it anyway

that they have taken from us! Look, here the place is prepared! Even the farms are all prepared," she said. "Besides, here I stand for them (in their place)! Do we live by them? Why! We ourselves maintain our own lives," she said. "Do things with all your might, my Young Girls, my Children! Time will tell what will come of it!" she said.

Up to this time she spoke to all her young girls, encouraging them. Here, on the side of those who had crossed over, he also spoke. First Man did. "Those of you who are chiefs, keep your position and rank here just as you have held in the past," he told them. "The things about which you have spoken and planned in the past, let these very same be the subject of your speeches and plans," he said. "As you see, within the hearing of you all, opposite of us, a loud-sounding speech (is being made)," he said. "All right, just that way let it be done," said those who were chiefs. And when dawn appeared yonder, the first in rank began to speak: "Arise! There are any number of things we should do! Get up and build the fires!" he announced. About the time when it was well warmed up, the second in rank also spoke. The next one also spoke when it had warmed up and the time for work had arrived. The very last one in rank went around among the men and also spoke. He spoke about the farms to be laid out.

For this purpose some men placed themselves at his disposal and began clearing the farm land that was to be, while some men started out on the hunt. As for the *nádleeh*, he nursed (along) each one of the children, some of whom were babes. Here, where they had volunteered for the land, quite a large tract was cleared by sunset. The parties who had gone on the hunt brought in their burdens. At (the place of the) *nádleeh* the pots were boiling. The skin part of a deer udder, after nicely removing its interior, he would fill with broth to be used in raising the children. In this manner he prepared them (the udders). You see, he had made them for the purpose of raising the children with it. On the other side, as soon as one was born of those still in the womb and left behind at the time of the Boating-across, they would tell about it. "Over here there is another one born with his testicles hanging up," they would say, and at once it was brought across here on the float. Whenever those that had been pregnant gave birth, the males were all brought across (and separated) from them.

Here on this side, it seems, where the farm land was being cleared, quite a large tract had been prepared. At the hunting (camp) that Granduncle-Grandmother of theirs would scrape (the hides). Buckskins in large numbers were heaped up by him. A crowd followed him like chickens wherever he went, after those children (whom he nursed) had grown up (and were able to walk). Those, already referred to, on the other shore knew no bounds for meanness. She (Woman Chief) would lead them to the shore and from where they would shout to them: "First Ma-a-n! Do you see this, perhaps?" they would say and, turning their backs to them they would stoop over and pull their dresses up from their backs. Doing this, there, they began to bother them with this. . . .

➤ ➤ ➤

Four seasons of planting follow. Each year the men plant larger fields, while the women plant fewer. In the fourth year, the women plant no crops at all, and they begin to get desperate, not only for food but for sex as well. Some are driven crazy by desire and rush into the river, only to drown. Others attempt to have sex with various unlikely objects and with animals. The men, too, are driven to distraction by sexual need. Four more years pass this way.

One day, a hunter is about to have intercourse using the liver of a deer when Owl stops him. "What ye have done is altogether out of place," Owl tells him, and he gives him a message to take back. The men must settle their differences with the women, or "the earth and sky will disappear." When the assembled men and their chiefs hear this message, they agree to follow Owl's advice.

➤   ➤   ➤

The four chiefs (each in turn) spoke out: "This (seems) good to us. True things have been told us. Should we, who are men, alone continue living here, the end of the (life) line would be reached. Truly there would be no way out of it. So the truth was told to us," they said. "Now you who are assembled, each one of you, how do you think of it?" Meanwhile First Man had not spoken, but the discussion had simply gone along so far in his presence. After that, however, My! what a noise of talking men there was in that crowd! "This is good (news) to us! Let it be done so without fail! Real, true (facts) have been told to us, my Chief, please!" they said. "From morning till night we are worrying for those with whom we formerly lived and for our children. You, First Man, please let it be, the bringing across! Don't let me plead in vain with you." So each one tore loose. He sat there without speaking. After that he spoke: "Does your Granduncle, the *nádleeh*, happen to be in," he asked. "No, he has not entered," was said. "Tell him to come! Exactly as he says it shall be, since he it was who prepared our land," he said.

When he was notified, he entered. Those things which they had told each other were related to him up to the very end, while he sat there, all attention, simply thinking it over, until all had been told to him. "I see, so it is, yes, my Children! But what do you say?" he asked. "What shall we say! Exactly just so let it be done! By all means let it be the bringing across; (that) we have been saying and begging our chief," they told him. "But what does my son say, he who is First Man?" he asked. " 'When you have entered it shall be done exactly as you say,' he says to you, my Granduncle-Grandmother," they told him. "So it is, then, my Child, my Babe! You have spoken of me as having the decision," he said.

"Look, here I am seated as you are looking at me! A new start cannot be made through me!" he said. "I am pleased with this. In the past I was worried about it, my Children," he said. "You have spoken of me as now being master of that. Let it now be the bringing across," he said. "And as Woman Chief (continues) to lead them to the shore, she again pleads there, you see! Look and listen to them! What will come of it, my Son, my Babe?" said that *nádleeh*. After that, finally, First Man said: "It is true that I put this authority in you for good, my Grandmother-Granduncle. Be it so! Now then let the bringing across be done, that is settled," he said. My! How this gladdened the men as soon as he spoke this! "Now get busy with the float till sunset. As soon as it is fixed up, bringing across will take place," he said.

At once they began and were occupied with this very

thing for four days. After four nights had passed, the crossing began. On the farther side they were massed together. My! How the people tumbled about (in each other's embrace)! saying "my Dear," to one another, and what a weeping went up! That Woman Chief entered (the float) first. But First Man was right at (his) home, he had not gone across with the others, they say. It (the boat) floated out into the stream with them and reached the shore for some more. When it was rowed back again, that Woman Chief and her daughter started off together, on a run. At the First Man's home the two had entered.

"My dear Husband," she said as she embraced the old man. That Woman Chief also said: "My Dear, my Babe, my Son," and embraced First Man. "It is true, you are the one by whom things do exist, not I. Not through me do they exist," she said. "It is true, you are indeed the holy highest one, while I am not that," she said. "Now exactly as you may direct, that same shall be, just following you it shall be," she said. "At no time will I take the decision away from you," she said. "All right, I hope you really mean this," said First Man. In this manner people made up with each other. "Be sure that, as you walked for us before, so now you continue to stand up firmly for us!" she said. From the other side all had been brought across, it was learned.

TEXT Berard Haile, *Women versus Men: A Conflict of Navajo Emergence* (Lincoln: University of Nebraska Press, 1981), pp. 18–20, 21, 22–23, 31–33.

S   P   I   R   I   T   S

I'm Going
to Have
You

Although the prudishness of Victorian observers often leaves us in the dark about the sexuality of Native American two-spirits, there is no reason to assume that they did not have active sex lives. In fact, a few accounts of two-spirit sex have been preserved, and they suggest that these "queens" were hardly retiring flowers. According to psychologist Erik Erikson, warriors among the Sioux Indians sometimes slept with a two-spirit the night before a war party in the belief that this contact with another male increased their virility. The Sioux medicine man Lame Deer, in the selection included earlier, relates how *winkte* gave the men they had sex with obscene nicknames, which were considered good luck. A famous painting by George Catlin depicts the annual "dance to the berdache" held by the Sauk and Fox Indians. Only those who had had sex with a two-spirit in the previous year were eligible to dance. In Catlin's painting, there doesn't appear to be any shortage of eligible men.

In the early twentieth century, a chief of the Pacific Northwest Kwakiutl tribe, who told his life story to Clellan S. Ford, related this account of his encounter with an especially avid two-spirit named Frances.

➤   ➤   ➤

I only knew well one of these men that wears women's clothing. There are others like that I know, but they used men's clothing. They are mostly Quatsino Indians. I will tell you about the one I knew. This man, her name was Frances. The first time I saw her, he came to Fort Rupert and I was young. This was long before I was married. The Quatsino Indians came and camped at Fort Rupert on their way to Fraser River. I saw this man with woman's clothing, but she had a man's voice. We went to see the people in the house where they were staying, and she began to look at us, and she spoke to me and says, "You, young fellow, I'm going to have you for my sweetheart." She had long hair like a woman's. They didn't stay long, so I didn't get to know her then. When they came home from Fraser River, they called at Fort Rupert, and they stopped there for a couple of months. During the time, she called me to go and see her at the house where she was, and when I went there, she caught hold of me, and when I went there she throwed me right into her bed. My, she was strong—awful strong! She told me she want me to lie with her. Before that I was told that she was a man, and I was kind of scared to lie down with her, but I couldn't help it because she was so strong and held me down. She opened her legs and pulled me in, taking hold of my pecker and putting it in. I didn't work; she done all the work. After I went out of the house, I told all the boys that she was a woman, and that I laid down with her, and all the boys went after her because she was free.

TEXT Clellan S. Ford, *Smoke from Their Fires: The Life of a Kwakiutl Chief* (New Haven, Conn.: Yale University Press, 1941), pp. 129–30.
OTHER SOURCES Erik H. Erikson, "Childhood and Tradition in Two American Indian Tribes," *Psychoanalytic Study of the Child* 1 (1945): 319–50; George Catlin, *Letters and Notes on the . . . North American Indians* (New York: Dover, 1973), 2:214–15.

S   P   I   R   I   T   S

There

Was Great

Rejoicing

Pretty Shield was a respected Crow elder when she related this story, primarily in sign language, to Frank Linderman in the early 1930s. She had been a young woman in the summer of 1876, when several warriors of her tribe had volunteered to join the American soldiers in a war against their traditional enemies, the Lakota and Cheyenne. Among them was a two-spirit named Osch-Tisch, or Finds-Them-and-Kills-Them, then in his early twenties. The Crow warriors fought with General Crook at the battle of the Rosebud, which ended in a standoff just ten days before General Custer's terrible defeat at the Little Bighorn. Linderman's transcription of Pretty Shield's account captures the cadence and style of Native American storytelling. Through her young woman's eyes we can really feel the excitement of seeing the Crow warriors returning from battle led by a wild woman and a two-spirit. Although the traditional life of the Crow Indians came to an abrupt end a few years later, Finds-Them-and-Kills-Them remained a prominent and respected member of the tribe until his death in 1929.

➤   ➤   ➤

"Did the men ever tell you anything about a woman who fought with Three-stars on the Rosebud?"

"No," I replied, wondering.

"Ahh, they do not like to tell of it," she chuckled. "But I

will tell you about it. We Crows all know about it. I shall not be stealing anything from the men by telling the truth.

"Yes, a Crow woman fought with Three-stars on the Rosebud, *two* of them did, for that matter; but one of them was neither a man nor a woman. She looked like a man, and yet she wore woman's clothing; and she had the heart of a woman. Besides, she did a woman's work. Her name was Finds-them-and-kills-them. She was not a man, and yet not a woman," Pretty-shield repeated. "She was not as strong as a man, and yet she was wiser than a woman," she said, musingly, her voice scarcely audible.

"The other woman," she went on, "was a *wild* one who had no man of her own. She was both bad and brave, this one. Her name was The-other-magpie; and she was pretty. . . .

"During the fight on the Rosebud both these women did brave deeds. When Bull-snake fell from his horse, badly wounded, Finds-them-and-kills-them dashed up to him, got down from her horse, and stood over him, shooting at the Lacota as rapidly as she could load her gun and fire. The-other-magpie rode round and round them, singing her war-song and waving her coup-stick, the only weapon she had. When the Lacota, seeing Bull-snake on the ground, charged to take his scalp, The-other-magpie rode straight at them, waving her coup-stick. Her medicine was so strong that the Lacota turned and rode away; and Bull-snake was saved. All the men saw these things, and yet they have never told you about them.

"Both these women expected death that day. Finds-them-

and-kills-them, afraid to have the Lacota find her dead with woman-clothing on her, changed them to a man's before the fighting commenced, so that if killed the Lacota would not laugh at her, lying there with a woman's clothes on her. She did not want the Lacota to believe that she was a Crow man hiding in a woman's dress, you see.

"Yes, Sign-talker, there was a woman and a *half*-woman who fought on the Rosebud with Three-stars. The woman, I remember, wore a stuffed woodpecker on her head, and her forehead was painted yellow. Her coup-stick was big medicine that day, and she rode a black horse. She went to the war because her brother had lately been killed by the Lacota. She wanted to get even, and she did. Riding straight at the Lacota, with only her coup-stick, she spat at them: 'See,' she called out, 'my spit is my arrows.' She rode against a Lacota's horse, even struck the Lacota with her coup-stick, counting a coup on him, just as Finds-them-and-kills-them fired with her gun, and killed him. When the Lacota fell The-other-magpie took his scalp. She was waving it when I saw her coming into the village with the others. Yes, and I saw her cut this scalp into many pieces, so that the men might have more scalps to dance with."

Pretty-shield had been speaking rapidly, her dark eyes snapping. Now she leaned back in her chair. "Ahh," she said a little bitterly, "the men did not tell you this; but *I* have. And it's the truth. Every old Crow, man or woman, knows that it is the truth."

And then as though she feared that she might have been unfair, "I am sure that your friend, Plenty-coups, has told you only the truth. But if he left *this* out he did not tell you all of the truth," she added quite severely. "Two women, one of them not quite a woman, fought with Three-stars, and I hope that you will put it in a book, Sign-talker, because it is the truth.

"The return of the Crow wolves [warriors] and these two women to our village was one of the finest sights that I have ever seen," she continued, excitement gone from her eyes. "I felt proud of the two women, even of the wild one, because she was brave. And I saw that they were the ones who were taking care of Bull-snake, the wounded man, when they rode in.

"Ahh, there was great rejoicing. . . ."

TEXT Frank B. Linderman, *Red Mother* (New York: John Day, 1932), pp. 227–31.

OTHER SOURCES Will Roscoe, "That Is My Road: The Life and Times of a Crow Berdache," *Montana: The Magazine of Western History* 40, no. 1 (Winter 1990): 46–55.

His Appearance

Is Brilliant

(Asushunamir)

The following excerpt is from the epic known as the Descent of Ishtar, inscribed in the Akkadian language of the Assyrian people of Mesopotamia around 1000 B. C. E. It is based on an even older myth concerning Ishtar's Sumerian counterpart, Inanna. In this myth, Inanna/ Ishtar travels to the land of the dead to attend the funeral of her sister's husband. But her arrival infuriates her sister, Ereshkigal, the queen of the underworld. Ereshkigal kills Inanna/Ishtar and turns her into a water skin, which she hangs from a nail on the wall. Meanwhile, the disappearance of Inanna/Ishtar causes all life on the surface of the earth to come to a halt. Animals no longer mate, men and women no longer have sex. The messenger of the gods, Papsukkal, begs for help from Ea, king of the gods, and Ea creates a being named Asushunamir.

Like many of the other two-spirit figures in this chapter, Asushunamir is a light bearer. Yet his radiance is not that of a solar father god but the intermediate, changeable light of the moon. His name has been translated as "his appearance is bright or splendid," which is also said of the sun or stars, meaning, in effect, "his face is pretty." Others have translated his name as "his rising is brilliant" or "his appearance is bright," which is similar to the terms used for the crescent moon and a play on the name of the moon god. Yet other lunar connections are brought into the myth by the figure of Papsukkal, the messenger of the gods, who is the son of the moon god Sin.

In the Akkadian tablets, Asushunamir is referred to as an *assinnu*; in another version, he is called a *kulu'u*. In the Sumerian version, Enki (counterpart to the Assyrian Ea) creates, instead of Asushunamir, two beings called a *kurgarrû* and a *kalatur*. All these terms refer to priestly offices, some of which can be traced back as far as the third millennium B.C.E. The *assinnu*, *kurgarrû*, and *kulu'û* (also spelled *kalû*) were singers, ritual performers, and priests, usually in the service of goddesses like Ishtar. They, too, had luminary and lunar associations. In one text, the *kurgarrû* are described as pouring out their "terrifying brightness" as they kindle fires and brandish torches. Other texts prescribe that on the occasion of lunar eclipses the king should touch the head of an *assinnu*. Overall, these priests share many characteristics with the *galli* of the Greco-Roman world and the *hijra* of India.

These priests were also involved in what scholars have termed *temple prostitution*. Unfortunately, we know very little about the real purpose of sex magic in Mesopotamian societies. In some ceremonies, the king, who represented Dumuzi or some other god, had sex with a priestess, representing Inanna, to encourage fertility. But individuals might also visit a temple on their own to have sex with a priestess or a priest. According to omen texts, one purpose of such a visit was to escape bad luck and deprivations. In the Sumerian and Akkadian languages, the term for describing luck and good fortune literally means "to acquire a god." Thus, having sex with one of these priests was a way of acquiring a god and, thereby, good fortune.

The following myth also credits these figures with the ability to cross the boundary between the living and the dead. In the Sumerian version, they pass through Ereshkigal's gates unnoticed, like flies. In the Assyrian account that follows, it appears that Asushunamir's beauty and radiance cause the gates to open. The most important skill possessed by these figures, however, is that of psychological healing. In the following myth, Asushunamir calms the "insides" of Ereshkigal, and this leads her to make a promise of hospitality that Asushuna-mir then uses to free Ishtar. The Sumerian version offers an even clearer description of how the *kurgarrû* and *kalatur* heal Ereshkigal.

Ereshkigal was moaning:
"Oh! Oh! My inside!"
They moaned:
"Oh! Oh! Your inside!"
She moaned:
"Ohhhh! Oh! My outside!"
They moaned:
"Ohhhh! Oh! Your outside!"
She groaned:
"Oh! Oh! My belly!"
They groaned:
"Oh! Oh! your belly!"
She groaned:
"Oh! Ohhhh! My back!!"
They groaned:
"Oh! Ohhhh! Your back!!"
She sighed:
"Ah! Ah! My heart"
They sighed:
"Ah! Ah! Your heart!"
She sighed:
"Ah! Ahhhh! My liver!"
They sighed:
"Ah! Ahhhh! Your liver!"

In other words, they use the power of empathy to heal Ereshkigal.
Counselors and therapists refer to this technique as *active listening*. It
is one of the simplest and most effective ways of expressing concern.
The listener paraphrases the feelings and sentiments expressed by the
speaker without judging or commenting on them. Active listening
encourages others to speak freely on an emotional level. Many times
this alone brings a sense of release and comfort, and little other inter-
vention is needed. But, as suggested in the preceding passage, an even
deeper level of this process is that, by reflecting Ereshkigal's pain in
this way, the *kurgarrû* and *kalatur* actually re-create it within themselves. This has the effect of drawing the suffering out and away from
the goddess, a procedure that ultimately has its roots in the magics of
shamanism. Shamans "suck out" objects from their patients' bodies
that are the sources of their illness. Further, being empathic, the *kurgarrû* and *kalatur* are also intuitive. They know each other's thoughts,
so they say the same things at the same time. In this regard, they provide an excellent example of the subject-SUBJECT relationship of
Divine Twins.

What is the connection between the power of empathy and being
neither male nor female? The ancient texts do not tell us the answer in
so many words, but I think we can venture one today. Men and women
are always defined against each other. Their sense of self depends on
this "otherizing." Individuals in two-spirit roles, however, know two
worlds and two sets of experiences, those of men *and* those of women.
For such people there is no "opposite" sex, no one who must be seen as
"other" so that they can define themselves.

One other theme of pertinence to gay men can be drawn from this story. Asushunamir's descent in search of Ishtar can be seen as symbolic of bringing the repressed, internalized image of the mother into consciousness. Of course, issues with "mom" are relevant to all men—no one has yet shown a connection between child raising and sexual orientation. Gay men, however, have distinct experiences with their mothers. If our fathers are absent, or if they pull away from us because of our gayness, mom is often the only parent left to identify with. Even when there are two parents around, we often find that our own emerging sense of self is better reflected in our image of mom than in our image of dad. Mom may even encourage this identification. So, for some boys, assuming a persona like mom's provides a way of attracting dad (and, later, other men). The gay man who typifies this pattern is likely to be an avid fan of Barbara Cartland novels and romance in general because he can identify with female heroines. His ideal man might not have to be heterosexual, but he should "take charge."

Other gay boys, however, seem to get the idea that the way to attract dad is to be *like* him, not different. When they grow up, you can find them exploring bars and social scenes where costumed masculinity is the favored style. In either case, making ourselves conscious of our mother's voice within us and of the reactive ways we respond to it (sometimes submitting, sometimes rebelling) is a liberating rite of passage. More often than not, if we have hang-ups about sex, it's mom's voice speaking to us as the voice of morality.

Like many gay boys, I idealized and sympathized with my mother, who raised me as a single parent. It has been difficult for me as an adult to acknowledge her negative as well as her positive influences (which I see being represented in the following myth by Ereshkigal and Ishtar, respectively). Only slowly have I been able to see her as a fully dimensional person—with fears and weaknesses as well as strengths—for whom being "both a father and a mother," as she felt she had to be, did not come naturally.

➤   ➤   ➤

PLAYERS AND PLACES

Asushunamir   "his appearance is bright or splendid"

Ishtar   in Sumerian, Inanna, goddess of sexuality and war, referred to as the "Lady of Heaven"

Ereshkigal   Ishtar's sister, "queen of the Great Below"

Papsukkal   also called Ninshubur, associated with the constellation Orion, minister of the great gods

Sin   moon god, father of Papsukkal

Ea   in Sumerian, Enki, god of wisdom who brought the arts of civilization to humans

Shamash   city on the Euphrates River above Babylon

Namtaru   a demon of the underworld and minister of Ereshkigal

Egalgina   a place in the underworld

Anunnaki   underworld deities

Papsukkal, the messenger of the Great Gods, his face
 downturned, his countenance sinister,
dressed in mourning clothes, bearing sores.
He went to Shamash there, weeping before Sin, his
 father,
before Ea, the king, his tears flowing.

S   P   I   R   I   T   S

"Ishtar has descended to the Land of No Return, and has
   not come up again!
Since Ishtar has descended to the Land of No Return,
the bull no longer mounts the cow, the ass does not
   impregnate the she-ass,
the man does not impregnate the girl on the street,
the man sleeps at his place,
the girl sleeps on her side."
Ea created in his wise heart an image,
he formed Asushunamir, an *assinnu*.
"Go there, Asushunamir, set your face to the gate of the
   Land of No Return!
The seven gates shall be opened before you!
Ereshkigal will see you and she will be glad at the sight of
   you.
After her insides calm and her mood cheers up,
let her swear the oath of the great gods.
Hold high your head, set your thoughts on the water skin,
   saying,
'Now then, oh mistress, give me the water skin, that I
   drink water from it!'"

When Ereshkigal heard this, she hit her thigh, she bit
   her finger.
"You have desired from me a wish, which one may not
   wish for.
Go, Asushunamir, I will curse you a mighty curse:
May the food of the troughs of the city be your food!
May the sewers of the city be your drink!

May the shadow of the city wall be your home!
May doorways be your seat!
May thirsty drunkards strike your cheek!"

Ereshkigal opened her mouth and spoke,
saying to Namtaru, her messenger, the words:
"Go there, Namtaru, knock at the Egalgina!
Adorn the doorways with coral stone!
Lead out the Anunnaki and seat them on the golden
    throne!
Spray Ishtar with the water of the life and take her away
    from my sight!"
Namtaru went forth, he knocked at the Egalgina,
he adorned the doorways with coral stone,
he led the Anunnaki out and set them on the golden
    throne,
he sprayed Ishtar with the water of the life and he took
    her away.
Through a gate he led her out and gave her back her
    breechcloth.
Through a second gate he led her out and gave her back
    the birthstone girdle of her hips.
Through a third gate he led her out and gave her back the
    rings around her arms and feet.
Through a fourth gate he led her out and gave her back
    the breastplates of her chest.
Through a fifth gate he led her out and gave her back the
    chains around her neck.

Through a sixth gate he led her out and gave her back the
rings on her ears.

Through a seventh gate he led her out and gave her back
the great crown on her head.

TEXT Peter C. A. Jensen, *Keilinschriftliche Bibliothek*, vol. 6, pt. 1,
Assyrisch-Babylonische Mythen und Epen (Berlin: Reuther & Reichard,
1900), pp. 87–91 (my translation).

OTHER SOURCES Diane Wolkstein and Samuel N. Kramer, *Inanna:
Queen of Heaven and Earth: Her Stories and Hymns from Sumer* (New York:
Harper & Row, 1983), pp. 65–66; Stephanie Dalley, *Myths from Mesopo-
tamia* (Oxford: Oxford University Press, 1991), pp. 158–59; A. Leo Op-
penheim, "Mesopotamian Mythology III," *Orientalia* 19, no. 2 (1950): 134–
35; W. F. Albright, "Some Cruces in the Langdon Epic," *Journal of the
American Oriental Society* 39 (1919): 65–90; Anne D. Kilmer, "How Was
Queen Ereshkigal Tricked? A New Interpretation of the Descent of Ish-
tar," *Ugarit-Forschungen* 3 (1971): 299–309; Erica Reiner, "City Bread and
Bread Baked in Ashes," in *Languages and Areas: Studies Presented to George
V. Bobrinskoy* (Chicago: University of Chicago Press, 1967), pp. 116–20;
Svend A. Pallis, *The Babylonian Akitu Festival, Danske Videnskabernes Sel-
skab, Historisk-Filologiske Meddelelser*, vol. 12, no. 1 (Copenhagen: Bianco
Lunos Bogtrykkeri, 1926); Thorkild Jacobsen, *The Treasures of Darkness: A
History of Mesopotamian Religion* (New Haven, Conn.: Yale University
Press, 1976), and *The Harps that Once . . . : Sumerian Poetry in Translation*
(New Haven, Conn.: Yale University Press, 1987), pp. 205–32.

S   P   I   R   I   T   S

Hurrah

for the

Mahu!

Mahu is the term used in Hawaii and Tahiti to refer to nonmasculine males who prefer the work of women and the sexual companionship of other (non-*mahu*) males. They are the Polynesian counterparts of North American two-spirits. Similar roles, known by other terms, have been documented throughout Oceania. The missionaries who were determined to convert Polynesians to Christianity were horrified by the openness of such practices. As was the case with the North American two-spirits, *mahu* came under pressure to abandon their ways, and, on many Pacific islands, they seem to have disappeared along with other aspects of traditional culture.

But, like Native American two-spirits, *mahu* have not disappeared. Today there is a revival of the role under way in Hawaii, much as lesbian and gay Indians are reviving the two-spirit role in North America. According to Carol Robertson, "The *mahu* population today embraces an astounding variety of individuals. It can designate women who dress and work as men, men who dress and work as women, women or men who dress and act so as to obscure their biological classification, women who will only associate with other women, men who dress 'festively,' men who undergo hormone treatments and/or eventually change their sex surgically, true hermaphrodites, and women and men who might, in English, call themselves 'gay.' Any of these people may choose to procreate or to raise children through the traditional adoption arrangement known as *hanai*. In fact, parents sometimes put their children in the care of *mahu*, for mixed-gender individuals are recognized as special, compassionate, and creative."

Although missionary accounts rarely speak of a religious dimension to *mahu* status, evidence suggests that this third-gender role did at one time have religious significance. In the Maori, Mangaian, and Samoan languages, terms related to *mahu* have the meaning of "to heal" and "to be healed" as well as "homosexual." Hawaiian oral tradition links *mahu* to the origins of the hula dance, which is based on an ideal of male/female balance. According to one Hawaiian traditionalist, a "handed-down tale tells of hermaphrodites who came from some unknown spot and landed on what is now Waikiki Beach. . . . The hermaphrodites—also referred to as *mahu*—were respected men; talented priests of healing and of the *hula*." Today, *mahu* are intimately associated with the revival of the hula tradition in Hawaii. As Robertson reports, "This tradition was handed down primarily through women and *mahu*."

The following description of a Tahitian *mahu* comes from the 1920 journal of American artist George Biddle. Biddle was part of a circle of talented American artists and anthropologists who visited Polynesia in the early twentieth century, many of whom were gay and lesbian. Biddle's ability to appreciate the *mahu* role and his endorsement of androgyny reflect the early stirrings of a gay consciousness.

➤ ➤ ➤

The Tahitian word for a "pansy" is *mahu*. I first heard the word at the Fourteenth of July celebrations in Papeete. The Papeete dance chorus was led by an old retainer of Queen

Marau's—her butler and majordomo. The performance of
the dancers was at times ragged and uninspired. The old fellow ran up and down the line of the dancing girls, urging
them to greater efforts. If a girl fell slightly out of line, if the
fury of her movements slackened, he did not hesitate to
switch her legs with a bamboo twig. His function reminded
me of that of the drum majorettes at our football games. The
dancers broke into a happy roar of approval: "*Aue te mahu e!
Mirimiri i te mahu!*—Hurrah for the *mahu*! Just look at the
mahu!"

Let me describe a typical *mahu*. He may be a pansy, but
the word has not necessarily the ugly connotation of our "homosexual." It designates a social type. . . .

Pua is an attractive young *mahu*, sixteen or seventeen
years old. He has a thin treble voice, sways his hips coquet-
tishly when he walks, and snatches for a broom at the slight-
est pretext. He accompanies the girls when they set off up
the valley after oranges. He is adept, too, at juggling them
and can keep four or five in the air at once. Nor does he truss
up his *pareu* about the loins; he wears it becomingly like a
short skirt an inch or two below the knees. When he grows
older he will doubtless let his beard grow like old Marau's
retainer. With the exception of the *mahu*, and occasionally
the missionaries, Tahitians always shave.

But the *mahu* is not necessarily a sex deviationist. He
could better be defined as a third sex, with the emphasis on
the social functions which he fulfills. In our own society—
probably in every society—there is such a need. But only in
Polynesia and other primitive cultures is the *mahu* openly

accepted and distinguished by a different manner of dressing. With us he is the cotillion leader, the fellow who can always strum out a tune on the piano, make any party a success. He is the confidant of men and women, because he understands the problems of each. He can help a girl with her knitting, or a man in the selection of a tie. He is the middleman and broker of the arts. Throughout the ages he has been witch doctor, priest, and prophet.

Perhaps all of us have at bottom a little of the *mahu* in us. I should like to think so. A hundred percent man or woman is a very trying person and I don't think quite fits into our modern world.

TEXT George Biddle, *Tahitian Journal* (Minneapolis: University of Minnesota Press, 1968), pp. 63–64.

OTHER SOURCES Carol E. Robertson, "The Mahu of Hawai'i," *Feminist Studies* 15, no. 2 (1989): 313–26; Mary K. Pukui, E. W. Haertig, and Catherine A. Lee, *Nana I Ke Kumu (Look to the Source)* (Honolulu: Queen Lili'uokalani Children's Center, 1972), 2:108, 110; David F. Greenberg, *The Construction of Homosexuality* (Chicago: University of Chicago Press, 1988), pp. 62–63; Stephen O. Murray, *Oceanic Homosexualities* (New York: Garland, 1992).

Respect

With an estimated fifty thousand members in India, the cult of the *hijra* is one of the most important continuing third-gender traditions today. A society of ritual performers whose origins may go back three thousand years or more, *hijra* are devotees of the Bahuchara Mata, an Indian mother goddess. Their key religious function today is the performance of a blessing rite that bestows fertility on newlyweds and male infants. It is believed that *hijra* have the power to foretell the future, to bring rain, and, if provoked, to utter fearful curses. Occasionally, they serve as temple personnel. Before the arrival of the British, they enjoyed guaranteed begging rights and titles to lands granted them by Indian and Muslim rulers. Having lost these rights during the colonial period, life today is more uncertain. *Hijra* survive largely by begging and through fees for their rites. Many resort to prostitution. Although their place in Indian society is well recognized, they are viewed with ambivalence, a combination of fear and awe.

In Indian terms, *hijra* are defined as males who lack male sex organs, either from birth or, more often, through castration, although many postpone this procedure until later in life. Not only does castration serve to render *hijra* gender ambivalent, it enables them to achieve *nirvan*, the state of inner calm and receptivity associated with higher consciousness. When anthropologist Serena Nanda asked *hijra* whether they identified as male or female, they typically responded by jumping to their feet, lifting their skirts, and displaying the results of their emasculation. "See," they insisted, "we are neither men nor women!" The ancient Sanskrit term for this status, *trhytīyām prakrhytim*, literally means "third nature."

The *hijra* illustrate a characteristic contradiction in Hindu religion by occupying both poles of an ascetic-erotic dichotomy. Although defined as religious celibates, they are infamous for their lewd public behavior and their involvement in prostitution. Some *hijra* even form long-term relationships with "husbands," establishing households and raising adopted children. *Hijra* can manifest such a contradiction because, having been stripped of gender *and* desire by their castration, they are "empty" and can serve as vehicles for the fertile power of the Mother Goddess herself. The sexual aura that surrounds them is not theirs in an individual sense but that of the Goddess.

Why do individuals choose to become *hijra*? In the answers that Nanda received, the most common reason was homosexuality. "I'll tell you about us hijra," Nanda was told. "We dress like girls because of the sexual desire for men. Why else would we wear saris? . . . We are born as a boy, and we grow up. One in a hundred people will know we are not a boy, but a hijra. Someone who has already had a relationship with a hijra, he will come to us and show us the state of his desire. Then we are attracted." Another explained, "See, we are all men, born as men, but when we look at women, we don't have any desire for them. When we see men, we like them, we feel shy, we feel some excitement." In other words, even though *hijra* are defined in terms of gender by Indian society, their own accounts of themselves emphasize homosexuality.

But these motives never appear in the origin stories and tales told by *hijra* and others. Homosexuality is portrayed only indirectly, as the *absence* of heterosexual desire. As one *hijra* told Nanda, "Only men who have not spoiled any lady or got any children should come into the

hijra company. You should not have had any affairs with ladies, not
have loved ladies, or done any sexual thing with them or have married
a lady. We true hijra are like this from childhood." This is really just
another way of saying homosexual without having to say it.

The following story, in which two *hijra* gain respect by demonstrat-
ing their powers, was collected by Nanda from a *hijra* in the early
1980s. It offers a rare opportunity to hear the voice of a traditional
third-gender person.

➤   ➤   ➤

One time there was a king in Hyderabad. There was a great
drought during his reign. There were two hijras sitting in
the road. . . . The people of the country went and told the
king, "Do something about the drought, the whole country
is famished and the people are dying." The king said, "What
can I do? I can't do anything, you people must approach
those two hijras who are sitting there by the roadside." The
people spoke to the king with contempt and said, "Why
should we ask them instead of you?" The king said, "If anything at all can be done, only they can do it, not me."

So then the king himself went to the hijras and told them,
"There is a drought, people are dying, and the city wants
rain. If you make rain, you can live here; if the rain doesn't
come you must go outside the city to live." The two hijras
who were sitting together were mother and daughter (elder
and junior). The daughter said, "Look, mother, so many
people have come, let us tell some lies and run away." But the
mother said, "Wait, please, I'll do something. God will look
after me." So she took the cloth from the upper part of her

body and dipped it in a cup of water and gave it to the people
to take with them. Then, she said, the rain will come.

Immediately the lightning and thunder came and rain
started pouring down; everyone was neck deep in water, it
was such a heavy downpour. Then the mother said "enough"
and the rain stopped. The people came back to see the hijras
but they were gone, and the place they had been sitting in
was submerged in water. So the king ordered that wherever
hijras were seen in that city they should be respected, and
that is why that city is full of hijras.

TEXT Serena Nanda, *Neither Man nor Woman: The Hijras of India* (Belmont, Calif.: Wadsworth, 1990), pp. 31–32.

OTHER SOURCES Will Roscoe, review of *Neither Man nor Woman: The
Hijras of India* by Serena Nanda, *Journal of Homosexuality* 21, no. 3 (1991):
117–25.

Wearing Rings on My Ears

and Bangles on My Wrists

(Arjuna)

The *Mahābhārata*, based on oral traditions dating back to 1000 B.C.E., is the longest heroic epic in any language. Written in ancient Sanskrit, its ninety thousand verses cover a great number of subjects, but the overriding theme is the rivalry between two sets of cousins, the Pānda-vas and the Kauravas, which eventually results in an apocalyptic battle.

Contemporary *hijra* claim two of the epic's heroes as their forebears, Bhīsma and Arjuna. Bhīsma is the son of a king and a river goddess who makes a vow of lifelong celibacy so that his father can marry a beautiful maiden and ensure that her children will inherit his king-dom. Later, he raises both the Pāndavas and the Kauravas. The *hijra* also make a lifelong vow of abstinence (although, in practice, this applies primarily to heterosexual relations). The other hero of the *Mahābhārata* claimed by the *hijra* is Arjuna. Arjuna is the fiercest of the Pāndava warriors, but, as the following selection relates, he passes for a year dressed as a member of the "third sex," living in a harem and teaching women the arts of dancing and singing. This occurs when the eldest of the five Pāndava brothers gambles away all their property, including their personal freedom. The brothers agree to be exiled for a period of thirteen years, the last of which they are required to live in disguise in another country. (Other heroes in Indo-European myths who pass a period of time dressed as women include Hercules, Achilles, Theseus, and Loki.)

The disguised Arjuna is described as a "fire within a well"—fire being a male element and water female. What strikes me most about the following account is the almost campy way in which Arjuna's hypermasculinity is juxtaposed to his third-sex costume. When I try to picture this, I get the image of a body builder wearing see-through harem pants—a very sexy Androgyne.

Back in the 1970s in San Francisco, it seemed like everyone was determined to be a star in some way. Given a stage—or a warehouse or a storefront—groups like the Cockettes and the Angels of Light put on lavish musical extravaganzas on shoestring budgets. And, if you couldn't get on a stage, you used the streets. One of my favorite groups was a troupe of gay belly dancers who used to appear at "Hibernia beach," an area in front of what used to be a Hibernia Bank, at Castro and 18th. Dressed like Arjuna, with flowing scarves, earrings, bangles, and finger cymbals, and dancing to wild drums, they were one of the most enchanting and erotic sights I've ever seen. They didn't seem to be imitating women to me—the difference between male and female hips ensured that. They were projecting an androgynous, gay masculinity that I find very appealing. One of these belly dancers was very beautiful, with dark eyes and hair, a small mustache, and a heart tattooed on his upper arm. Boy, did I have a crush on him! Now I realize that it was the archetype I loved—the archetype of Arjuna as the seductive, gay-masculine two-spirit.

The following excerpt opens with Arjuna's declaration of the disguise that he intends to assume. The second passage describes his arrival at the palace of King Virata, in whose service the disguised Pāndavas have placed themselves for their thirteenth year of exile.

➤ ➤ ➤

Yudhishthira said,—"And what office will be performed by that mighty descendant of the Kurus? . . ."

Arjuna replied,—"O lord of the Earth, I will declare myself as one of the neuter sex. O monarch, it is, indeed, difficult to hide the marks of the bow-string on my arms. I will, however, cover both my cicatrized arms with bangles. Wearing brilliant rings on my ears and conch-bangles on my wrists and causing a braid to hang down from my head, I will, O king, appear as one of the third sex. Vrihannala by name [also spelled Brhannada]. And living as a female I will (always) entertain the king and the inmates of the inner apartments by reciting stories. And, O king, I will also instruct the women of Virata's palace in singing and delightful modes of dancing, and in musical instruments of diverse kinds. And I will also recite the various excellent acts of men and thus conceal myself, O son of Kunti, by counterfeiting disguise. And, O Bharata, should the king enquire, I will say that *I lived as a waiting maid of Draupudi in Yudhishthira's palace*. And, O foremost of kings, concealing myself by this means, as fire is concealed by ashes, I will pass my days agreeably in the palace of Virata!"

.   .   .

Next appeared at the gate of the ramparts another person of enormous size and exquisite beauty decked in the ornaments of women, and wearing large ear-rings and beautiful conch-bracelets overlaid with gold. And that mighty-armed individual, with long and abundant hair floating about his neck, resembled an elephant in gait. And shaking the very earth with his tread, he approached Virata and stood in his court. And beholding the son of the great Indra, shining with exquisite lustre and having the gait of a mighty elephant,—that grinder of foes having his true form concealed in disguise, entering the council-hall and advancing towards the monarch, the king addressed all his courtiers, saying, "Whence doth this person come? I have never heard of him before." And when the men present spake of the newcomer as one unknown to them, the king wonderingly said,—"Possest of great strength, thou art like unto a celestial, and young and of darkish hue, thou resemblest the leader of a herd of elephants! Wearing conch-bracelets overlaid with gold, a braid, and ear-rings, thou shinest yet like one amongst those that riding on chariots wander about equipped with mail and bow and arrows and decked with garlands and fine hair! I am old and desirous of relinquishing my burden. Be thou like my sons, or rule thou like myself all the Matsyas! It seemeth to me that such persons as thou can never be of the neuter sex!"

Arjuna said,—"I sing, dance, and play on instruments. I am proficient in dance and skilled in song. O lord of men, assign me unto (the princess) Uttara. I will be dancing-master to the royal maiden. As to how I have come by this form, what will it avail thee to hear the account which will only augment my pain? Know me, O king of men, to be Vrihannala, a son or daughter without father or mother!"

Virata said,—"O Vrihannala, I give thee what thou desirest! Instruct my daughter, and those like her, in dancing. To me, however, this office seemeth unworthy of thee! Thou deservest (the dominion of) the entire earth girt round by the ocean!"

The king of the Matsyas then tested Vrihannala in dancing, music, and other fine arts, and consulting with his various ministers forthwith caused him to be examined by women. And learning that this impotency was of a permanent nature, he sent him to the maidens' apartments. And there the mighty Arjuna began giving lessons in singing and instrumental music to the daughter of Virata, her friends, and the waiting-maids, and soon won their good graces. And in this manner the self-possessed Arjuna lived there in disguise, partaking of pleasures in their company, and unknown to the people within or without the palace.

TEXT *The Mahabharata or Krishna-Dwaipayna Vyasa*, vol. 3, *Virata and Udyoga Parva*, trans. Pratap C. Roy (Calcutta: Data Bose, n.d. [1890s]), pp. 3–4, 18–19.

OTHER SOURCES George T. Artola, "The Transvestite in Sanskrit Story and Drama," *Annals of Oriental Research of the University of Madras* 1975: 57–68; Alf Hiltebeitel, "Siva, the Goddess, and the Disguises of the Pandavas and Draupadi," *History of Religions* 20, nos. 1/2 (1980): 147–74.

Strap
of My Bra,
Hem of My Pants

In Brazil, slaves brought from the Guinea coast of Africa (especially Dahomeans and Yorubans) continued practicing their native religion. Over time, they absorbed influences from Catholicism, Indian religions, and spiritualism, and their membership came to include individuals of mixed and Indian, as well as African descent. Today, a wide array of Afro-Brazilian possession cults flourish throughout the country, three of the leading ones being Candomblé, Macumba, and Umbanda.

In the northeastern Brazilian city of Salvador (more commonly known as Bahia), cult houses, each with a "mother" or a "father," can be found in almost every neighborhood. Ceremonies involve offerings to deities called *orixás*, who live in the house, and dancing, during which priestesses and sometimes others become possessed by the *orixás* or one of their more individualized manifestations called *exus*. The *orixás* and *exus* speak through the possessed person, foretelling the future, prescribing cures, and offering advice. Whether they are initiated or not, many Brazilians visit cult houses to seek advice and aid from the spirits and from the "mother-of-saint" or "father-of-saint" who runs the house.

In the early twentieth century, a new cult called *caboclo* developed in Bahia based on the Candomblé tradition. *Caboclos* are bawdy spirits of mixed Indian-European descent. Their introduction led to the relaxation of many of the stricter rules of Candomblé, and the cult became accessible to a larger portion of the population. Instead of years of training, individuals could become "sons" or "daughters" of a saint (i.e., initiated members of a house) after just seven days. Even those who do not "receive a saint" (enter trances) were initiated. The most controversial departure of *caboclo* worship from earlier cults was to allow men to become leaders. Those who did so were predominantly homosexual. According to anthropologist Ruth Landes, they came primarily from the lower classes and, more often than not, were of mixed blood. Most were devotees of Yansan, an African goddess, identified with St. Barbara and described as "the man-woman."

In the 1980s, Jim Wafer, a gay anthropologist, participated in Candomblé worship in Bahia. As he relates, gay Candomblé members are experts in a form of stylized verbal abuse called *baixa*. *Baixa* are typically uttered against an antagonist in public settings, but there is also a special, religious form that is delivered during relaxed moments at cult festivals. Many of the figures introduced in this book—the *hijra, galli,* and in some cases North American two-spirits—are credited with the power to utter fearful curses against those who offend them. In the argot of North American gay camp, we call this *reading the beads*, giving someone a good tongue-lashing. But we have few examples of such curses uttered by queens with recognized spiritual powers.

The following are two *baixa* recorded by Wafer. The first is typical of the curses uttered by drag queens and transvestite prostitutes in the streets of Bahia; the second was uttered in jest at a Candomblé religious festival. The comments in parentheses are Wafer's.

➤ ➤ ➤

What nonsense is this? So you want to bad-mouth me, eh? Who are you, by chance?—strap of my bra, hem of my pants, carpet of the office, street where the whores walk in

Maciel, bottomless chamber pot, pillow where I lie down
with my man, remains of my man's sperm, used rag of my
menstruation!

Who are you? Do you want to bad-mouth me, eh? Do you
want to get into a fight? I don't even know who you are—
door for knocking, gate for receiving (clients in a brothel),
abī (uninitiated person) without pot (vessel used to hold
water during initiation), dancer (in the circular dance of
Candomblé rituals) without father or mother (-of-saint), *iaô*
daughter-of-saint) shaved by *iaô* (a daughter-of-saint's head
must be shaved by a father- or mother-of-saint, not by a fellow daughter), *exua* badly "seated" at the back of my house
(the *exus* should be "seated" at the front of a house)!

TEXT Jim Wafer, *The Taste of Blood: Spirit Possession in Brazilian Candomblé* (Philadelphia: University of Pennsylvania Press, 1991), pp. 36–37.
OTHER SOURCES Ruth Landes, "A Cult Matriarchate and Male Homosexuality," *Journal of Abnormal and Social Psychology* 36, no. 3 (1940):
386–97; Peter Fry, "Male Homosexuality and Spirit Possession in Brazil,"
in *The Many Faces of Homosexuality*, ed. Evelyn Blackwood (New York:
Harrington Park, 1986), pp. 137–53; Seth Leacock and Ruth Leacock,
Spirits of the Deep: A Study of an Afro-Brazilian Cult (New York: Doubleday
Natural History, 1972).

S   P   I   R   I   T   S

A
Different
World

Whereas the previous selection provided an example of gay talking, the passage that follows illustrates a complementary talent that gay men often have—that of listening. The indomitable Quentin Crisp, one of the great observers of gay men's ways, describes this skill in his autobiography, *The Naked Civil Servant*.

➤ ➤ ➤

Homosexuals have time for everybody. This is not only an instance of the known law that all outsiders are polite to insiders because at best they secretly revere them or at worst fear that they may one day need them. Homosexuals are sincerely interested. They will sit for hours on stairs while chars complain about their rheumatism; they will stand at street corners while postmen rage against the handwriting of correspondents; they will pay extra fares to hear conductors rail against their wives. Every detail of the lives of real people, however mundane it may be, seems romantic to them. Romance is that enchantment that distance lends to things, and homosexuals are in a different world from the "dead normals" with many light years dark between. If by some chance an hour of pointless gossip makes fleeting reference to some foible, some odd superstition, some illogical preference that they find they share with the speaker, homosexuals are as amazed and delighted as an Earthman would be on learning that Martians cook by gas.

TEXT Quentin Crisp, *The Naked Civil Servant* (New York: Holt, Rinehart & Winston), 1977.

Auld

Scratty'll

Git Thi

Gods who play tricks, who don't really act like gods at all, crop up in myths and tales from every part of the world—as poltergeists and hobgoblins, in the form of the Greek god Hermes and figures like Pinocchio, and as animals such as the raven or the hare and insects such as spiders. Perhaps the most well-known trickster figure is Coyote, the ubiquitous antihero of countless Native American folktales. Both gullible and curious—a dangerous combination—Coyote is always getting into trouble or causing problems for others, although in some tribes he is credited with powers that include the creation of the world. The typical Coyote story portrays him as the victim of his impulses, especially for food and sex, with an infant's fascination with bodily processes, especially defecating and urinating. Coyote displays a casual disregard for his own body, giving away his eyes in a bet or storing his penis and testicles, in the wrong order, in a box. Typical of tricksters, Coyote has the power to transform himself into other animals and humans. If he wants to pass as a woman, he makes a vagina out of an elk's liver or a gourd—and this never fails to fool his unwitting victims.

Jung attributed great importance to the trickster figure: "In picaresque tales, in carnivals and revels, in sacred and magical rites, in man's religious fears and exaltations, this phantom of the trickster haunts the mythology of all ages, sometimes in quite unmistakable form, sometimes in strangely modulated guise. He is obviously a 'psychologem,' an archetypal psychic structure of extreme antiquity. In his

clearest manifestations he is a faithful copy of an absolutely undifferentiated human consciousness, corresponding to a psyche that has
hardly left the animal level."

This in part accounts for the often childish and slow-witted character of many tricksters. When figures like this appear in our dreams,
they often represent what Jung termed the *shadow*, a projection of
repressed aspects of one's own personality (in my own dreams, this
role is often played by my dog, now deceased, or by anonymous "home-
less" people). Jung goes on to argue, however, that the trickster is the
forerunner of the savior figure, a being that is god, human, and animal
all at the same time. "He is both subhuman and superhuman, a bestial
and divine being, whose chief and most alarming characteristic is his
unconsciousness." In fact, he is so unaware of himself that he has no
sense of his body as a unity, hence his propensity to give away or
detach his bodily parts. This aspect of the trickster figure echoes the
experience of shamans, who are dissected or torn asunder in the
course of their spirit journeys.

The ability to change gender is a common trait of tricksters. Rather
than claim all tricksters as "gay," however—since most are pansexual,
having sex not only with males and females but even animals, trees,
and stones—I would say that two-spirit figures are sometimes tricksters and that tricksters are sometimes a little queer.

What are the traits of the Queer Trickster? I think of Andy, whom I
first met when he was roommates with my friend Prissy after Prissy's
move to San Francisco. Not yet twenty-one, Andy was a streetwise gay
hustler who had spent most of his life in foster homes or on the meat
rack of San Francisco's Polk Street. It was the late 1970s, and the ideal
was to avoid having to get a regular job. (Andy, in any case, had few
real job skills and, as I gradually realized, couldn't read or write.)

Getting on "crazy welfare"—social security payments for those declared mentally disabled—was one way to do this. All you had to do was convince a psychiatrist that you were crazy, and, given the gender-bending fashions of the 1970s and the willingness of shrinks to see gay people as mentally ill, it wasn't hard. Alternatively, you could support yourself in the "underground economy," selling drugs, for example. Andy did both. He got on crazy welfare by dating his psychiatrist, and he sold Quaaludes on the streets and in the bars.

(Quaaludes were the favored drug of the 1970s. Intended to sedate, they produced a kind of peppy but relaxed and very horny state when taken in combination with alcohol. There's a story that when the president of the Bay Area Physicians for Human Rights asked Harvey Milk, San Francisco's first gay supervisor, what his group could do for the gay community, Harvey replied, "Prescribe more Quaaludes.")

The Queer Trickster is unpredictable, undependable, rebellious, impulsive, charmingly and irritatingly adolescent, catalytic, and charismatic. Two-spirit drag is only one of the forms and shapes he can assume—he can cross class lines, race lines, and national borders and on occasion convince you that he's heterosexual. To me, coming from an inhibited, small-town, middle-class background, Andy was all these things, everything I was not. He was the one who could show me how to unleash the queen, my true gay spirit; he could teach me to be spontaneous and free. And so, for several months, I spent my weekends following him around on his adventures in the streets of San Francisco. The Queer Trickster taught me many lessons about moving through the layers of the urban landscape, about being honest when it came to my feelings and desires, and about confronting my fear of being judged by gays and nongays alike. I often wonder now if I gave back as much as I got because in the end Andy was unable to get past the impulsiveness of the trickster. No sooner did he seem to stabilize his life than some form of self-destructive behavior caused everything to blow up in his face. He died of an overdose of pills (or a suicide—we never knew) in 1981.

The next three selections provide examples of the Queer Trickster and his powers.

Old Scrat was the English version of a pre-Christian trickster known throughout Germanic Europe. According to Jacob Grimm, the *scrat* or *schrat* was "a wild, rough, shaggy wood-sprite, very like the Latin faun and the Greek satyr, also the Roman *silvanus*." Elsewhere Grimm described the *scrat* as "a frolicking, dancing, whimsical homesprite, rough and hairy to look at . . . rigged out in the *red little cap* of a dwarf, loving to follow his bent in kitchens and cellars." *Scrat* and *schretlin* were worshiped with offerings as late as the sixth and seventh centuries. They may have been portrayed with masks. According to Grimm, certain trees and temples were dedicated to them.

Various European folk sayings referred to these figures. If a baby's nipple became inflamed, for example, it was said that "the *schrättli* have sucked it dry." Other sayings refer to *schrätel* who weigh on sleepers, like the incubus and succubus demons who were believed to have sex with sleeping women and men, respectively. In southern Austria, *scrat* were said to be visible in the play of sunbeams on walls, in blue flickers, or as a red face appearing in a cellar window—all of which reminds me of the Navajo god Begochídíín, who appears in a later selection.

Sadly (and typically), we know almost nothing about the figure of Scrat at that ancient time when he was formally worshiped. Most of the surviving references come from the period of history in which the old pagan deities of Europe had been reduced to hobgoblins and bogey figures to scare children—or made into versions of the devil. Old dictionaries are often the only source of information. The following list, for example, shows that versions of the word *scrat* existed in many languages throughout Europe. The various meanings of these terms underscore the identification of Scrat as a queer trickster.

➤ ➤ ➤

GERMAN

scrat, scrato, scraz   "hairy shaggy elves," *pilosus* (Latin)
schrate, schraz, schrag   goblin, elf
waltschrate   satyr
schrättlin, schretlin   a spirit light as the wind and the size of
   a child, household spirits
schrata, schretel   butterfly

SLAVIC

screti, scretti (Old Bohemian)   *penates intimi et secretales*

SCANDINAVIAN

skratte, skratti, skrati (Old Norse)   evil spirit, goblin, monster
skratti (Old Icelandic)   wizard, goblin, monster
skratta (Swedish), *skratte* (Danish)   to laugh loudly
scratt (Swedish)   fool, jester

ENGLISH

scritta, skratt   hermaphrodite
scratte, scrate, skrat   a hermaphrodite; hermaphroditism; a goblin,
   monster

scrat, skratt (Scotch) a puny, stunted, or shrunken person

Old Scrat, Scratch (Scotch and English dialect), *Scrat* (English dialect),
  Scrat-Harry (dialect), *Scraty, scratti* (English dialect) a name for
  the devil, "Be a good bairn or Scrat'll be sewer to cum for thee," "Go
  to the old Scratch" (1777); a hobgoblin or bogey, "By goy! but auld
  Scratty'll git thi if thoo doesn't come in"; a hermaphrodite

scarth (from scrat) an abortion, monster; a hermaphrodite, "full of
  rebaldrie" (1508)

➤ ➤ ➤

In his 1786 treatise on Priapus, Richard Payne Knight provides a brief
account of Scrat, linking him to the ancient phallic deity worshiped by
the Greeks and Romans.

➤ ➤ ➤

There were personages connected with the worship of Priapus who appear to have been common to the Romans under
and before the empire, and to the foreign races who settled
upon its ruins. The Teutonic race believed in a spiritual
being who inhabited the woods, and who was called in old
German *scrat*. His character was more general than that of
a mere habitant of the woods, for it answered to the English
hobgoblin, or to the Irish cluricaune. The scrat was the
spirit of the woods, under which character he was sometimes called a *waltscrat*, and of the fields, and also of the
household, the domestic spirit, the ghost haunting the
house. His image was probably looked upon as an amulet, a
protection to the house, as an old German vocabulary of the
year 1482, explains *schraetlin*, little scrats, by the Latin word

penates. The lascivious character of this Spirit, if it wanted more direct evidence, is implied by the fact that *scritta*, in Anglo-Saxon, and *scrat*, in old English, meant a hermaphrodite. Accordingly, the mediaeval vocabularies explain *scrat* by Latin equivalents, which all indicate companions or emanations of Priapus, and in fact, Priapus himself.

TEXT Richard P. Knight, *A Discourse on the Worship of Priapus* (Secaucus, N.J.: University Books, 1974), pp. 151–52.

OTHER SOURCES C. G. Jung in Raul Radin, *The Trickster: A Study in American Indian Mythology* (New York: Schocken, 1972), pp. 200, 203; Jacob Grimm, *Teutonic Mythology*, trans. James S. Stallybrass (New York: Dover, 1966), 2:478–81, 4:1424; "Schrat," *Handwörterbuch des Deutschen Aberglaubens* (Berlin: de Gruyter, 1935/1936), vol. 7; *Oxford English Dictionary*; B. Kirkby, *Lakeland Words: A Collection of Dialect Words and Phrases* . . . (East Ardsley/New York: EP Publishing and British Book Centre, 1975); Francis H. Stratmann, *A Middle-English Dictionary* (Oxford: Clarendon, 1891); William Grant and David D. Murison, eds., *The Scottish National Dictionary* (Edinburgh: Scottish National Dictionary Association, 1971); Samuel Johnson, *A Dictionary of the English Language* . . . (London: W. Strahan, 1775); Robert E. Lewis, ed., *Middle English Dictionary* (Ann Arbor: University of Michigan Press, 1986); Joseph Wright, ed., *The English Dialect Dictionary* (Oxford: Henry Frowde, 1905); Arthur R. Borden, Jr., *A Comprehensive Old-English Dictionary* (Washington, D.C.: University Press of America, 1982); Richard Bernheimer, *Wild Men in the Middle Ages: A Study in Art, Sentiment, and Demonology* (Cambridge, Mass.: Harvard University Press, 1952).

S   P   I   R   I   T   S

Why Lizard's Head

Is Always Moving

Up and Down

The following story was told by Ojong Itaroga, a man of the Ekoi (or Yakö) people of southern Nigeria and recorded by P. Amaury Talbot. It offers an interesting combination of gay-related themes—including elements of the Twins, the Queer Trickster, and the Two-Spirit.

Two sons of Tortoise (Ared and Affion) borrow female sexual parts from Lizard to play a trick on the god Obassi Nsi. But the tortoise boys decide that they like Lizard's parts and don't want to give them back. Typical of tribal folktales, the story concludes with a moral explaining a relatively trivial aspect of lizard behavior—but the foibles and weaknesses of human personality are the story's real focus.

The god, Obassi Nsi, is also interesting. Talbot recorded a conversation that he had with an Ekoi man concerning this figure. Obassi Nsi is the earth deity—although in most cultures the earth is considered female. His counterpart is Obassi Osaw, the sky god, also male. Talbot's informant explains that the two gods are friends: "They talk together and eat together. I think that Obassi Nsi is really our mother and Osaw our father. For whenever we make offerings we are taught to say Nta Obassi (Lord Obassi) and Ma Obassi (Lady Obassi). Now I think that the lord is Osaw, and the lady Nsi. Surely Nsi must be a woman, and our mother, for it is well known to all people that a woman has the tenderest heart."

➤ ➤ ➤

In the old days, when all the beasts could speak like men, Obassi Nsi married many wives. These were the daughters of nearly all animals on earth, and each creature who gave his daughter in marriage to Obassi received a very rich gift in exchange.

Now Tortoise also wanted a gift like the rest, but he had only sons and no daughter. He took a long time to think over the matter; at length he made a plan. He called two of his sons and told them that he was about to give them to Obassi as wives, so they must take care never to let anyone see their nakedness. After warning them in this way, he dressed them in very rich robes, like girls, and they set forth.

When Tortoise and his two seeming daughters reached the hall where Obassi was sitting, he stood forth and said:

"I am the best of all your friends, for the rest have given you each a wife, but I alone bring two."

Obassi thanked him, and gave him in return twice as great riches as he had given to the others. "Lord," said Tortoise, "there is one thing which I must tell you. No one must see my daughters' nakedness, else they will die."

"What a thing to say!" answered Obassi; "since you have told me this, there is no danger of such a thing."

On this Tortoise went away, rejoicing in his success, while Obassi handed over the two new wives to his head wife that she might look after them, never thinking that they were boys.

Not long after, their mistress found out the true state of the case. She went secretly to Obassi and told him that the two girls whom Tortoise had given him in marriage possessed the masculine nakedness.

Obassi questioned the woman very earnestly if she meant

what she said, and when she assured him that it was true, he replied quietly:

"Do not speak of this any more, lest the two Tortoises should overhear and flee away to their father."

Obassi fixed a day on which to make known to all the trick which had been played upon him. He sent around to his fathers-in-law to tell them that he was about to give a great show, and that he expected all those who were invited to be present and in good time. By this invitation he meant to have Tortoise punished, and perhaps even killed, for his deceit.

The two sons of Tortoise suspected what was going on, so they sent for Lizard, and from her they borrowed the feminine nakedness. When, therefore, the day came round, and Obassi went very early in the morning to ascertain the fact that his two young wives were boys, he found them girls after all.

The guests came in great multitudes and sat down in companies, eager to see the wonders which Obassi had promised. The latter was very angry, and began scolding his head wife for lying to him, not knowing that all she had said was true. Then he went to the audience hall, and simply told the people that there would be no show, for his wife had disappointed him. So all departed with much discontent.

Three days later Lizard went to the boys to ask for the parts she had lent them, but they only asked her to take a seat and eat a few balls of fu-fu. Later they begged her to come again in a few days' time, when they would do as she asked.

Over and over again Lizard came, but each day she was

put off in the same manner. At length one day she began to sing loudly, and her song was as follows:

Ared Tortoise, give me secret parts mine.
Affion Tortoise, give me secret parts mine.
I die, I die, for secret parts mine.
Also, if I live life, I live for secret parts mine.

The people in the compound heard the singing, and ran to see who it was who could make such a song. Tortoise boys (now girls) begged Lizard to take a seat once more and eat a few fu-fu balls as usual. She sat down and began eating. One of them then said, "Let us each make fu-fu balls for the others to swallow," and all agreed to the fun. One of our well-known two then rolled a fine ball and secretly put some pricking fish-bones within it, dipped it in the soup-pot, and put it in poor Lizard's mouth. The latter tried to swallow it, but it stuck in her throat, where the pin-like bones held it fast. Lizard lay on the ground voicelessly stretching her neck, and trying in vain to swallow the ball or eject it.

This is the cause why Lizards are seen to raise and let fall their heads. They are still trying to get rid of the fu-fu ball given them by the sons of Tortoise.

That is the reason why Tortoise's trick has never been discovered up to this day, and thus it is that Lizard lost her voice and her "Ndipp" [secret parts], and only gained in exchange the habit of lifting her head up and down.

TEXT P. Amaury Talbot, *In the Shadow of the Bush* (London: William Heinemann, 1912), pp. 17, 378–80.

S   P   I   R   I   T   S

Son

of the Sun

(Begochídíín)

The Navajo Indians who today live in Arizona and New Mexico were originally a people of the far north, from Alaska and Canada. At some unknown time in prehistory, they began migrating southward, and sometime between 1000 and 1400 C. E. they arrived in the Southwest. Here they found the Anasazi people living in pueblos and tending farms. Although the Navajos adopted a great deal from the religion and culture of the Anasazi, one of the gods they brought with them was Begochídíín. In his oldest form, Begochídíín (spelled here Be'gochí and Begochiddy) was a trickster who had power over game animals and was, therefore, the patron of hunters.

Here is how one Navajo described him:

➤ ➤ ➤

Be'gochí was the son of the sun. The sun committed adultery with everything in the world. That was how so many monsters were born. After this, the sun was put a way off so that this could not happen again. But as the sun came up he touched a flower which became pregnant and gave birth to be'gochidí. He was the youngest son of the sun, and the sun spoiled him. He was put in control of many things, such as game and domestic animals. He was a berdache and the first pottery-maker.

He could also move about invisibly and change into different forms at will: a rainbow, wind, sand, water, etc. He was named be'gochidí because he would make himself invisible and sneak up on young girls to touch their breasts, shouting "be'go be'go" (breast). He especially annoyed men who were hunting. When a hunter had taken his aim and was ready to shoot, be'gochidí would sneak up behind him, grab his testicles, and shout "be'go." This spoiled the hunter's aim every time. The worst was when a man and woman lay down to have intercourse. He was always touching one or the other and shouting "be'go."

➤   ➤   ➤

Before their arrival in the Southwest, the Navajos were primarily hunters and gatherers. When they began to shift to agriculture and herding, Begochídíín's character changed as well. He was credited with the creation of domestic as well as game animals and with being the source of the first seeds. He was said to be the inventor of pottery and the first two-spirit.

One of the most interesting aspects of Begochídíín is his relationship to his father, the sun. So often, gay-related gods lack fathers and fall outside the usual kinship system. Navajo society is matrilineal, however. Sons do not inherit their name or property from their fathers, for these are passed through the mother to her daughters. As a result, the father-son relationship in matrilineal societies has a different tenor. It is not so fraught with the repressed fears of the father that his son will replace him and the resentment of the son toward the father because of his power over him. Thus, Begochídíín's most significant parent is his father, a distinctly nonpatriarchal father who indulges his youngest son and seems indifferent to his third-gender nature. In the traditional psychoanalytic model, these traits—overprotectiveness and indulgence—are usually attributed to the mothers of homosexuals.

Begochídíín evolved into a complex figure. Having been born from sunlight, he was usually invisible, but he could appear at any time and take many forms. He was the source of a medicine made from flowers, and his home was sweet smelling. He had power over wind and insects. Various accounts describe him as an old man, or as a boy who turns into a man, or as alternating between old and young—much as the term *nádleehé*, or "the one who constantly changes," suggests.

In the 1920s and 1930s, the Navajo *nádleehé* Hastíín Klah worked with the wealthy patron of Navajo religion and arts Mary Cabot Wheelwright to record his extensive knowledge of Navajo myths, prayers, and songs. In Klah's version of the Navajo origin myth, Begochídíín plays a central role as a creator god and a culture bearer, while his earlier traits as a trickster god are missing. When the goddess Changing Woman travels to her home in the Pacific Ocean, she is greeted by Begochídíín. According to Klah, "His hair was shining and little rays of light shone and sparkled from him." Elsewhere, Klah described him as fair skinned, with yellow hair and blue eyes (which are female colors in Navajo symbolism), and dressed like a woman. In other words, Begochídíín bridges not just gender but *all* forms of social difference—including those of race.

The following story comes from the myth of the Hail Chant ceremony, transcribed by Mary Wheelwright. Hastíín Klah was the last Navajo medicine man who knew how to perform this ceremony, which was concerned with control of the elements—hail, lightning, and wind, in particular. The passage begins at a point when the people of the god Black Thunder have just made peace with the people of White Thunder after fighting a war. The Black Thunder people decide to make a journey to the home of White Thunder. Along the way they encounter Begochídíín disguised as a boy who turns into an insect. When they attempt to touch the insect, it unleashes swarms of stinging insects—a dramatic image of the return of the repressed. In this case, the people are unable to recognize the god in his malignant form. By offering him the proper prayer stick, they signify their recognition of this unconscious aspect of Begochídíín and, therefore, of their own unconscious. At the end of the myth, this trickster figure becomes a transcendental savior who lives in the sky and watches over his people.

➤ ➤ ➤

When the Black Thunder people came to Standing Rock, the leader of the Black Thunder people looked back at the long line of his people, and far off in the distance he saw a boy throwing dust and dirt high into the air. Black Thunder went on again and then a little later stopped once more and looked back, and again saw the boy throwing dust and dirt into the air. This happened four times and the leaders wondered what it meant. Finally they stopped and talked it over and at last, becoming very curious, they decided to send someone back to see what the boy was doing, so Black Thunder told some people to run back and find out, and when they arrived at the place where the boy had last been seen, they could find nothing there but a yellow worm about three inches long.

The people all crowded together to look at it, and as nothing else was to be seen there they said it must be the boy. [When Hastíín Klah narrated this myth to Gladys Reichard, he omitted a part at this point because it was "too dirty" to tell to a woman.]

The leader told one of the men to pick up the worm, and as he reached down the worm leaped high in the air, as high as the men standing about. They were frightened at this and stepped back, and the worm jumped again and again until it had jumped four times, and at the fourth jump it turned into a man, and quantities of bees poured out of his mouth and lighted on all the people, getting into their hair, eyes, and ears, and stinging and frightening them badly. They begged the man to stop sending these bees to torment them, but he did nothing but laugh and laugh, and sent forth more bees in swarms until the people were in great agony.

At last they gave the man a Yellow Kehtahn [prayer stick] and he drew in his breath and sucked all the bees back into his mouth. This was the first time that any of the people had seen bees, and there were all kinds, honeybees, hornets, and bumblebees, and every kind of bee, big and little.

Then they saw that the man was Begochiddy, and were greatly amazed. The Kehtahn which they gave him was filled with tobacco and the end stuffed with sacred pollen, and this has been Begochiddy's Kehtahn ever since. Begochiddy told the people that he would go with them and watch over them, and the people were glad and went on their way, when suddenly Begochiddy disappeared from their midst and they did not see him go, so they knew that he had gone up into the sky.

TEXTS Willard W. Hill, *The Agricultural and Hunting Methods of the Navaho Indians*, Yale University Publications in Anthropology 18 (New Haven, Conn.: Yale University Press, 1938), p. 99; Hasteen Klah, "N'Dlohe, or Hail Chant," in *Hail Chant and Water Chant*, ed. Mary C. Wheelwright, Navajo Religion Series, vol. 2 (Santa Fe: Museum of Navajo Ceremonial Art, 1946), pp. 15–16.

OTHER SOURCES Hasteen Klah, *Navajo Creation Myth: The Story of the Emergence*, comp. Mary C. Wheelwright, Navajo Religion Series, vol. 1 (Santa Fe: Museum of Navajo Ceremonial Art, 1942); Gladys A. Reichard, *The Story of the Navajo Hail Chant* (New York: Gladys A. Reichard, 1944).

S   P   I   R   I   T   S

A

Vast

Hermaphrodite

For the mystical English poet William Blake, the vision of the hermaphrodite was a terrifying one. In his writings, the man-woman represents chaos, a lack of differentiation that is the opposite of creation and life. This is a fair metaphor for the negative side of the Two-Spirit archetype, the danger of allowing the "queen" within to take over completely. Such total identification with an archetype invariably leads to inflation of the ego, arrogance, self-centeredness, and power trips.

The following passage comes from *Vala or the Four Zoas*, completed in 1804. It deals with the four powers or faculties that Blake believed existed within each person (also the four mighty creatures who stand around the throne of God and the principle of fourfoldness in general). In the poem, these powers are at war with each other. Urizen, one of the Four Zoas, stands for the power of abstract reasoning, law, and materialism.

➤ ➤ ➤

> Terrified & astonish'd, Urizen beheld the battle take a
>   form
> Which he intended not: a Shadowy hermaphrodite, black
>   & opake;
> The soldiers nam'd it Satan, but he was yet unform'd &
>   vast.

Hermaphroditic it at length became, hiding the Male
Within as in a Tabernacle, Abominable, Deadly.
. . . .

The war roar'd round Jerusalem's Gates; it took a hideous
   form
Seen in the aggregate, a Vast Hermaphroditic form
Heav'd like an Earthquake lab'ring with convulsive groans
Intolerable; at length an awful wonder burst
From the Hermaphroditic bosom. Satan he was nam'd,
Son of Perdition, terrible his form, dishumaniz'd,
   monstrous,
A male without a female counterpart, a howling fiend
Forlorn of Eden & repugnant to the forms of life,
Yet hiding the shadowy female Vala as in an ark &
   Curtains,
Abhorr'd, accursed, ever dying an Eternal death,
Being multitudes of tyrant Men in union blasphemous
Against the Divine image, Congregated assemblies of
   wicked men.

TEXT William Blake, *Vala or the Four Zoas*, 8.102–6, 8.247–58.

The

Divine

Twins

Oh, I knew that all the other kids around me were thinking of girls as sex objects, *to be manipulated—to be lied to in order to get them to "give in"—and to be otherwise treated with contempt (when the boys were together without them). And, strangely, the girls seemed to think of the boys as objects, too. But that was it! Writing in 1976, I was remembering vividly how, in that long-ago fantasy, he whom I would reach out in love to was indeed projected as being another me—*and the one thing we would not be doing *was making objects of each other. Just as in my dream (which I would go on having for years), he'd be standing just before dawn on a golden velvet hillside . . . he'd hold out his hand for me to catch hold of, and then we would run away to the top of the hill to see the sunrise, and we would never have to come back again because we would now have each other. We would share everything, and we'd always understand each other completely and forever!*

Harry Hay, "A Separate People Whose Time Has Come"

Harry Hay's description of subject-SUBJECT love as the ideal of our boyhood fantasies was like the Pied Piper's flute to me when I first heard it at a gay men's spiritual gathering in 1979. Years of adolescent insecurity—and all those books by psychiatrists and psychologists, those truly dirty books, that were the only writings on homosexuality that my hometown library allowed me to see—had tarnished the dream of my childhood, the dream of finding another boy just like me, who shared all my interests and, indeed, my every feeling and thought. One other boy would be all that it took to create a safe harbor, a space in which to breathe and grow. That dream had kept me going through some lonely, scary times.

What Harry helped me realize is that this fantasy of an equal relationship with another boy contains within it a complete set of values and ideals—for equality and mutuality in relationships, for respect toward the inherent dignity of others, for self-determination and individual freedom, and more. All the values that would later attract me to progressive politics and social change were already there within my fantasies of being with a boy just like me.

Harry's ideas concerning subject-SUBJECT consciousness and Mitch Walker's exploration of the psychological dynamics of "magickal twinning" have led me to pay close attention to myths involving twin figures. These myths do not always indicate the sexuality of the figures involved, and it would be anachronistic simply to label them *gay*, with our present sense of that term. But these stories do speak to anyone who has been involved in an intense same-sex relationship, and today most of us who have had these experiences are gay. Even so, nongay men sometimes form intense relationships with each other, and I think that myths like those of Gilgamesh and Enkidu and of Baldr and Loki have something to offer them as well.

We can relate to the myths of Divine Twins in various ways. For some, the Twins can be a source of images for a social identity, much as the Two-Spirit archetype is reflected in third-gender roles. One doesn't have to be in a "twin" relationship to relate to the images and stories of this archetype. You might see yourself in the controlling Gilgamesh or the wild, unruly Enkidu; in the proverbial good boy Baldr or in the trouble-making trickster Loki. Similarly, in the powers associated with these Divine Twins, you might see a reflection of your own particular skills and contributions.

As these stories reveal, gay love unleashes powerful creative forces, no less than the gender-bending magic of the Two-Spirit. The Divine Twins are often culture bearers, associated with healing, law, poetry, and the slaying of monsters—like the Greeks Eurybatus, who slew a monster to save his beloved Alcyoneus, and Harmodius and Aristogiton, who together slew the tyrant Hippias. What unleashes their powers, what enables them to invent their arts, is that the Twins *heal each other*. Today our opponents demand to know, What are gay people good for? Well, first and foremost, we are good for each other. We heal and restore each other through sex, humor, and devoted friendship. This, in turn, unleashes our powers to create. When these creative projects are shared with a partner—whether through something as mundane as decorating a home or as noble as fighting together for social justice—our bonds grow even deeper. In fact, there is a clue here to the secret of long-term gay relationships—the need for shared, creative interests above and beyond sexual attraction, a third thing, forged together, that then calls on the couple to be a couple, even when they might feel otherwise.

So, when heterosexuals ask why they should grant us our privacy and the freedom to satisfy our emotional and sexual needs without interference, our answer is that meeting these needs is what enables us to make the social contributions that everyone benefits from, whether through our careers, our creative projects, our volunteer service, or our relationships with families and nongay friends—every time we share the insights gained by leading a life off the beaten path.

Heterosexuals often have a hard time understanding how relationships between two men or two women could have any value since they can't, on their own, produce children. If society privileges heterosexual relationships, it's because society benefits from the production of children. Who benefits from a gay relationship? These myths are a direct answer to this question: gay relationships release creative cultural and social energies that are just as valuable as the bodies of children. Yet another heterosexual presumption is that the male-female model of bonding—of two complementary halves making a whole—is the only way of forming a mature, adult relationship. Again, these myths answer with images of men, already aware of masculine and feminine within them, forming relationships based on supplementing, enhancing, and amplifying, rather than complementing or completing, each other.

The dynamics of the Divine Twins often come into play at that point in our lives when we begin to explore relationships. The subject-SUBJECT ideal expressed by Harry Hay is widely sought by gay men. Even queens, leather daddies, and bottoms want their relationships to be based on mutual attraction and consensual decision making! This reflects an important historical change in the area of human relationships. In the past century, in Western societies and many other parts of the world, age-old customs of arranged marriages have given way to the ideal of freely choosing one's partner on the basis of mutual attraction. (In fact, it may be that, because they were outlawed and therefore escaped these customs, gay relationships provided the model for more equal and romantic relationships.) This was a profound change for women in particular, who, before this, rarely enjoyed emotionally satisfying relationships with men. In terms of gay relationships, it means that, if the partners engage in role playing, if one acts "feminine" and does the housework and the other brings home the "bacon," they do so out of choice, not out of social pressure or custom. For this reason, I think that the psychological dynamics symbolized by the Divine Twins are important for most gay men today.

The following stories include both positive and negative examples of the archetypal Twins. In this sense, it's a misnomer to say that they are always "divine." The relationship of archetypal Twins, however, is always potent—whether the ill-fated, ultimately destructive bond between Baldr and Loki or the competitive but ultimately positive relationship of Gilgamesh and Enkidu. The chapter concludes with poetic accounts of same-sex devotion from ancient Chinese literature and the Persian mystic Rūmī, in which love for the other who is a reflection of oneself becomes the basis for an elevated spiritual and ethical outlook.

SOURCE Harry Hay, "A Separate People Whose Time Has Come," in *Gay Spirit: Myth and Meaning*, ed. Mark Thompson (New York: St. Martin's, 1987), p. 286.

Becoming One

Instead of

Two

Of all the speeches in praise of Eros that appear in Plato's *Symposium*, or discourse on love, Aristophanes' is the most playful, if not outright fantastic. If you miss the humor at first, just try to picture the original humans as he describes them—they must have looked like inflated surgical gloves rolling about like tumbleweeds!

The joke is that, as Aristophanes points out, *androgyne* was a term of derision among the Greeks of his day—like calling a man a *sissy*. But, in the fable he relates, the Androgyne turns out to be the origin of heterosexual men and women, while homosexual men originate from an all-male double being. What is involved here is the secret male fear that contact with women somehow dilutes a man's masculinity, expressed here as gay male chauvinism. I read Aristophanes as saying, "You may claim that gay men are less masculine, but you straight men originate from and end in androgyny. When you are whole you are half-female." It's the kind of joke gay people like to tell about heterosexuals. You know, "How many heteros does it take to change a lightbulb?" Aristophanes' answer is three.

What this tale accounts for is specifically the origin of *sexual preference*. Although Aristophanes' story is clearly comic, it *presumes* that the three sexual preferences it describes—heterosexual, homosexual, and lesbian—make sense to the audience. What is fantastic about the tale is not the three forms of love but the way in which they originated. Although recent scholars have made a great deal of the fact that the classical Greeks had no word exactly equivalent to our *homosexual*, they certainly did seem to be aware that individuals had prevailing emotional/sexual orientations. All forms of same-sex love were viewed in terms of the pattern of *paederastia*, or love of youths by men, but notice that Aristophanes speaks of male couples "who spend their whole lives together." The notion of age difference becomes something of a formality when both partners are in their forties or fifties.

In fact, focusing as it does on the desire of lovers to become "one instead of two," Aristophanes' tale offers some extraordinary images of "magickal twinning." I think that it conveys especially that passion that characterizes the beginning of a relationship, when you can't seem to get close enough or spend enough time with your lover. At another level, this desire for union is an essentially spiritual yearning to erase all differences and distance, even the boundaries of the ego itself.

➤ ➤ ➤

"Indeed, Eryximachus," said Aristophanes, "it is my intention to speak in a different vein from you and Pausanias. Men have never understood the power of Eros. If they did understand, they would have built splendid temples and altars, and honored him with sacrifices, but this is not done, although it should be done. Of all the gods, he is the most human friendly. He cures those ills of men that are the greatest obstacle to the happiness of the human race.

"I will try to explain his power to you, so that you can share this teaching with the rest of the world. You must begin with the nature of man and his misfortunes. Our original form was not like the present, but otherwise. First there were three kinds of humans, instead of two; man and woman, and a third, a combination of the other two, whose name survives but not the thing itself. The Androgyne was then in form and name a unity, of both kinds, sharing in male and female equally, although now the term is only a put-down.

"Second, each human was round, his back and sides forming a circle. Each had four hands and legs, and one head with two faces looking opposite ways set on a round neck. There were four ears, two sets of genitals, and all the other parts to go along. He could walk upright as now, in either direction, as he pleased. When he started running fast, he rolled over and over like an acrobat, whirling around with arms and legs sticking out, only there were eight limbs to speed him around and around.

"There were these three kinds because the male was originally born from the Sun, the female from the Earth, and the one partaking of both from the Moon, because the Moon also partakes of both. They were round in shape as in their way of walking, taking after their parents. Their energy was great, and their thoughts were so grand that they even conspired against the gods, and the story was told of them that Homer told of Ephialtes and Otus, who attempted to mount heaven and lay hands on the gods.

"Zeus and the other gods debated what to do. They could not slay them like the Giants, whom they had struck with thunderbolts—it would only serve to eliminate the honors and offerings that men gave them—still they could not allow such licentious behavior.

"Then Zeus, gathering his thoughts, spoke, saying, 'I

have a plan that, without doing away with them entirely, will end the licentiousness of men by lessening their strength. I propose to cut each one into two. At the same time that we make them weaker, they will become more useful by their multiplication. And they will walk upright on two legs. If they continue acting licentiously, I will do it again,' he said. 'I will slice them in two and then they will have to go hopping on one leg.'

"So saying, he sliced each person into two, just like an apple cut in half for pickling, or an egg cut with a hair. And as he cut them, he asked Apollo to turn the face and half neck to the side, so that they might see the work of the knife and be more orderly as a result, and then to heal them up. Apollo turned their faces around and pulled their skin together over what we call the stomach, just like a purse with a drawstring, and he tied this mouth at the center in a knot, making what we know as the navel. He smoothed away the wrinkles and formed the breast, like a shoemaker smoothes leather. He left a few around the area of the belly and the navel, however, as a vestige of the original state.

"Now when this form had been cut in two, each half, yearning to embrace its other, would throw its arms around the other and entwine together, wishing to grow together, refusing to eat until they began to die of hunger and laziness, but refusing to do anything apart. Whenever one of them died and left the other half alone, it went seeking to embrace any half of the whole woman, which now we call a woman, or man it came across. In this way they were dying off.

S   P   I   R   I   T   S

"Zeus, taking pity, offered a new plan. He moved their genitals to the front. Until then they had been on the outside, like everything else, and they did their begetting and bearing not with one another but on the earth, like crickets. These parts he now shifted to the front, to be used for reproducing with each other, by the male in the female, so that if in their entwinings a man should come upon a woman there would be conception and an engendering of their kind. And also if male met with male there would be satisfaction at least engendered from their union, so that they might return to their work and to everyday life.

"Thus love for one another is anciently implanted in mankind, seeking to bring together into one form the two and heal the nature of mankind. Each of us is thus only a half-token of a man, like a flat-fish showing the traces of having been cut in two, each one looking for the token that will fit him. All those men who are parts of that combined one that at first was called Androgyne are woman lovers [*philogunaikes*]. Adulterers, too, are mostly descended from that kind, as well as philandering women [*gunaikes philandroi*]. On the other hand, all the women who were parts of the woman are not at all drawn toward men, but turn toward women. The lesbian prostitutes [*hetairistriai*] are descended from this kind.

"Men who are parts of the man pursue the masculine, and, as long as they are boys, show that they are truly male by making friends with men and rejoice in lying together with them and being clasped in the embraces of men. These are the finest boys and youths for they have the most manly

natures. Some say that they are shameless, but falsely.
Their behavior is not due to shamelessness but to daring,
manliness, and virility, since they are eager to greet their
kind. Evidence of this is the fact that on growing up these
men alone become statesmen. On reaching the status of a
man, they are youth lovers [*paiderastousi*], and in their nature have no interest in wives or begetting children, and only
do these things under compulsion. They are happy to live on
with one another unmarried.

"In any case, a man of this sort is born to be a lover of
youths and fond of having lovers, eager to greet his own kind.
When one of them meets the other, whether a lover of youth
or a lover of another kind, they are marvelously stricken
with love and friendliness and desire, and cannot be separated from one another for even a little time. These are the
ones who spend their whole lives together, yet cannot say
what it is they desire of one another. No one could assume
that this is mere aphrodisia, that this alone could be the reason they rejoice in each other's company with so much zest.
Plainly the soul of each is wishing for something that it is
unable to say, only divining or suggesting and speaking in
riddles.

"Suppose that Hephaestus with his tools should come and
stand over them as they lay together and say, 'What do you
wish, O mortals, to bring forth from one another?' They
would be unable to explain. And if he asked them again, 'Do
you desire to be united into a single whole so that you will
not be deprived of each other by night or by day? If that is
what you desire, I am ready to fuse and weld you into one,

so that from two will come forth one, and for as long as you live, the two of you will share a single life, and when you die you will also be one in Hades by sharing a single death. I ask you, is this what you desire and would you be satisfied with this lot?' Not one man among them would deny or fail to acknowledge that this is what they wish for. Each would affirm that this is what he had been wishing for all along—to be joined and fused into one with his beloved, thus becoming one instead of two.

"The cause of all this is that our ancient form was as I have said, and we were whole. The craving and pursuit of wholeness is called Eros. . . . I say, and this applies to the whole world of men and women, that the way to bring happiness to our race is to fulfill our Eros and to find our own favorite and thereby return to our ancient form. If this is the best thing of all, the best acts we can choose are those that bring us closest to it—that is, to find a favorite who naturally suits our mind. If we would praise the god who makes possible this great boon, we must praise Eros; it is proper that we celebrate him. Not only does he supply great hope, if we worship the gods piously, he will return us to our ancient form and heal us and create for us the happiness of the blessed."

TEXT Plato, *Symposium* 189C–191D (my translation).

The Divine Twins

None Like Him

(Kepakailiula

and Kaunalewa)

Traditional Hawaiian culture recognized not only a gender-based form of homosexuality in the *mahu* role—emotional and sexual relationships between men who were not *mahu* were recognized as well. Both partners were referred to as *aikāne*, a term that is usually translated as "friend" but that is actually derived from *ai*, or "coition," and *kāne*, "male," and has also been translated as "sodomy" and "cohabitation." (Similarly, in the following text, the reference to the two heroes "living together" might be better translated by our euphemism "sleeping together.") Often, these relationships were between older and younger or higher- and lower-status men, but they also occurred between individuals of similar age and social status.

References to *aikāne* in the journals of the Cook expedition (1776–80) to Hawaii all attribute a sexual dimension to this status. As one diarist, John Ledyard, wrote:

> It is a disagreeable circumstance to the historian that truth obliges him to inform the world of a custom among them contrary to nature, and odious to a delicate mind . . . ; the custom alluded to is that of sodomy, which is very prevalent if not universal among the chiefs. . . . The cohabitation is between the chiefs and the most beautiful males they can procure about 17 years old. . . . These youths follow them wherever they go, and are as narrowly

> looked after as the women in those countries where
> jealousy is so predominant a passion; they are extremely
> fond of them, and by a shocking inversion of the laws of
> nature, they bestow all those affections upon them that
> were intended for the other sex.

Being an *aikāne* was still not quite the same as having a gay identity in today's terms. Many men in *aikāne* relationships were also married to women. Similarly, just because sexual relations *could* occur does not mean they always did. Nonetheless, they did provide an institutionalized outlet for homosexual desires for those so inclined, one that was highly idealized. According to an ancient Hawaiian proverb, an *aikāne* was like "a nest of fragrance."

The following story, collected by Abraham Fornander in the mid-nineteenth century, deals with a semilegendary Hawaiian hero named Kepakailiula, "one of the strongest of the sons of Hawaii." In his time, Kepakailiula became king of Hawaii, Maui, Oahu, and Kauai. Like other Hawaiian heroes, Kepakailiula formed both *aikāne* and heterosexual relationships. It was while living with his *aikāne*, however, that he performed some of his most famous feats. Like other Divine Twins, the bond of love between these two men releases powers of healing and leads to the slaying of a tyrant.

The story of Kepakailiula's birth is revealing. According to Hawaiian legend, he was hatched from an egg. Missing or obscure fathers are a common trait of the figures represented in this collection—Dekanawida, Enkidu, and Loki all lack one or more of the parents necessary for full participation in heterosexual kinship systems, and, as such, they are problematic. Typically, they are abandoned at birth and raised outside the dominant social order, or they are thrust out of the community when their unique natures become apparent.

Figures like Kepakailiula represent the emergence of formerly repressed possibilities. They are prodigies who stand for a different way of being. Many of them are described as literally shedding light. But their light—and this is key—is never the light of the sun, the father god. Rather, theirs is the light of the moon—a moon "which the sky ne'er saw," in the words of the poet Rūmī. Kepakailiula's light, for example, is compared to that of a volcano. Unlike the sun, however, his red glow can be seen both day and night.

Kepakailiula is raised by foster parents, a common Hawaiian practice, except that both these parents are men. Their names distinguish them on the basis not of gender but of relative activity—one stays at home, the other travels incessantly. Like other twinned figures in mythology, it takes the two of them together to make a complete personality. Later in the story, they are given a wife to share, but they still retain their identity as a couple. Their association with agriculture and husbandry makes them typical culture bearers.

Fornander collected two accounts of Kepakailiula. The first describes his birth and his male parents. The second relates his adventures as a young man.

➤ ➤ ➤

PLAYERS AND PLACES

Kepakailiula   "Born with red skin"
Ku   father of Kepakailiula
Hina   mother of Kepakailiula

S   P   I   R   I   T   S

Kiinoho "Ki'i staying," and *Kiihele*, "Ki'i going,"
 Kepakailiula's foster fathers
Makolea wife of Kepakailiula
Kaunalewa *aikāne* of Kepakailiula
Kaikipaananea king of Kauai
Kukaea "manure," servant of Kaikipaananea
Paliuli the Hawaiian paradise

Kepakailiula was born in Keaau, Puna, Hawaii, in the form originally of a chicken egg. His father was Ku and his mother was Hina. . . . Kiinoho and Kiihele were the brothers of Hina.

All Kiinoho did was to sit in one place and very seldom moved around; he was, however, a very great fortune teller and could predict coming events that happen in the very near future as well as events afar off. All that Kiihele did was to travel. He was a great runner and could make the circuit of Hawaii in one day, starting from home in the morning and arriving home before sunset of the same day. . . .

One night Kiinoho had a dream, wherein he was instructed by a spirit as follows: "You two must go to Paliuli and live there, you and Kiihele; you will find all your needs supplied without fatigue."

Kiinoho dreamed the same thing for three nights before he spoke of it to Kiihele. Kiihele was, however, very indifferent about the matter and did not believe in what Kiinoho told him. Shortly after this they both had the same dream repeated to them. At daylight they talked the matter over and decided that they must accept the invitation and go and live in Paliuli. They then made their preparations and procured certain things by the *lau* (four hundred), such as hogs, awa, fish, fowls, kapas and malos. That night they retired early and at the second crowing of the cock in the early dawn, while it was still dark, they got up and started for Paliuli without the knowledge of their sister or people.

It is said in this story that this was the first time that Paliuli was found by man, through the direction of the gods. Afterwards it was again taken away from man by the gods and it has been hidden ever since.

Upon their arrival at Paliuli, they looked and saw that it was a very good land, flat, fertile and well filled with many things desired by man; the ohias were as large as breadfruit; they saw a fish pond within the land stocked with all kinds of fish of the sea with the exception of the whale and the shark, so they made their home there. They began to cultivate the soil, raised different animals until the place was filled with everything imaginable. . . .

One day Kiihele said to Kiinoho: "How queer of us to care for all these things! Who is going to eat them?"

Kiinoho replied: "Our son Kepakailiula. Let us go and bring him here."

They then proceeded from Paliuli and went down to Keaau, where their sister Hina was living.

Before these two went to Paliuli, however, Hina showed signs of being with child. Upon their return she was almost ready to be confined. After greetings were exchanged and their weeping ended, Hina rose and went out to relieve her-self. As Hina rose to go out, Kiinoho requested Kiihele to go out, saying: "Go out and get the child."

Kiihele asked: "Where is it?" "At the place where Hina is sitting." When Kiihele came to the place he saw an egg lying on the ground. He took it up and wrapped it in a feather cape; and they returned to Paliuli, where Kiinoho exercised all his powers and at the expiration of ten days and nights he unwrapped the feather cape and saw the egg had formed into a beautiful child; after inspecting it they concluded there was none like him.

The child was again wrapped up in the feather cape and left for a period of forty nights before they again looked at it. When they did they saw that the child had grown more beautiful; no pimples, no deformities, straight back, open face; its skin and eyes were as red as the feather cape which enwrapped him. Thus did Kepakailiula become the fire that lighted up Paliuli by day and by night, whose only equal was Pele of Kilauea. Pele gave light from the crater of Kilauea, while Kepakailiula gave light from Paliuli, giving Puna and Hilo two red objects to view by day and by night. Kepakai-liula was therefore called "The first-born of the beloved one of Paliuli." Kepakailiula would not touch either ordinary food or meat; all he ate was bananas, one bunch for each meal. . . .

When Kepakailiula reached the age of twenty years, it was seen that he was very handsome and pleasant to look upon. He was without blemish; he was perfect from the soles of his feet to the crown of his head. Because of this

great beauty, Kiinoho sent Kiihele to travel around Hawaii
in search of a wife for Kepakailiula.

➤   ➤   ➤

After rejecting several possible spouses, Kiihele eventually finds Makolea, who is "without blemish and was so beautiful that she was like
the full moon." Unfortunately, Makolea is already engaged to the king
of Maui. Kepakailiula eventually kills the king and marries not only Makolea but also the daughter of another local king. Kepakailiula's repu-
tation spreads, and the king of Oahu, hoping to avoid conflict, sends
emissaries inviting him to take possession of his island. Kepakailiula
travels with his wives and his foster fathers, Kiinoho and Kiihele, and
their shared wife to Oahu, where he places the foster fathers in charge
of the island. One day, while surfing, Makolea is spotted by two servants of the king of Kauai, who are seeking a wife for him. They seize
her and take her to Kauai.

➤   ➤   ➤

Kepakailiula then set sail for Kauai, and on the morning of
the next day he reached Waimea. As soon as he landed he
took his canoe and broke it into pieces, then after this was
done he went to the first house he saw, where lived one of
the chiefs of Kauai, Kaunalewa by name, a very rich and
honored man. When Kaunalewa saw the goodly appearance
of Kepakailiula he called him, and when he arrived before
him he urged that they become friends, saying: "I want you
to become my friend [aikāne] and whatever you request of
me I will grant it."

After they had been living together for about three days,

the voices of the people and the king were heard shouting and yelling. Kepakailiula therefore asked his friend Kaunalewa: "What is this shouting up above here?"

Kaunalewa replied: "It is our King Kaikipaananea playing honuhonu [a wrestling game], also wrestling, boxing and such other games. Some one must have been thrown, hence the shouting."

Kepakailiula then said: "Can't the place be visited?"

The friend answered: "And why not?"

They then went up to the place and to the very presence of Kaikipaananea surrounded by a vast multitude. When the people saw Kepakailiula they all shouted their admiration, for he was such a handsome looking fellow. After the shouting the people began to take pity on him for they were sure he would be killed by Kaikipaananea. He was the king of the whole island of Kauai, and was considered the strongest man in his day, and he was especially noted for his great skill in boxing. . . .

When Kaikipaananea saw Kepakailiula, he called out to him: "Say, stranger, come this way and join in the games with the sons of the soil [island natives]; the honuhonu, the mokomoko, wrestling and boxing."

Kepakailiula replied: "I don't know anything about the game of honuhonu."

Kaikipaananea said: "Not knowing that game, let it be the game of wrestling then."

"I don't know that game even."

"Let it be boxing then."

"Yes, I believe that I can do a little of that, for I have acquired a little learning in that game, but I never was declared an expert at it. I am willing to try conclusions with the son of the soil in that game, however. . . ."

At the acceptance of the challenge to box, they both stood up facing each other. Kaikipaananea then asked of his opponent: "Who shall have the first chance? Shall it be the son of the soil or the stranger?"

Kepakailiula answered: "Let the son of the soil have the first chance and the stranger the last."

As soon as this point was settled, Kaikipaananea struck at Kepakailiula, hitting him and causing him to stagger from dizziness and he almost fell to the ground. With the exception of the staggering Kepakailiula was otherwise unaffected. He then with one great effort braced himself up and in a moment he was himself again. He then struck at Kaikipaananea, hitting him and knocking him down, causing him to make water, to twist his feet and to become unconscious for a period of time sufficient for the cooking of two umus [a long time]. After lying down for this length of time, Kaikipaananea came to and said boastingly: "Say, but it was fine fun! Here you have made it worth while at last."

When Kaikipaananea was knocked down, however, the people shouted and yelled of the great strength exhibited by Kepakailiula, and all said: "No man was ever found strong enough to knock Kaikipaananea down and here you have gone and done it."

After this Kepakailiula and his friend, Kaunalewa, proceeded home. On the next day the two again went up to the grounds where the games were being held, and this time

they had a wrestling match in which both arms of Kaikipaananea were broken. Three days after this encounter,
Kaikipaananea sent out his servant Kukaea, to go and notify
everybody to come together at the king's palace to find the
king's riddle.

Kukaea was the personal servant of Kaikipaananea; his
food was the excrement of Kaikipaananea and the water he
drank was the king's urine. Because of his living on these
things he was called Kukaea. This was the only food he ever
tasted from his birth until the day when he was sent out to
make a circuit of Kauai, to make known the king's decree.

The proclamation was called out in the following manner:
"All the people are commanded to come to the king's palace
and solve the king's riddle. If it is found he will be saved from
the oven of hot stones; if it is not found he will be thrown to
his death into the oven. No man, woman, child or those
weak from old age shall remain at home; only those who do
not wink when you poke your finger at their eyes. If any one
remains at home on that day, his house shall be burned down
and the king's punishment shall be meted out to him, from
the parents to the children, relations, and to the last connection and even to a friend [*aikāne*]. This will be the punishment meted out to any person who remains at home this
day."

In the course of the journey taken by Kukaea, to issue the
king's decree, he came to the house where Kepakailiula was
living, still calling out the king's proclamation at the top of
his voice.

When Kepakailiula heard the call he asked his friend: "Who is this man that is making that call?"

The friend replied: "It is Kukaea, the personal servant of Kaikipaananea. He is on his way calling everybody to come to the king's palace to solve the king's riddle. If a person gives the right answer he will be saved, but if he makes a mistake he will be thrown to his death into the oven of hot stones."

When Kepakailiula heard this, he said to his friend: "Then call him to come here, for I wish to see him."

Because of this wish Kaunalewa called to Kukaea to come. Kukaea then turned toward them and when at some distance away, he said: "It is not proper for me to come any nearer, for I am not fit for your company; I smell bad, for I have had nothing else for food except the king's excrement, to this day."

Kepakailiula, however, called out to him: "Come here, don't be afraid or have any fear."

When Kukaea came up Kepakailiula asked him: "Open your mouth?" Kukaea then opened his mouth and Kepakailiula poured water into his mouth and on his body and told him to wash himself and be rid of the foul odor of his body. Kepakailiula then gave him some kapas and a loin cloth, and set food and meat before him. Kukaea then sat down and ate until he was satisfied. When he finished his meal, he turned and said to Kepakailiula: "What shall I give you as payment for this great kindness? Here I have lived from my birth to this day with my king and have just completed the circuit of Kauai, but no one has ever given me food to eat. I have at last

found that food and meat are indeed pleasant to the taste.
Therefore here is what I shall give you in return for your
kindness. I will give you the answer to the king's riddle, for
I am the only person that knows the answer. . . ."

➤ ➤ ➤

Kukaea tells the two friends the solution to the riddle and instructs
them to seize the king at a key moment and throw him into his own
oven. The heroes follow these instructions. When the king's followers
come to his aid, Kukaea joins Kaunalewa and Kepakailiula to defeat
them. Kepakailiula now recovers his wife and goes to the home of
Kaunalewa, where he tells his *aikāne*: "You shall be the king of the
whole of Kauai. You shall be the king of the things above it and the
things below it, the things in the uplands and the lowlands, the things
that are cooked and uncooked. You shall be the ruler of the land and
Kukaea shall rule under you."

TEXT Abraham Fornander, *Fornander Collection of Hawaiian Antiquities
and Folk-lore*, Memoirs of the Bernice Pauahi Bishop Museum, vols. 4 and
5 (Honolulu: Bishop Museum, 1918–19), pp. 498–517, 384–405.
OTHER SOURCES John Ledyard in Robert J. Morris, "*Aikāne*: Accounts of Hawaiian Same-Sex Relationships in the Journals of Captain
Cook's Third Voyage (1776–80)," *Journal of Homosexuality* 19, no. 4 (1990):
21–54; David Malo, *Hawaiian Antiquities*, trans. N. B. Emerson (Honolulu: Hawaiian Gazette Co., 1903); Mary K. Pukui, *'Olelo No'Eau: Hawaiian Proverbs and Poetical Sayings* (Honolulu: Bishop Museum, 1983);
Martha Beckwith, *Hawaiian Mythology* (Honolulu: University of Hawaii
Press, 1970).

He Is an Equal

to You

(Gilgamesh and Enkidu)

The hero Gilgamesh is believed to have been a king in Sumer sometime between 2800 and 2500 B.C.E. By the end of that millennium, however, he had become the subject of myths and legends that portrayed him as the culture hero of the city of Uruk. Sometime in the early second millennium B.C.E., these stories were combined to create the world's oldest literary epic.

As the fragments of the tablets containing this story were pieced together in the beginning of the twentieth century, it became clear that same-sex love was a central theme. Gilgamesh, the unruly ruler of Uruk, and Enkidu, the wild man of the plains, may be the original example of Divine Twins. But the legacy of Gilgamesh and Enkidu is a complex one. The moving account of their love unfolds against a background of conflict—between Gilgamesh and his people and, even more sharply, between Gilgamesh and the goddess Ishtar.

Ishtar, as she was known to the Assyrians and Babylonians, or Inanna, as she was called by the Sumerians, held an extremely important position in Mesopotamian religions from the earliest times. Although the social organization of Sumer appears to have been patrilineal (descent traced through fathers and wives living in their husbands' homes), women were esteemed in religion. In ceremonies and literature, female sexuality was unabashedly celebrated. Temples, which were economic and cultural centers, were staffed by various classes of female functionaries. Becoming a priestess represented a meaningful alternative role for women to a much greater extent than in ancient Greece and Rome.

That is why, when we read of Gilgamesh brazenly challenging the goddess Ishtar, it should give us pause for reflection. As the story unfolds, it becomes clear that the events related reflect a crucial transition in human history. The opening scenes establish the fact that Gilgamesh is a new kind of man with a new kind of psychology. He builds walls around the city of Uruk—much as the patriarchal male builds walls around his ego and seals off the openings of his body—and he insists on the patriarchal right to use those weaker than him, the boys and girls of the city, for his sexual pleasure. The people of Uruk appeal to Aruru, the mother of the gods, and she creates a rival to Gilgamesh, the wild man, Enkidu.

The unfolding relationship between Gilgamesh and Enkidu is the most interesting part of the epic. Initially, as the following passage relates, these two heroes contend with each other. After a wrestling match that ends in a draw, they decide that they are equals. The passage that follows this opens with the two heroes kissing each other to seal their friendship. Then, like Kaunalewa and Kepakailiula, they proceed to slay a monster. After this, Gilgamesh defies Ishtar by rejecting her sexual overtures. Her lovers always seem to have bad luck and short lives, he complains, and he fears she will treat him the same. But what Gilgamesh is really rejecting is a basic principle of female-centered religion—the right of the goddess to choose her own lovers.

One of the most ancient ceremonies observed in the temples of Sumer was the sexual union of the king and a priestess. That mortals could have contact with the gods by having sex with a priest or priestess was a central belief of Sumerian religion. In this sacred marriage, the priestess represented the Earth Mother, the most important and constant element of fertility. The male figure, on the other hand, represented by the king in the ceremony and by the god Dumuzi in

mythology, was seen as a variable factor. He served to stimulate the
Earth Mother's fertility, and then by dying he symbolized the har-
vested crop. As the myths tell it, Dumuzi, like a male Demeter, spent
part of the year in the underworld and part in the world of the living.

But Gilgamesh rejects this version of the male principle. He does
not want to be secondary or interchangeable. Given the role of sexuality in Mesopotamian religions, it's not surprising that he redefines his
relationship to Ishtar by forming an alternative relationship. At this
point in time, this has to be a relationship with another man—female
deities willing to be dutiful wives have not yet been invented. From
another point of view, men's power over women is based on the bonds
that men have with each other, their willingness to aid and support
each other in asserting their superiority over women. If this myth
really does reflect a historic change, it's not surprising that the emphasis should be on this male bond. It must be strong to overcome the loy-
alties men might otherwise feel toward women, who are, after all,
their mothers, sisters, and wives.

We know that the Sumerian cities of Mesopotamia were slowly
overtaken by the nomadic Semitic-speaking people of the surrounding
deserts, who would have seemed like "wild men" to city dwellers. Perhaps this story partly reflects an alliance between the males of these
two groups that resulted in a reduced role for goddesses like Ishtar. In
any case, in the myth, male cooperation serves to defeat the forces that
Ishtar sends against Gilgamesh and Enkidu.

This story is more than patriarchal propaganda, however, because it
clearly warns against the arrogance exemplified by Gilgamesh, which
results from denying the feminine. Beyond this, the relationship of the
two heroes leads to real growth for Gilgamesh. The emotions aroused
in him by Enkidu lead him out of the blind aggression and one-
sidedness of patriarchal identity to a more balanced and sensitive form

of masculinity. On the very night following his triumph over Ishtar, Gilgamesh dreams that the gods have decided that Enkidu must die. Initially angry, Gilgamesh realizes that there is nothing he can do to alter this fate, so he says good-bye to his friend in a moving speech. With Enkidu gone, Gilgamesh sinks into hopeless despair, wandering the countryside, wailing like a woman (or like the third-gender *kalû* priests, whose official job was to wail at funerals). He tries to enter the underworld to rescue his friend, but fails. After a long series of trials, he resigns himself to the fact of mortality, his own and Enkidu's, taking comfort in the accomplishments he will leave behind him as the ruler of Uruk.

In contrast to Gilgamesh, Enkidu represents a different kind of masculinity, more connected to the feminine, in the sense of being more instinctive. He is created by the mother goddess, Aruru, and a woman initiates him before his entry into the city (whether she was an official "holy woman," what scholars like to call a temple prostitute, or a commercial prostitute is not clear; both statuses are known to have existed). He is described with words that are puns on terms for various priests, including the two-spirit *assinnu*. (In an earlier story, Asushunamir was also described as an *assinnu*.) In other words, the feminine is not eliminated entirely from the picture but placed at a point once removed, with Enkidu serving as an emissary from this archetypal domain. Only later, when the image of a strong, erotic, warrior woman like Ishtar had long been forgotten, would myths be able to do away with Enkidu and rely on figures of helpless maidens, stout wives, and evil temptresses to represent the reduced, patriarchal vision of the feminine.

When I read the story of Gilgamesh and Enkidu, I think again of my friendship with Andy, whom I described earlier. As a street-savvy gay youth, he was everything I wasn't. I was an inhibited, middle-class college graduate from a small town who hadn't had his first sexual experience with a man until he was twenty. Andy had been having sex since he was fourteen and slipping into gay bars since he was sixteen. While I was taking tests in college, he was mastering all the ins and outs, the fashions and fads, of San Francisco in the 1970s. Everywhere we went together he had friends or made friends; I never knew where we might end up by the time the night was over. Andy taught me, most of all, how to enjoy the gay scene, how to stop worrying about picking up men and to allow it to happen naturally as part of just having a good time.

For many of us, the first euphoria of coming out is lost when we realize how inhibiting the gay cruising scene can be. And today the need for caution due to the HIV virus can also lead to inhibition. That's why I think there is still a place for wild men like Enkidu and my friend Andy—to help untie the knots of emotional and sexual repression.

I would like to think that the story of Gilgamesh and Enkidu doesn't always have to end with the death of the wild man. Rather, the lesson is that we must integrate what Enkidu represents into our conscious selves, to make him a part of our self-image. When this happens, the symbol, in the form of the projection of Enkidu that we sometimes make on others, *does* die—or, rather, its outer, separate existence falls away as we absorb it into our own psyches. This is what happens when Gilgamesh grieves the loss of Enkidu later in the story—the outcome of grieving is to make the ones we have lost a part of ourselves, to make their attitudes and characteristic behaviors our own.

Because the Gilgamesh myth is available in various editions, I am including only a brief passage here, from a new translation by David F. Greenberg, which describes the initial confrontation between Gilgamesh and Enkidu. This is from the Old Babylonian version of the epic, originally inscribed in the early second millennium B.C.E. It includes several homosexual innuendos and puns—for example, the word for meteorite, *kiṣru*, is probably a pun on *kezru*, a term for male prostitute, and axe, *ḫassinu*, plays on *assinnu*, one of the priests of Ishtar.

➤   ➤   ➤

PLAYERS AND PLACES

Anum   "Sky," the god of Uruk, his temple is called *Eanna*

Uruk   a city founded by Sumerians in southern
    Mesopotamia

Enkidu   a primitive man created by the Mother Goddess,
    Aruru

Shamḫat   term for a class of priestesses of Ishtar, used
    here as a personal name

Ishḫara   another name for Ishtar, the goddess of love,
    marriage, and birth

Ninsunna   "Lady Wild-Cow," mother of Gilgamesh

Ellil   head of a younger generation of Sumerian and
    Akkadian gods, whose worship was centered in Nippur

COLUMN I

Gilgamesh rose for the purpose of revealing a dream.
He says to his mother:
"Mother, this very night
I was a male prostitute, walking around
in the midst of the youths.
The stars of the heaven appeared to me.
A meteorite of Anum fell toward me.
I lifted it and it became too heavy for me.

S   P   I   R   I   T   S

I moved it but I was not able to set it in motion.
The people of Uruk were gathered around it.
The youths were kissing its feet.
I leaned my forehead against it.
They supported me;
I lifted it and carried it to you,
O mother of Gilgamesh who knows everything."
She said to Gilgamesh:
"Perhaps, Gilgamesh, someone like you
was born in the steppes.
The hills raised him.
You will see him and you will rejoice.
Youths will kiss his feet.
You will embrace him.
You will lead him to me."
He lay down. He has seen another.
He tells the dream to his mother.
"Mother, I have seen another.
I was looking at what happened. In the street,
in the city square of Uruk,
an axe was lying.
They were gathered around it.
The appearance of the axe was unusual.
I myself saw it and rejoiced.
I loved it.
I was caressing it
like a wife.
I took it and placed it at my side,
O mother of Gilgamesh, who knows everything."
She tells Gilgamesh:

Q U E E R

COLUMN 2

"Because he is a rival to you,"
she interprets the dream to Gilgamesh.
Enkidu is sitting before a (female) prostitute.
They are making love with one another.
Enkidu has forgotten where he was born.
Six days and seven nights
Enkidu was being aroused.
He had intercourse with the prostitute.
The prostitute opened her mouth, and
said to Enkidu:
"I look at you; your appearance is like a god.
Why are you traversing the steppes
with wild animals?
Come! Let me lead you
to the heart of Uruk, the market town,
to the pure temple, the dwelling of Anum.
Enkidu get up! Let me lead you
to Eanna, the dwelling of Anum
where Gilgamesh . . . deeds
and you . . . (like?)
you will ? . . . yourself
Come get up from the ground.
The poverty of a shepherd."
He listened to her word; he accepted her command.
The advice of the woman
fell on his heart.
She tore (her) garment.
(With) the first (part) she dresses him;
with the second she dressed herself.

S P I R I T S

Q   U   E   E   R

Holding his hand,
she leads him like a child
to the hut of a shepherd,
to the place of the cattle-pen.
The shepherds gathered around him.

. . . .

COLUMN 3

He used to suck
the milk of wild animals.
They placed bread before him.
He squinted; he stares
and looks at it.
Enkidu did not recognize it.
He had not been taught
to eat bread,
to drink beer.
The prostitute opened her mouth, and
said to Enkidu,
"Eat the bread, Enkidu.
It is necessary for life.
Drink the beer! It is the custom of the country."
Enkidu ate the bread
until he was satisfied.
He drank
seven pitchers of beer.
(His) liver became loose [he relaxed]. They sang gleefully.
His very heart rejoiced;
his face brightened.
He has smeared . . . (his) body hair(?).

S   P   I   R   I   T   S

He has rubbed
his hairy body with oil.
He became like a human.
He put on a garment.
He was becoming like a man.
He took his weapon.
He attacks the lions
(so that) the shepherds could lie down at night.
He chased away the wolves.
He drove away the lions
(so that) many shepherds could lie down.
Enkidu was their watchman,
an alert man,
a singular youth.

. . . .

COLUMN 4

. . . .

He had intercourse.
He raised his eyes;
he saw a man.
He said to the prostitute,
"Prostitute, go to the man.
Why did he approach?"
"Let me hear his name."
The prostitute called to the man.
She is going to him and has spoken to him:
"Youth! where are you hurrying?
What arduous task are you undertaking?"
The youth opened his mouth.

The Divine Twins

Q   U   E   E   R

He said to Enkidu:
"They invited me
to the wedding house
that is established for the people
to choose bridehood.
I am going to heap up a fancy buffet
onto the cult distribution table of the wedding house
for the ruler of Uruk, the market town.
The canopy of the people is open for marrying.
For Gilgamesh, the ruler of Uruk, the market town,
the canopy of the people is open
for the purpose of marrying.
He is copulating with the purchased wives.
He first, and
the husband afterward.
By the spoken instructions of Anum,
at the cutting of his umbilical cord
it was decreed for him."
At the utterance of the youth
his face turned pale.

COLUMN 5

Enkidu was walking in front
and Prostitute behind him.
He entered the heart of Uruk, the market town.
A crowd gathered around him.
He took his stand in the street
of Uruk, the city square.
People gathered, and
said about him,

S   P   I   R   I   T   S

"He is one whose physique is equal to (that of) Gilgamesh.
The stature is short
(but) very strong of bone.
A youth, where he was born
he ate plants of the spring pasture.
He used to suck
the milk of wild animals."
Offerings were constant in Uruk;
The youths cleansed themselves.
A hero has been placed
for the youth who has fair (?) countenance,
for Gilgamesh who is like a god.
A counterpart has been set for him.
A bed for Ishḫara
has been lain down.
In the night, Gilgamesh
coupled with Ishḫara.
He went to her, and then
Enkidu stood in the street.
He blocked the way
Of . . . Gilgamesh.
. . . very strongly.

COLUMN 6

. . . the road
Gilgamesh . . .
. . . around . . .
He became angry.
He rose . . .

Q U E E R

Before him . . .
They confronted one another in the city square of the
  land.
Enkidu blocked the gate
with his feet (or foot).
He did not allow Gilgamesh to enter.
They grabbed each other. Like bulls
they bent over.
They destroyed the doorpost.
The wall shook.
Gilgamesh and Enkidu
grabbed each other.
They bent over like bulls.
They destroyed the doorpost.
The wall trembled.
Gilgamesh kneeled,
his foot on the ground.
His anger became appeased and
he turned away from him.[1]
As soon as he turned away from him,

1. There is ambiguity in the text as to what is going on. If we translate *ikmisma Gilgamesh* as "Gilgamesh kneeled," it appears that Enkidu has been victorious, which is odd given that Gilgamesh is the central figure in the epic and is hailed by Enkidu immediately after the fight. Perhaps Gilgamesh kneeled *on* Enkidu. It is also unclear whose anger is appeased. Enkidu's anger has been mentioned previously, but one has to go back to line 8 to find his name mentioned explicitly. Gilgamesh has not been described as angry; perhaps it was taken for granted that Gilgamesh would have been angry at Enkidu for having blocked his way. [DFG]

S P I R I T S

Enkidu said to him,

to Gilgamesh,

"Like a unique one your mother

bore you.

A wild cow of the stock-pen,

Ninsunna

elevated your head over (that of other) men.

Ellil has decreed to you

the kingship of the people."

TEXT Translated by David F. Greenberg, with thanks to Daniel Fleming, Eva von Dassow, and his fellow students in Akkadian.

OTHER SOURCES Anne Drafkorn Kilmer, "A Note on an Overlooked Word-Play in the Akkadian Gilgamesh," in *Zikir Šumim: Assyriological Studies Presented to F. R. Kraus on the Occasion of His Seventieth Birthday*, ed. G. van Driel, Th. J. H. Krispijm, M. Stol, and K. R. Veenhof (Leiden: E. J. Brill, 1982), pp. 128–32; Stephanie Dalley, *Myths from Mesopotamia* (Oxford University Press, 1991); Jeffrey H. Tigay, *The Evolution of the Gilgamesh Epic* (Philadelphia: University of Pennsylvania Press, 1982).

All Ills

Grow Better

(Baldr and Loki)

The story of Baldr and Loki as related in Scandinavian myths is a rich source of gay themes. The most complete account of them appears in the *Prose Edda* of Snorri Sturluson (1178–1241 C.E.). Sturluson was an Icelandic chief and scholar who drew on oral tradition, genealogical records, old songs and lays, and poems of court poets to create his mythological epic. The *Edda*, also known as the *Gylfaginning* (The beguiling of Gylfi), begins with the story of the Swedish king Gylfi, who has been tricked out of his land by the Æsir, mythical descendents of the Trojans who have migrated to Scandinavia. Gylfi decides to visit the Æsir disguised as a beggar. In response to Gylfi's questions, the gods tell him stories about their history and their deeds, including the following account of Loki and Baldr.

Loki and Baldr drew my attention for two reasons. Taken together, they provide an interesting example of a pair of complementary figures similar to Gilgamesh and Enkidu. That is, it takes the qualities of both to make a single personality in both its conscious and its unconscious aspects. But Loki can also be viewed as a two-spirit, gender-transgressing Trickster, while Baldr has qualities of a culture bearer. Clearly, the story of these two gods involves a complex set of symbols and dynamics.

Baldr is the son of Odin and Frigg. The Norse poets refer to him as the God of Tears and the Bleeding God. According to the *Edda*, "He is best, and all praise him; he is so fair of feature, and so bright, that light shines from him. . . . He is the wisest of the Æsir, and the fairest-spoken and most gracious; and that quality attends him, that none may gain-say his judgments. He dwells in the place called Breida-blik [Broad-gleaming], which is in heaven; in that place may nothing unclean be." Loki, on the other hand, is the son of the giant Fárbauti and a woman named Laufey (or Nál), about whom nothing else is known. In the *Edda* he is called Loki Laufeyarson, after his mother, which is a striking reversal of the usual Scandinavian practice of nam-ing sons after their fathers. He is called the Evil Companion and Bench-Mate of Odin; the Thief; the Forger of Evil; the Sly God; the Slanderer and Cheat of the Gods; and, as a consequence of his Prome-thean fate, the Bound God. According to the *Gylfaginning*, "Loki is beautiful and comely to look upon, evil in spirit, very fickle in habit. He surpassed other men in that wisdom which is called 'sleight' and had artifices for all occasions; he would ever bring the Æsir into great hardships, and then get them out with crafty counsel." A kind of male Pandora, Loki is credited with fathering the Fenris-Wolf, the Midgard Serpent, and other monsters.

Like other Queer Tricksters, Loki is a flaky, shape-shifting trouble-maker who symbolizes the personality fixed at a preadult level. In var-ious stories, he transforms himself into a bird, a fish, a fly, a flea, and, in at least three stories, a female. His name has been linked to the Swedish word for spider, *locke*, and various Scandinavian sayings and beliefs associated with spiders reinforce Loki's trickster nature. In the *Lokasenna* (Loki's wrangling), a contest of insults in which Loki taunts the assembled gods and goddesses, Odin accuses Loki of being unmanly. Hadn't he spent eight winters beneath the earth, "milking the cows as a maid, and giving birth to a brood"? Loki responds that Odin himself is said to have woven spells and passed among humans dressed as a witch. In the poem *Hyndluljoth*, Loki is described as eating the half-cooked heart of a woman, becoming pregnant, and then giving birth to the monsters that plague men. In the *Asgaðr* myth, he turns himself into a mare and gives birth to Odin's horse, Sleipner. If this weren't enough to indicate Loki's attitude toward gender, there is the story in which he ties his genitals to the beard of a goat and attempts to castrate himself to make the giantess Skadi laugh.

Loki displays a casual disregard concerning the integrity of his body typical of shamans and tricksters. That this indifference should include his male sex organ suggests a very different mind-set from that of patriarchal males, for whom possession of a working phallus is essential to their gender identity. Indifferent to these values, Loki plays tug-of-war with his penis. The episode makes more sense when placed next to the example of the *galli* and *hijra*. Both are priests of the Goddess whose radical rejection of patriarchal values took the form of self-castration.

All this is to say that *both* Baldr and Loki can be seen as gay-related archetypes. In Baldr, I see the "best little boy in the world," the almost-perfect gay boy who is the darling of his parents, who tries to make up for his one hidden defect by overcompensating in everything he does. Loki, on the other hand, is the bad gay boy, too different, too obvious, too queer ever to fit in. He's the kind of gay boy who runs away from home to become a hustler or a drag queen. This gay boy can't help but feel envy and resentment toward the overcompensater.

Yet another dimension of this story has to do with Baldr and Loki's relations to Odin. Baldr is Odin's perfect son; Loki is Odin's blood brother and "bench-mate" and, according to one account, his adopted son. It's easy to imagine that competition for the love of this father figure is behind Loki's deviousness, but the key point is that both gay boys clearly need their father's love. Gay men, I think, often carry this need into their adult lives. Our ambivalent feelings toward our fathers, who loved us only to leave us once they sensed our gayness, can end up haunting our relationships with lovers and friends alike.

The dynamics we see between Baldr and Loki—competition, resentment, closetry—often creep into gay relationships. For anyone who grew up with brothers and sisters, it's easy to slip into good child/bad child roles. This may be especially true for those of us who have gay brothers. In my family, at least, my older gay brother got pegged with being a bad boy, while I, even though I sensed what I had in common with my brother, wholeheartedly embraced the good-boy role, overachieving and overcompensating in every way I could to win love from my parents, all the while feeling secret guilt about the way in which my brother was losing out in this competition. I also feared my brother, not only because he knew my secret, but because our destinies were somehow linked—whatever his gay life would be, mine would be, too.

A gay reading of Baldr and Loki is only one of the many possible interpretations of these figures. One can detect, for example, a conflict of cultures—represented by Baldr, who is linked with the cyclic life of vegetation, and Loki, whose shamanistic-trickster qualities are more typical of the hunting, gathering, and herding peoples of northern lands. Various myths, for example, associate Loki with fishing, with the invention of the fishnet, and with pastoral pursuits.

Considering that Baldr ends up living in hell and that Loki ends up in a living hell, with snake poison dripping on his face, it's not a very happy story—although, according to one account, Baldr returns after the final destruction of the world, when the Earth Mother rises again from the sea and "all ills grow better." Even so, it would seem that our original, child-like brilliance is doomed to be tarnished when we find

that others fear or envy us because of our difference. In the sequel to
Baldr and Loki, I would hope that the favored child and the rebellious
queer manage to get together so that the desire for perfection begins to
get comfortable with a little chaos.

➤   ➤   ➤

PLAYERS AND PLACES

Baldr   son of Odin and Frigg

Loki   son of *Laufey* and a giant, companion/brother of
      Odin

Frigg   "the Beloved," wife of Odin, mother of Baldr; lives
      in Fensalir, "the Ocean Halls"

Fensalir   "sea-halls," home of Frigg

Höðr "war," Baldr's blind brother

Hermóðr   son of Odin

Nanna   Baldr's wife

Fulla   a goddess, Frigg's sister or handmaid

Thökk   "thanks," a giantess

Hel   (1) abode of the dead; (2) a daughter of Loki

Thing   assembly, meeting

Ásgard   fortified dwelling place of the Æsir

Skadi   daughter of the giant Thjazi

Sigyn   Loki's wife

Now shall be told of those tidings which seemed of more
consequence to the Æsir. The beginning of the story is this,
that Baldr the Good dreamed great and perilous dreams
touching his life. When he told these dreams to the Æsir,
then they took counsel together: and this was their decision:

to ask safety for Baldr from all kinds of dangers. And Frigg took oaths to this purport, that fire and water should spare Baldr, likewise iron and metal of all kinds, stones, earth, trees, sicknesses, beasts, birds, venom, serpents. And when that was done and made known, then it was a diversion of Baldr's and the Æsir, that he should stand up in the Thing, and all the others should some shoot at him, some hew at him, some beat him with stones; but whatsoever was done hurt him not at all, and that seemed to them all a very worshipful thing.

But when Loki Laufeyarson saw this, it pleased him ill that Baldr took no hurt. He went to Fensalir to Frigg, and made himself into the likeness of a woman. Then Frigg asked if that woman knew what the Æsir did at the Thing. She said that all were shooting at Baldr, and moreover that he took no hurt. Then said Frigg: "Neither weapons nor trees may hurt Baldr: I have taken oaths of them all." Then the woman asked: "Have all things taken oaths to spare Baldr?" and Frigg answered: "There grows a tree-sprout alone westward of Valhall: it is called Mistletoe; I thought it too young to ask the oath of." Then straightway the woman turned away; but Loki took Mistletoe and pulled it up and went to the Thing.

Hödr stood outside the ring of men, because he was blind. Then spake Loki to him: "Why dost thou not shoot at Baldr?" He answered: "Because I see not where Baldr is; and for this also, that I am weaponless." Then said Loki: "Do thou also after the manner of other men, and show Baldr honor as the other men do. I will direct thee where he stands; shoot at him with this wand." Hödr took Mistletoe and shot at Baldr, being guided by Loki: the shaft flew through Baldr, and he fell dead to the earth; and that was the greatest mischance that has ever befallen among gods and men.

Then, when Baldr was fallen, words failed all the Æsir, and their hands likewise to lay hold of him; each looked at the other, and all were of one mind as to him who had wrought the work, but none might take vengeance, so great a sanctuary was in that place. But when the Æsir tried to speak, then it befell first that weeping broke out, so that none might speak to the others with words concerning his grief. But Odin bore that misfortune by so much the worst, as he had most perception of how great harm and loss for the Æsir were in the death of Baldr.

➤ ➤ ➤

Hermódr the Bold, another son of Odin, agrees to offer the goddess Hel a ransom for the release of Baldr, and he rides off on Odin's horse, Sleipnir. The goddess is willing to release Baldr on one condition.

➤ ➤ ➤

But Hel said that in this wise it should be put to the test, whether Baldr were so all-beloved as had been said: "If all things in the world, quick and dead, weep for him, then he shall go back to the Æsir; but he shall remain with Hel if any gainsay it or will not weep." Then Hermódr arose; but Baldr led him out of the hall, and took the ring Draupnir and sent

it to Odin for a remembrance. And Nanna sent Frigg a linen
smock and yet more gifts, and to Fulla a golden finger-ring.

Then Hermódr rode his way back, and came into Ásgard,
and told all those tidings which he had seen and heard.
Thereupon the Æsir sent over all the world messengers to
pray that Baldr be wept out of Hel; and all men did this, and
quick things, and the earth, and stones and trees, and all
metals,—even as thou must have seen that these things
weep when they come out of frost and into the heat. Then,
when the messengers went home having well wrought their
errand, they found, in a certain cave, where a giantess sat:
she called herself Thökk. They prayed her to weep Baldr out
of Hel; she answered:

Thökk will weep   waterless tears
    For Baldr's funeral;
Living or dead,   I loved not the old man's son;
    Let Hel hold to that she hath!

And men deem that she who was there was Loki Laufeyarson, who hath wrought most ill among the Æsir. . . .

➤   ➤   ➤

And so, Loki finally triumphs over Baldr, who remains in the domain
of Hel until the end of the earth. Loki, however, suffers a horrific punishment for his actions. Despite his shape-shifting powers, the Æsir
finally capture him at Fránangr Falls.

➤   ➤   ➤

S   P   I   R   I   T   S

Now Loki was taken truceless, and was brought with them into a certain cave. Thereupon they took three flat stones, and set them on edge and drilled a hole in each stone. Then were taken Loki's sons, Váli and Nari or Narfi; the Æsir changed Váli into the form of a wolf, and he tore asunder Narfi his brother. And the Æsir took his entrails and bound Loki with them over the three stones: one stands under his shoulders, the second under his loins, the third under his houghs [the back of the knees]; and those bonds were turned to iron. Then Skadi took a venomous serpent and fastened it up over him, so that the venom should drip from the serpent into his face. But Sigyn, his wife, stands near him and holds a basin under the venom-drops; and when the basin is full, she goes and pours out the venom, but in the meantime the venom drips into his face. Then he writhes against it with such force that all the earth trembles: ye call that "earthquakes." There he lies in bonds till the Weird of the Gods.

TEXT *Gylfaginning*, in Snorri Sturluson, *The Prose Edda*, trans. Arthur G. Brodeur (New York: American-Scandinavian Foundation, 1916), pp. 36, 41–42.

OTHER SOURCES *Poesy of Skalds*, in *The Prose Edda*, pp. 91–92; *Voluspo* and *Lokasenna*, in Henry A. Bellows, trans., *The Poetic Edda* (New York: American-Scandinavian Foundation, 1926); and in Lee M. Hollander, trans., *The Poetic Edda* (Austin: University of Texas Press, 1962); Anthony Faulkers, ed., *Edda* (Oxford: Clarendon, 1982).

When You Piss,

I Shall Piss

As Well

The German anthropologist Günther Tessmann, who observed the Fang and Pangwe peoples of West Africa at the turn of the century, found that they practiced an unusual form of sex magic.

> It is noteworthy that homosexual intercourse is included among the medicines for wealth because it is believed that through the intimate contact the medicine of one will be transferred to the other. In a case known to me in Ebaän-gon, the passive party possessed the medicine and the active party wanted to acquire it. . . . In actual fact it might turn out that the effect of the medicine consists in the mutual support the two "friends" render each other, based chiefly on the consciousness of common guilt and the endeavor not to let this guilt be known.

Unfortunately, Tessman's account is heavily colored by his homophobic reaction to these practices. He reports that this "medicine" is danger-ous and that its practitioners often contract fatal or debilitating dis-eases. The untoward fate of the two homosexual protagonists in the following story is, according to Tessman, "punishment" for their sex-ual practices. But he presents no evidence that this is the native view.

I include this story primarily because of the striking way in which one of the four suitors declares his love for the father, saying, "When you piss, I shall piss also." It reminded me of something I've noticed whenever I've bonded closely with another man. At some point in the process of getting to know each other physically and emotionally, when infatuation is at its highest, we start having mutual orgasms. There's a kind of biological synchronization that occurs between two people in close emotional contact. In a similar way, lesbian friends of mine have told me that women living in collectives often have their periods at the same time. Yet another concrete manifestation of magickal twinning is when the partners start dressing alike or wearing matching jewelry, tattoos, and so forth. A friend of mine once found this happening quite unconsciously with a man he was getting to know and, at first, wondered if he was in danger of losing his identity within the relationship. That danger always exists when infatuation is involved, but, as the following tale suggests, I think that these gestures are natural processes of gay bonding, of the emergence within the psyches of both partners of the Divine Twin archetype.

The following has been translated from the German. Because of the length of the character's names, they appear abbreviated after their first use.

➤   ➤   ➤

PLAYERS AND PLACES

Bongo-be-ntúudumo   father of *Akúkedanga-be-bongo-be-*
   ntúudumo, "One who is more beautiful than a snail,"
   a young woman of marriageable age
Scho-bo-schua   not translated, the first of the four suitors,
   who ends up declaring his love for the girl's father
Scho-bö-ngönne-ma-kö-make   "I go out in order to come
   back," the second suitor
Scho-bö-kaa-jem-bodscho-melang   "He knows no
   wickedness," the third suitor

S   P   I   R   I   T   S

Scho-bo-num-e-kub-b'ogbuale-ba-jem-e-kidi-a-lenne "Hen
  and quail, they know when the morning starts," the
  fourth suitor

The story of Scho-bo-num-e-kub-b'ogbuale-ba-jem-e-kidi-
a-lenne and Akúkedanga-be-bongo-be-ntúudumo.

There was once named a man Bongo-be-ntúudumo, who
had a daughter who was called Akúkedanga-be-bongo-be-
ntúudumo and was very beautiful.

Once upon a time, four lovers met on a path who were all
walking to their beloveds. When they asked each other, "To
whom do you go?" it was answered on all sides, "To Akúke-
danga!" Then said they, "Well then, let us go together and
see whom the girl loves."

The lovers, all from different families, were called thus—
the first Scho-bo-schua, the second Scho-bö-ngönne-ma-
kö-make, the third Scho-bö-kaa-jem-bodscho-melang, and
the fourth Scho-bo-num-e-kub-b'ogbuale-ba-jem-e-kidi-a-
lenne.

So the four lovers came into the village, where they sought
the father of the girl. He said, "Oh! how is it that four men
have arrived when there is but one girl! But we can indeed
see that it is so."

The mother likewise said, "Oh! four men! I know surely
that this or that lover has come, and if the girl loved him, he
slept with her; if she loved him not, then he went home
again. But four men all at once?"

Then the young men said, "We will see whom the girl
loves."

The girl loved only the Scho . . . lenne, while the father

loved the Scho-bo-schua, the mother loved the Scho . . . make, and the brother of the girl loved the Scho . . . melang. So they all slept together in the cottage, and the girl slept with the Scho . . . lenne in bed. But when Scho . . . lenne wanted to embrace the girl, one of the other three from the other beds would said, "Oh! how lecherous this girl is! Immediately on the first day she lets her lover embrace her!"

Then the girl said, "O! how this man speaks! Stop, we must choose another day."

At night, however, the lover of the girl asked, "Don't you want to marry me?" The girl consented, but they decided that the lover should not steal her at night, since the other young men might notice this, but rather by day. They would say they were going bathing. And so it happened.

The husband went the next day ostensibly to the water, where the girl followed him. Then both walked to the village of the lovers.

When in the afternoon the two didn't come back, and it became obvious that Scho . . . lenne had abducted the girl, Scho . . . make addressed the mother, the one he liked, and reproached her. But the mother said, "Oh! what do I know of it? I don't occupy the skin of the girl!" Then Scho . . . make became angry, seized a bush knife, and drove it into the mother. She died on the spot. Then he went straight home.

As Scho-bo-schua was unwilling to be satisfied with that, the father went to the lover who had abducted the girl and demanded from him a bride-price. Scho . . . lenne gave it to him, and the father took it back and said to Scho-bo-schua, "Here is the money; I will compensate you with it."

But Scho-bo-schua said, "No! I don't want it."

So then the father took one of his wives and the money and tried to offer them to Scho-bo-schua as compensation. But he would not take it, saying, "No! I don't want it; instead, we shall always be together. When you piss, I shall piss as well; when you defecate, I shall be near; when you sleep, I shall sleep in the same bed with you."

Thus Scho-bo-schua did it, and both slept together. In the end, however, both became sick from frambosia and died.[1] Scho . . . melang slept with the brother of the girl in one bed, and both got leprosy, and they, too, died.

TEXT Günter Tessman, "Gleichgeschlechtliches Leben der Pangwe" (1909, MS), quoted in Ferdinand Karsch-Haack, *Das Gleichgeschlechtliche Leben der Naturvölker* (Munich: Ernst Reinhardt, 1911), pp. 152–54 (trans. Bradley Rose and Will Roscoe).

OTHER SOURCES Günter Tessman, *The Fang Peoples: An Ethnographic Monograph on a West African Group*, trans. Richard Neuse (New Haven, Conn.: Human Relations Area File, 1959), pp. 131–34.

1. Frambosia or yaws is a disease spread by skin-to-skin contact and caused by the same spirochete as syphilis. Once thought to have originated in the New World, syphillis is now believed to have mutated from African yaws. This folktale seems to moralize a disease to make a statement against homosexuality, much as HIV has been exploited in recent years. Whether this is the attitude of the Fang people, however, or of the anthropologist who recorded the story is not clear.

Linked

Jade

Disks

Homosexuality has an interesting place in Chinese history. All the values and social structures of traditional Chinese culture were geared toward the production of sons to carry on the family name, to take care of parents when they are old, and to maintain the cult of family ancestor worship. There was little or no room for a committed or exclusive same-sex lifestyle. In fact, traditional Chinese culture was so preoccupied with heterosexual reproduction and the assumption that everyone shared this obsession that it doesn't seem to have considered homosexuality a threat. The subject provoked humor more often than horror. One finds little prejudice against same-sex love until modern times. Instead, it is portrayed as being just as capable of expressing the ideals of fidelity, chastity, loyalty, self-sacrifice, and beauty as heterosexual love.

Chinese literature provides evidence of homosexuality among men and women at all levels of society. The one restriction, and not a small one, was that a man's homosexual affairs not interfere with his marriage to a woman and the production of a male heir. As in Japan, one can find both age- and gender-based forms of same-sex love, although neither pattern was formalized, and examples of relationships between men of similar backgrounds and ages can be found as well. Homosexual prostitutes, who often cross-dressed, and the numerous eunuchs of the Chinese court, who were assumed to be homosexual, existed alongside idealized relationships between two men, neither of whom were seen as being feminine.

The following passages from Liu I-ch'ing's *A New Account of Tales of the World* reveal that the appreciation of male beauty and friendship was well developed in the era of the Chin dynasty (265–420 C.E.). The comments following some of the passages were written by later Chinese writers.

➤ ➤ ➤

P'an Yüeh and Hsia-hou Chan both had handsome faces and enjoyed going about together. Contemporaries called them the "linked jade disks" (*lien-pi*).

COMMENTATOR: Yüeh and Chan were sworn brothers and consequently like to wander about together.

P'ei K'ai possessed outstanding beauty and manners. Even after removing his official cap, with coarse clothing and un-dressed hair, he was always attractive. Contemporaries felt him to be a man of jade. One who saw him remarked, "Look-ing at P'ei K'ai is like walking on top of a jade mountain with the light reflected back at you."

Chih Tun characterized Wang Meng as follows: "Whenever he comes along adjusting his lapels, how light and airy his graceful soaring!"

COMMENTATOR: Wang Meng possessed an attractive bearing and appearance. Every time he viewed himself in a mirror he would say, "How on earth did Wang Na ever beget such a son?" His contemporaries considered it a perceptive remark.

During the reign of the Duke of Hai-hsi, each morning as the courtiers gathered for the dawn audience, the audience hall would still be dark. It was only when the Prince of

K'uai-chi, Ssu-ma Yü, came that all became radiantly light, like dawn clouds rising.

Someone praised the splendor of Wang Kung's appearance with the words, "Sleek and shining as the willow in the months of spring."

➤ ➤ ➤

When I began reading examples of traditional Chinese literature on same-sex love, it seemed at first as if there were few archetypal images or themes. Most stories recount love affairs between men, both good and bad, and conclude with brief moral commentaries on the appropriateness or the inappropriateness of their behavior. Of course, there are a great many subtleties of expression in Chinese writing, in which almost every concept consists of several other concepts linked together in metaphoric and visual ways, which one misses by reading translations. Chinese literature also tends to lack the focus on individual psychology that is so characteristic of modern Western literature. After spending more time with these stories, however, I realized that they involved values that were no less archetypal for traditional Chinese than Greek myths were for Greeks. The words translated into English as "filial devotion" or "self-constraint," and even the terms for same-sex love, evoke specific images often based on these classical stories. Terms like *cut sleeve*, referring to an emperor who cut off the sleeve of his robe rather than disturb the sleep of his lover, and *half-eaten peach*, referring to an aide who shared a peach with his lord, became synonyms for same-sex love and, in turn, served to link homosexuality to the archetypal themes and images of these stories.

In a story written around 1655, for example, Li Yu refers to homosexuality as the "Southern Mode" because, he says, it is common in the southern province of Fujian (a little like the Englishman who always imagines that customs are freer in southern countries like Italy). He goes on to draw from nature to create a memorable image of same-sex love: "Deep in the mountains grows the banyan tree, also known as the Southern Mode tree. If there is a sapling nearby, the banyan will actually lean over and try to seduce it. Eventually, when it has succeeded, its branches will be clutching the sapling in a tight embrace, as it folds the young tree into its bosom. The two will then form a single tree which is impossible to separate with knife, saw or chisel."

The following selection is one of the canonical stories of Chinese homosexuality. It comes from the collection *Chan-kuo Ts'e* (Intrigues of the warring states), which was compiled in the late Han period (300–221 B.C.E.). The name of one of the characters, Lung-yang (also spelled Long Yang), is still a synonym for *homosexual* used by Chinese today.

➤   ➤   ➤

LUNG-YANG

The king of Wei and Lord Lung-yang were fishing together from the same boat. When Lord Lung-yang had caught some ten fish he began to weep.

"What troubles you?" enquired the king, "and why don't you tell me of it since it distresses you this much?"

"I would not dare be distressed in your presence," protested Lord Lung-yang.

"Then why do you weep?"

"I weep because of the fish your majesty may catch."

"What does that mean?"

"Well, when I got my first fish I was delighted," said Lord Lung-yang. "But then I got one even bigger, so I wanted to throw the first one back. Then I thought: today, despite my bad auspices and offensive behaviour I have the privilege of straightening and brushing your majesty's mat. My rank is that of a ruler. When I am in court men step aside for me. On the road men clear the way for me. But within the four seas, oh how many beauties there must be! When they hear that the likes of me has gained the favour of the king, they will pick up their skirts and race to you. Then I will be the object of feelings such as I had toward the first fish I caught—I will be thrown back. How might I not weep at such thoughts?"

"Alas," cried the king of Wei, "why did you hesitate to tell me about it if this is what you felt!" Thereupon he had an order posted everywhere throughout his kingdom saying "Whoever shall dare to speak of beauties in my presence will have his whole clan extirpated."

TEXTS Liu I-ch'ing, Shih-shuo Hsin-yü: A New Account of Tales of the World, trans. Richard B. Mather (Minneapolis: University of Minnesota Press, 1976), pp. 310, 311, 315, 316, 317; J. I. Crump, trans., Chan-Kuo Ts'e (Oxford: Clarendon, 1970), p. 449.

OTHER SOURCES Li Yu, "A Male Mencius's Mother Raises Her Son Properly by Moving House Three Times," in Silent Operas (Wusheng Xi), ed. Patrick Hanan (Hong Kong: Renditions/Chinese University of Hong Kong Press, 1990), p. 101; Bret Hinsch, Passions of the Cut Sleeve (Berkeley and Los Angeles: University of California Press, 1990); Giovanni Vitiello, Review of Passions of the Cut Sleeve and The Great Mirror of Male Love, Journal of Homosexuality 25, no. 4 (1993): 137–47.

S   P   I   R   I   T   S

That Moon
Which the Sky
Ne'er Saw

Jalāl al-Dīn Rūmī (1207–73 C.E.) was born on the frontiers of Afghanistan in a well-established religious family. After his family moved to
Konya, Turkey, Rūmī received formal religious training and appeared
destined to follow his father's footsteps as an Islamic mullah. But at
the age of thirty-seven he encountered a wandering dervish named
Shams al-Dīn, a native of Tabriz, who had arrived in Konya in 1244
and attracted immediate attention by the fervor of his religious devotion. Rūmī became infatuated with Shams, discovering in his love for
the dervish a way of participating in the divinity of God himself. As
R. A. Nicholson relates:

> Jalāl al-Dīn found in the stranger that perfect image of the
> Divine Beloved which he had long been seeking. He took
> him away to his house, and for a year or two they remained
> inseparable. Sultān Valad (Rūmī's son and biographer) lik-
> ened his father's all-absorbing communion with this "hid-
> den saint" to the celebrated journey of Moses in company
> with Khadir, the sage whom Sufis regard as the supreme
> hierophant and guide of travellers on the Way to God.
> Rūmī's pupils resented their teacher's preoccupation with
> the eccentric stranger, and vilified and intrigued against
> him until Shams al-Dīn fled to Damascus. Rūmī sent his
> son to bring him back; but the tongues of his jealous tradu-

cers soon wagged again, and presently, perhaps in 1247,
the man of mystery vanished without leaving a trace
behind.

Rūmī made the search for his lost beloved a spiritual quest. To symbolize this, he invented the whirling dance of the Mevlevi dervishes,
performed to the music of flute, drum, and tambourine. Or perhaps
we should say that he recovered these forms, for the rites of the whirling dervishes have much in common with those of the ancient *galli*,
the priesthood of Cybele and Attis that originated in the same area
where Rūmī lived and died. Dancing and spinning night after night,
Rūmī paused only to recite extemporaneous strands of poetry, which
his pupils avidly transcribed. Over three thousand of these survive.
In them Rūmī continually repeats the name of his beloved, Shams
al-Dīn.

If I were writing a biography of Rūmī, I would face the usual problem of deciding whether to call him *gay* and whether his poetry, dedicated to a male beloved, means that he had sex (or desired to have sex)
with men or whether it merely reflected poetic convention. But, from
the perspective of gay mythology, these questions can be set aside.
Rūmī uses the language and images of same-sex love, words and pictures that express feelings that we all have had in our gay relationships. Further, his images are archetypal in that they transcend his
own particular time and place and resonate with images from around
the world. Here again we find the moon as a symbol of another mode
of masculinity, like that of Endymion, Asushunamir, and Begochídíín.

For Rūmī, contemplating the image of the beloved and of beauty in
general resulted in an appreciation of the unspeakable essence of God.

S   P   I   R   I   T   S

To achieve this appreciation was to participate directly in the nature of God himself, to be filled with his holiness. This is a beautiful illustration of the psychic process involved when two gay men, who see themselves in each other, form a bond of love. The sense of sameness, of complete identification with the other, erases ego boundaries. When the one you love and desire is a reflection of yourself, who is to say where you stop and he begins? A lot of people have taken a lot of drugs to achieve this state of consciousness, the sense of oneness with the world around you. Heterosexuality can sometimes lead men and women to this awareness, but homosexuality does so much more powerfully, profoundly, and regularly.

It is in this space—the space of recognizing one's self in another— that the kind of relating that Harry Hay calls subject-SUBJECT occurs. There is nothing to constrain the partners from seeing themselves in each other—the lack of physical difference between their bodies facilitates this—so there is no basis for objectification. This is the state to which Rūmī alludes in his line, "With two forms and with two figures but with one soul," and it is what Walt Whitman writes of in his poem "Of the Terrible Doubt of Appearances":

> When he whom I love travels with me or sits a long while
>   holding me by the hand,
> When the subtle air, the impalpable, the sense that words
>   and reason hold not, surround us and pervade us,
> Then I am charged with untold and untellable wisdom, I
>   am silent, I require nothing further.

The titles of the following poems are mine—Rūmī's poetic works are generally known by number only.

S P I R I T S

Q U E E R

➤ ➤ ➤

THAT MOON

That moon, which the sky ne'er saw even in dreams, has
  returned
And brought a fire no water can quench.
See the body's house, and see my soul,
This made drunken and that desolate by the cup of his
  love.
When the host of the tavern became my heart-mate,
My blood turned to wine and my heart to kabāb.
When the eye is filled with thought of him, a voice
  arrives:
"Well done, O flagon, and bravo, wine!"
Love's fingers tear up, root and stem,
Every house where sunbeams fall from love.
When my heart saw love's sea, of a sudden
It left me and leaped in, crying, "Find me."
The face of Shamsi Dīn, Tabrīz's glory, is the sun
In whose track the cloud-like hearts are moving.

A BEAUTY

A beauty that all night long teaches love-tricks to Venus
  and the moon,
Whose two eyes by the witchery seal up the two eyes of
  heaven.
Look to your hearts! I, whate'er betide, O Moslems,
Am so mingled with him that no heart is mingled with
  me.

S P I R I T S

I was born of his love at the first, I gave him my heart at
 the last;
When the fruit springs from the bough, on that bough it
 hangs.
The tip of his curl is saying, "Ho! betake thee to rope-
 dancing."
The cheek of his candle is saying, "Where is a moth that
 it may burn?"
For the sake of dancing on that rope, O heart, make
 haste, become a hoop;
Cast thyself on the flame, when his candle is lit.
Thou wilt never more endure without the flame, when
 thou hast known the rapture of burning;
If the water of life should come to thee, it would not stir
 thee from the flame.

HAPPY THE MOMENT

Happy the moment when we are seated in the palace,
 thou and I,
With two forms and with two figures but with one soul,
 thou and I.
The colours of the grove and the voice of the birds will
 bestow immortality
At the time when we come into the garden, thou and I.
The stars of heaven will come to gaze upon us;
We shall show them the moon itself, thou and I.
Thou and I, individuals no more, shall be mingled in
 ecstasy,
Joyful, and secure from foolish babble, thou and I.

S   P   I   R   I   T   S

Q U E E R

All the bright-plumed birds of heaven will devour their
  hearts with envy
In the place where we shall laugh in such a fashion, thou
  and I.
This is the greatest wonder, that thou and I, sitting here
  in the same nook,
Are at this moment both in 'Irāq and Khorāsān, thou
  and I.

TEXT *Selected Poems from the Dīvāni Shamsi Tabrīz*, trans. Reynold A.
Nicholson (Cambridge: Cambridge University Press, 1898), pp. 1–2, 27,
85, 153.

OTHER SOURCES A. J. Arberry, trans., *Mystical Poems of Rūmī: First
Selection, Poems 1–200* (Chicago: University of Chicago Press, 1968), and
Mystical Poems of Rūmī: Second Selection, Poems 201–400 (Boulder, Colo.:
Westview, 1979); Shems Friedlander, *The Whirling Dervishes: Being an Ac-
count of the Sufi Order Known as the Mevlevis . . .* (Albany: State University
of New York Press, 1992).

S P I R I T S

The

Way of

Initiation

I think one reason sex is so important for gay men is that every experience of orgasm reenacts the central emotional experience of our lives—coming out. Buildup and tension, the effort to hold back, then finally eruption, liberation, repose. In the physical release of every moment of coming, we reexperience our emotional triumph over shame, guilt, and self-hatred. What stronger challenge to everything negative put on us by society than this immeasurably pleasurable experience? Truly, being in the arms of another man is the safest space I know of. All lingering doubts about my sexuality vanish in an overwhelming feeling of rightness.

The symbolic and mythological counterpart of coming out is the rite of initiation. And, just as coming out is powerfully linked to sexuality, so are gay initiations. Here is the deeper meaning of our fascination with fantasy and sex play—the inner need for initiatory experience. If we reduced all the various roles that show up in gay erotica to a common denominator, it wouldn't be top/bottom or inserter/insertee, but "the one who shows" and "the one who sees," teacher and student, initiator and initiated. What the initiate learns to see is himself from the initiator's position. He acquires new vision by giving up his own and accepting that of another. There is a nonvoluntary aspect at a certain point of this process that is often hard for us to accept on an intellectual level. But the Way of Initiation seems to require this.

Gay erotica is filled with initiatory images and stories. The historical and cross-cultural myths that follow show the historical depth of these images and their connection with age-based patterns of homosexuality. As Robert Hopcke has pointed out, gay erotica, often written anonymously and filled with stock characters and scenarios, is really a kind of folklore, rich in archetypes that reveal gay psychological themes. A typical plot interweaves the sexual exploits of a main character with his coming out. At the same time that the protagonist learns sexual techniques, he learns self-acceptance. He must encounter and overcome homophobia and his own fears. This challenge is often personified by a powerful figure who is both erotic and oppressive. A series of increasingly intense sexual experiences becomes a metaphor for the process of overcoming these fears and demons.

The prevalence of these themes in gay erotica, from stories and novels to sexually explicit videos, reveals the relevance of the Initiation archetype in the imaginations of gay men today. Writer Sam Steward first noticed this fascination emerging in the 1950s, in the wake of the cult film *The Wild One*, in which Marlon Brando portrayed the moody leader of a gang of leather-jacketed misfits:

> In a sense the so-called leather movement began with this movie, and the pounding hearts of many persons sitting in darkened theatres told them that here was something they had been wanting for a long time. Suddenly through the dim and obscure shadowings surrounding the Death and Disappearance of the Hero there began to be seen the vague outlines of a new and exciting replacement. . . .
>
> There began to appear motorcyclists in leather—leather everywhere, jackets, pants, jockstraps, caps, boots and belts—and keys right and left, chains and silver studs. Often it seemed overdone: one elegant in full leather had

three inches of black leather filigree lacework sewed to the bottom of his leather pants to lengthen them.

John Preston was another writer who tapped into gay men's fantasies. His novel *Mr. Benson* became an underground hit in the 1980s. The story describes the initiation of a young man into a caring but physically severe relationship as the slave of a charismatic master named Aristotle Benson. According to Preston, "Far from being unnoticed, it made me something of a celebrity. I got to sell T-shirts by mail order that read: LOOKING FOR MR. BENSON. There were versions with or without a question mark. . . . I got fan mail and there were even fan clubs that met to read each installment and then act it out among themselves. There were people in all parts of the country that were actually doing the things I wrote about."

It would be hard to imagine a better example of an archetype and its influence than the dark image of the leatherman and the lengths to which gay men will go to identify with him, completely submerging their identity behind leather uniforms. But, as I pointed out in the introduction, the gay leatherman's hypermasculinity fosters a negation of gender. A world in which there is only one sex is a world that is sexually undifferentiated, in which roles are assumed on the basis of choice not anatomy. The gay leatherman, in other words, represents a different kind of masculinity—dark, nocturnal, alternately receptive and active—a "lunar masculinity" quite distinct from the "solar masculinity" of patriarchal, heterosexual male figures.

The anonymous leatherman often stands at the gateway of the path of Initiation for gay men. What is the nature of the experience he represents? Anthropologists have long noted that initiations incorporate three phases, with distinct rites pertaining to each. At the outset, initiates are withdrawn from normal social interaction, often in a dramatic way. This is followed by a period in which various ritual procedures, including trials and tests and sometimes extended training, serve to induct initiates into a new identity. A final set of rites reincorporates initiates back into the community. They often receive new names, clothing, body markings, or other insignia. Symbolically speaking, the entire proceeding enacts a ritual death and rebirth.

Joseph Henderson, a Jungian therapist, found similar patterns in the dreams of his patients—in the form of symbols such as pyramids, temples, and steps or ladders that lead upward (often seven in number) and in scenes involving symbolic woundings and shamanic dismemberment. Henderson termed the three phases *submission, containment*, and *liberation*. As an archetype, Initiation involves a *process* rather than a specific figure, and for this reason initiatory figures might be male, female, or third gendered. Henderson concluded that the appearance of initiatory images and themes in dreams and other creative activities expresses a psychological yearning for a symbolically marked passage into adulthood.

A friend of mine shared a dream with me recently that is a perfect illustration of this archetype. "I dreamt I was at a boys' camp, sort of like the one I went to as a kid, except that this was very severe and militaristic. Everyone was gay, including my father. There were all these exercises and tests we had to go through. In one part, I saw my father sinking into a swamp and disappearing completely. Then he slowly came back up, holding a flower in his hand. Then I dreamed we were watching this in one of those old super-8 movies, and when it was over we got up and walked out of the theater." I don't know my friend well enough to comment on the personal meaning of this dream for him, but the images he described all evoke the Initiation archetype—the separation and isolation into an all-male milieu, training and other tests, the father figure who withdraws but then returns. The image of the father emerging back out of the swamp (an appropriate symbol for the unconscious) bringing the gift of a flower is especially striking. Thinking about it gives me a feeling of reassurance and resolution—especially considering the gay associations with flowers (see the story of Apollo and Hyacinthus).

Henderson makes an important distinction between the pattern of psychological growth associated with the archetype of Initiation and that of the conventional hero's journey. For the male protagonist of the hero myth, sex is experienced as a triumph, even a conquest—both heterosexual and homosexual examples of this can be cited. In the Initiation archetype, however, sex is typically linked to the phase of submission. Submission, rather than conquest, is what leads us to communion and the final phase, liberation.

This is why I feel that the so-called hero's journey is not a useful myth for gay men. We are not heroes who seek adventures, like Achilles or the knights of the Round Table, we rarely defeat anyone, and mysterious, erotic females, whether goddesses or princesses, rarely appear to us. Our psychic experience is much more akin to that of the shaman, who does not triumph by strength of will or principle or anything, but *submits* and, as a result, is disintegrated, his ego shattered, only later to be reconstituted. Further, the supernatural beings that we encounter on these spirit journeys are typically powerful and frightening females, like the Warrior Woman of the Zunis or the possessive Mother of the Gods, Cybele. Few heterosexual men, on the other hand, are willing to experience sexual submission. But, for gay men, being able to drop our ego boundaries when threatened by others more powerful than we are is a survival skill. Sometimes I think that heterosexual men hate us for just this reason—because, despite their opinions of us, we survive by letting them think they have defeated us. They can't imagine why anyone would want to live without male privilege—but, then, they can't imagine the joys of being gay.

Rather than trying to create a gay version of the hero myth or simply ignoring our differences altogether and claiming that personal growth and mythology are the same for gay men and straight men, as Robert Bly and other leaders of the men's movement do, let's look for stories that *honor* the uniqueness of what we see and feel. Gay men are not straight men . . . *for a reason*. There is more than one path of growth, for heterosexual men as well as gay men. The myths show us that.

The stories that follow reveal the subtle interconnections between traditional patterns of mentorship and initiation, as found in such diverse cultures as native Borneo, ancient Greece, and medieval Japan, and contemporary examples of the gay erotic imagination.

SOURCES Samuel M. Steward, *Bad Boys and Tough Tattoos: A Social History of the Tattoo with Gangs, Sailors and Street-Corner Punks, 1950–1965* (New York: Harrington Park, 1990), pp. 53–54; John Preston, *Mr. Benson* (New York: Masquerade Books, 1992), and *Flesh and the Word: An Anthology of Erotic Writing* (New York: Penguin, 1992), pp. 7–8; Joseph L. Henderson, *Thresholds of Initiation* (Middletown, Conn.: Wesleyan University Press, 1967).

Gold Is Put

into

Our Eyes

The texts that follow describe a traditional rite of initiation, that of the *manang*, or shaman-priest, of the Iban people of Northern Borneo. The Iban recognize several grades of shamans, the highest being the *manang bali*, or "transformed shaman." Instructed by dreams from female spirits, the *manang bali* cross-dress and are usually homosexual. Their skills include healing and making predictions. They serve as mediators and peacemakers, and they perform funerary rites. In all this, they follow the mythical founder of the *manang* role, Menjaya Raja Manang, who also changed his sex. Similar religious third-gender roles have been documented throughout Borneo, Sulawesi, the Philippines, and Southeast Asia.

The initiation of a *manang bali* is officiated at by seven other shamans (a number Joseph Henderson found frequently associated with the Initiation archetype). They stage a mock battle in which they "die"—that is, they fall into a state of unconsciousness. While in trance, the initiate hopes to have a vision of a spirit who will help him find powerful, ceremonial objects. A chicken and a pig are sacrificed, and the liver of the pig is examined to determine the future success of the initiate. Then the initiate lies on the floor and is buried in rice. When he is raised up again, he is given a new name and recognized as a shaman. The other *manang* give him charms and instruct him in healing arts. The three phases of initiation—submission (mock death), containment (burial in rice), and liberation (receiving a new name and status)—are clearly evident.

Subsequent rites are performed when a *manang* is ready to acquire additional powers. According to an account in an 1896 ethnography by Henry L. Roth:

➤   ➤   ➤

> The *manangs* lead the neophyte into a private apartment cur-
> tained off from public gaze by long pieces of native woven
> cloth; and there, as they assert, they cut his head open, take
> out his brains, wash and restore them, to give him a clear
> mind to penetrate into the mysteries of evil spirits, and the
> intricacies of disease; they insert gold dust into his eyes to
> give him keenness and strength of sight powerful enough to
> see the soul wherever it may have wandered; they plant
> barbed hooks on the tops of his fingers to enable him to seize
> the soul and hold it fast; and lastly they pierce his heart with
> an arrow to make him tender-hearted and full of sympathy
> with the sick and suffering.

➤   ➤   ➤

The following description of the *manang bali* comes from the same source.

➤   ➤   ➤

> The *manang bali* is a most extraordinary character, and one
> difficult to describe: he is a male in female costume, which
> he will tell you he has adopted in obedience to a supernatural
> command, conveyed three separate times in dreams. Had he
> disregarded the summons he would have paid for it with his
> life. Before he can be permitted to assume female attire he

is sexually disabled. He will then prepare a feast and invite the people. He will give them tuak to drink, and he will sacrifice a pig or two to avert evil consequences to the tribe by reason of the outrage upon nature. Should he fail to do all this every subsequent calamity, failure of crops and such like, would be imputed to his conduct and he would be heavily fined. . . .

It is difficult to say at what age precisely a person may become a *manang bali*. One thing, however, is certain, he is not brought up to it as a profession, but becomes one from pure choice or by sudden inclination at a mature age. He is usually childless, but it sometimes happens that he has children, in which case he is obliged to give them their portions and to start afresh unencumbered in his new career, so that when he marries, if he be so minded, he can adopt the children of other people, which he frequently, nay, invariably, does, unless it so happen that his husband is a widower with a family of his own, in which case that family now becomes his.

The *manang bali* is always a person of great consequence, and manages, not unfrequently, to become the chief of the village. He derives his popularity not merely from the variety and diversity of his cures, but also largely from his character as a peacemaker, in which he excels. All little differences are brought to him, and he invariably manages to satisfy both parties and to restore good feeling. Then again his wealth is often at the service of his followers, and if they are in difficulty or distress he is ever ready to help. . . .

Bishop Chambers on once asking a *manang bali* how he

professed to recover a drowned spirit, received as answer: "We hold that in addition to the true spirit given by God to man, there is another spirit, the shadow, which ordinarily attends a man wherever he goes. This is the spirit which falls into the water. We are sent for. We place a platter filled with water before us. After incantations we fish in this platter with hawk-bells. We pull these out a few times with no result. At length the spirit comes up, is captured, and restored." "How is it you see this spirit when others cannot?" "Oh! we are the Illuminated (Bakliti). At our initiation gold is put into our eyes, hooks are stuck into our finger-nails, our skull is cleft open."

TEXT Henry L. Roth, *The Natives of Sarawak and British North Borneo* (London: Truslove & Hanson, 1896), 1:270–71, 280–81.

OTHER SOURCES Erik Jensen, *The Iban and Their Religion* (Oxford: Clarendon, 1974); Edwin H. Gomes, *Seventeen Years among the Sea Dyaks of Borneo* (Philadelphia: Lippincott, 1911); Charles Hose and William McDougall, *The Pagan Tribes of Borneo*, 2 vols. (London: Frank Cass, 1966); Stephen O. Murray, "Late-Nineteenth Century Reports of Manangs in Northern Borneo," in *Oceanic Homosexualities*, ed. Stephen O. Murray (New York: Garland, 1992), pp. 285–92.

Muscle
Bound

Almost any example of gay erotica would serve to illustrate the role of initiatory themes in the gay imagination. I recently found a short novel that especially captured my interest, called *Muscle Bound*, by "Christopher Morgan." The story's hero, Tom, is an all-American, blond-haired, Midwestern youth newly arrived in New York City. Although he had a gay relationship in college, Tom is still not comfortable with his sexual identity. He winces whenever he hears the words *gay* and *queer*, and he can't imagine coming out to his parents. He arrives in the big city innocent but eager and gets a job at the Gold Medal Gym.

I was attracted to this story because it is set in a gym. I don't know how other gay men feel about working out, but I definitely have a love-hate relationship with exercise. I often find myself struggling to arouse the motivation and willpower to work out, but I always love the feeling when I do, that heightened awareness of the body that only sore muscles can give you. It's very sexy. So I find myself eroticizing the gym as a place where pleasure and pain are combined. One of my favorite fantasies is to imagine being in a gym after hours with a friend and to combine sex play with our work out.

But back to our story. . . . Our hero, Tom, soon discovers that everything is not quite right at the Gold Medal Gym. The other workers and even the customers appear to be mysteriously under the power of the gym's owner, Mr. Marcus, and his ugly henchman, Frank. Tom soon discovers the reason. Marcus and Frank have videotaped all these men performing compromising sex acts. Unless the men do as they please, the tapes will be released to their families and distributed to videotape dealers. For Tom, Marcus possesses another source of power as well—a god-like body and total self-assurance, which Tom finds irresistibly attractive. The first excerpt that follows describes Tom's initial encounter with his new boss.

What I see in a description like this is not an adult fantasy of hyper-masculinity and power but a little gay boy catching his first glimpse of a naked adult man. It is the father's penis that appears so huge, desir-able, and forbidden in the gay boy's eyes. This is the gigantic penis that we see again and again in gay male visual art and literature. The huge phalluses in Tom of Finland's drawings, for example, remind me of nothing so much as my own first wide-eyed glimpse of adult male penises in the showers at the neighborhood swimming pool. If you pay attention, you'll notice how often these kind of erotic pictures are actually drawn from a perspective below the waist, at the height of a boy.

Tom is also blackmailed into becoming the obedient servant of Mar-cus and Frank, who form a pair of evil twins—not quite the same as the all-powerful father figures of patriarchal myths. Marcus and Frank organize a rigorous training program for Tom, including private workouts that combine weightlifting with heavy-duty sex. The low point for Tom—his ritual of submission—comes after the first of these sessions, when the ever-brutal Frank handcuffs him to a urinal in the gym's bathroom and brings in the other workers. The second excerpt below describes the scene that ensues. The use of the word *dissected* in this passage is revealing. One of the most common motifs of shaman-ism is an encounter with spirit beings who kill the shaman and tear his body to pieces. Fortunately, Tom's experience stops short of this!

Following this episode, Tom enters the phase Henderson terms *con-*

tainment, in which he is under the power of Marcus and Frank. Their power, however, is not physical but psychological. Literally and metaphorically, Tom is enslaved by his fears of being "outed." And he is enslaved because he believes Marcus has something he lacks. As Marcus tells Tom at the beginning of his initiation, "Be good and do the right thing. I know you will. You do really want this, boy, I can tell. You came to me of your own free will, and you will thank me one day." These two attitudes, fear and attraction based on a sense of lack, all too often characterize how we as gay men relate to our fathers.

The initiatory themes are most apparent in the sex scenes. Sexual punishments are made part of Tom's weightlifting program. Every scene involves a series of tests and barriers that he must overcome. By giving him strength and self-confidence, however, this training eventually enables Tom to challenge Marcus and escape his captivity. He is made into a "man," but in gay terms—as a "bottom" who "takes it like a man." His psychological growth is linked to a thorough transformation of his body. Of course, this is a common feature of tribal rites— the bodies of initiates are often marked with tattoos, scars, circumcision, shaving, and so forth.

The recoding of the bottom role as masculine rather than passive or feminine is one of the most interesting developments in the modern gay male imagination. A whole new sexual type has emerged, what I call the *aggressive bottom.* No one epitomizes this type better than the gay porn star Joey Stefano. The aggressive bottom does not pretend to be unwilling, weak, or conquered as the rationale for accepting penetration. He *likes* getting fucked. In fact, he can't get enough. His asshole swallows cocks, toys, ultimately, like a character from Rabelais, the entire world. When we remember that preserving the integrity of the male body has been a preoccupation in Western culture since the time of the Greeks, we can appreciate just how radical the aggressive bottom is as an unequivocal affirmation of gay pleasure. I only hope my hero Joey is always using condoms; I want to continue to enjoy his exploits for a long time to come. The author of *Muscle Bound* always has his characters use condoms.

Meanwhile, Tom falls in love with another young man at the gym, a Latino named Will. Although Tom continues to be a bottom to Will's top, their relationship is emotionally warm and supportive, and this provides a refuge for Tom during his initiatory period. Will, for his part, is inhibited by macho pretensions and hang-ups. While Tom gets "hardened," Will learns to "soften" a little. By the end of the story, they meet somewhere in the middle. In other words, they achieve the egalitarian ideal of the Divine Twin archetype—in emotional terms, at least, since they remain distinguished by race and by top/bottom roles. Their developing subject-SUBJECT relationship is contrasted to the subject-OBJECT relationship they find themselves in with Marcus and Frank, who, as evil twins, are their opposites.

The final phase of Initiation—liberation—occurs when Tom, Will, and the other men whom Marcus and Frank have blackmailed join forces to overthrow them. Just as Marcus is about to force Tom to fuck Will while the other men watch—a reversal of their usual roles as bottom and top that, in the world of gay erotica, is considered "unnatural"—the group tackles the evil twins and ties them up. They proceed to inflict on them the same treatment they had received. The scene ends with a striking image—Marcus and Frank handcuffed and bound together head to toe, like Greek wrestlers in a sixty-nine position, their cocks in each other's mouths, with the keys to the handcuffs dropped into condoms and inserted in their asses. The young men leave with a tape of the entire episode to ensure their future freedom.

S   P   I   R   I   T   S

One can't help but feel, however, that these two dark twins of gay psychology will escape their predicament and end up haunting many other erotic tales. Archetypes have a way of doing that.

➤   ➤   ➤

The hypnotic power of Marcus' voice brought Tom's head down over the bare feet, and he groveled like a dog and pressed his lips to them. Again, the sense of well-being flooded him; here too was the mark of a man, the smell and taste of one. Bent double, his dick pressed painfully against him, Tom licked and kissed Marcus' feet. Above him, he heard the clinking sound of a belt buckle being undone, and the sensuous sound of the leather slipping through the belt loops. He looked up to see the man drop the belt and beckon to him.

"You've got the right attitude, my boy," Marcus said, with satisfaction. "Get up here and get closer to what you really want."

Tom moved eagerly, and at the older man's direction, opened the trousers and lowered them over the strong hips and the thick, barrel shaped thighs.

Marcus wasn't wearing anything under the pants.

Tom stopped his sensual movements in absolute, amazed horror . . . and hunger.

Ron Marcus hefted his machine up in one hand, and shook it temptingly in Tom's face. "I didn't tell you to stop, boy. Get them off. You'll get enough of this, when I let you."

Tom shuddered and continued to undress the man. Was his mouth actually watering? He had never seen a cock so huge, so beautiful! It was thick, and heavy looking, running with curving veins, the head a perfect plum shape. As Marcus lifted one foot and then another, he grinned at the shaking youth on the floor before him. . . .

Tom couldn't think any more. Here was a million wet dreams come true, here was his man, his god, and all he could do was reach out and kiss those strong legs.

·   ·   ·

"Now, this is Mr. Marcus' new boy," Frank said, pointing toward him. "His name is Tommy. Say hello to Tommy, guys."

"Hello, Tommy!"

"Nice cocksucking, Tommy."

"Hiya, asshole!"

Tom hung his head. He couldn't bear to watch them standing in front of him, cocks hanging out, hunger in their eyes.

"He's also Mr. Marcus' new toy, so don't be playing with him without permission. We got special permission tonight. Mr. Marcus wants this shithead to understand what his place is around here. Look at me, shithead!"

Tom looked up, miserable.

"You are the lowest of the low, asshole. Any guy in this place is better than you, any fucking one. You belong to Mr. Marcus now, body and soul. Do you understand that, cocksucker!"

Tom nodded.

"Then say it!"

"I . . . I belong to Mr. Marcus."

"And say that you're an asshole."

"An-and I'm, an a-asshole."

The men laughed again.

"Well, I'm glad you know that, asshole, I surely am glad. 'Cause knowing that is your first step toward becoming a man, isn't it, guys?" They agreed, laughing and grinning and holding onto their cocks. "And all these guys wanna help you get out of that asshole status, don't they?"

"Yeah, eventually!" said Larry. "After he learns his manners!"

"Yeah, we're all gonna help you become a man, asshole. But first, you gotta learn what it's like not being one." Frank leaned over and unlocked the cuff attaching Tom to the urinal, and then pulled him up. Turning him around, he locked both of Tom's wrists behind his back and pushed him into the waiting arms of the other three men.

They caught him effortlessly, and fell immediately to exploring his body. Hands ran all over him, squeezing his jock, spreading his cheeks, pinching his nipples, slapping his ass . . . fingers invaded him, exploring his mouth and ass, and he cried out.

"What a baby," one of them said. . . .

Tom was manipulated down on his back, a pile of something soft under the base of his spine, his wrists pressed into the tile floor. From this new position, everyone looked like giants, huge, horny giants looking over their captive. They stripped off the rest of their clothing and stood, all marvelous specimens of manhood, all showing the effects of a dedicated program of training. Tom swallowed hard. In any other circumstances, this would be a wet dream. But instead, he was cold, and sore, and they were looking down at him like they were ready to dissect him. He decided not to waste any more breath trying to talk his way out.

TEXT "Christopher Morgan," *Muscle Bound* (New York: Masquerade, 1992), pp. 81–82, 137–140.

Snatched

Away

(Zeus and Ganymede)

The shocking story of Zeus (the Roman Jupiter) and Ganymede, in which the all-powerful god of Olympus kidnaps a mortal youth, may be based on the homosexual patterns of the island of Crete. According to Strabo, quoting Ephoros, Cretan men actually did kidnap youths as part of an extended initiation rite—the same term, *harpagēi*, is used in the following poem by Theognis to describe the capture of Ganymede. Or, rather, the procedure was *thought of* as an abduction. In practice the whole affair was pre-arranged.

Even so, the dramatic removal of initiates from the community followed by a long period of separation is reminiscent of initiations in tribal societies. The practice of living in the mountains and hunting during this period also shows up in the story of Apollo and Hyacinthus. At the end of this seclusion, the youth receives new clothes, a new name, and a new identity. Again, we see the familiar pattern of submission, containment, and liberation.

Recent archaeology offers evidence supporting Strabo's account. According to Robert Koehl, an excavated site in the mountains of Crete has yielded remains of animal bones and other artifacts that suggest it may have been the location for the feasting Strabo describes. A drinking cup, one of the gifts given to initiates mentioned by Strabo, was found painted with a scene depicting just such an exchange between a man and a youth. Other evidence of initiatory homosexuality among the Greeks comes from inscriptions dated to the fifth and sixth centuries B.C.E. on the island of Thera, a colony of Sparta. Here, on a rock face near the temple of Apollo and other shrines, men carved the names of their lovers. Although these scratchings look like simple records of sexual conquests, their location in the temple precinct and their subject fit the general pattern I've been describing, in which the initiators are thought of as capturing by force the young men they initiate. One of the longer inscriptions reads, "By the [Apollo] Delphinios, Krimon had sex here with a boy, the brother of Bathykles." Others state simply, "Pheidippidas had sex" and "Krimon had sex with Amotion here."

The relation of Cretan to later forms of Greek homosexuality is still unknown. It is not clear whether these practices were native to the Minoan civilization of Crete or were introduced by the Indo-European invaders, the Dorians, who arrived between 1100 and 1000 B.C.E. Although it seems logical that the idealized man-youth relationships of Plato's *Symposium* evolved from these older initiatory practices, there is no direct connection between them. Homosexual relationships in Plato's time were idealized, but they were pursued for personal and social, not religious, reasons.

Here is Strabo's account of the Cretan rite of initiation, followed by versions of the Ganymede myth as told by ancient and modern writers.

➤   ➤   ➤

> They have a peculiar custom with respect to their attachments. They do not influence the objects of their love by persuasion, but have recourse to violent abduction [*harpagēi*]. The lover apprises the friends of the youth, three or more days beforehand, of this intention to carry off the object of his affection. It is reckoned a most base act to conceal the youth, or not to permit him to walk about as usual, since it would be an acknowledgment that the youth was unworthy of such a lover. But if they are informed that the ravisher is

equal or superior in rank, or other circumstances, to the youth, they pursue and oppose the former slightly, merely in conformity with the custom. They then willingly allow him to carry off the youth. If however he is an unworthy person, they take the youth from him. This show of resistance does not end, till the youth is received into the Andreium [*andreion*, "men's house"] to which the ravisher belongs.

They do not regard as an object of affection a youth exceedingly handsome, but him who is distinguished for courage and modesty.

The lover makes the youth presents, and takes him away to whatever place he likes. The persons present at the abduction accompany them, and having passed two months in feasting, and in the chase, (for it is not permitted to detain the youth longer,) they return to the city. The youth is dismissed with presents, which consist of a military dress, an ox, and a drinking cup; the last are prescribed by law, and besides these many other very costly gifts, so that the friends contribute each their share in order to diminish the expense.

The youth sacrifices the ox to Jupiter, and entertains at a feast those who came down with him from the mountains. He then declares concerning the intercourse with the lover, it took place with his consent or not, since the law allows him, if any violence is used in the abduction, to insist upon redress, and set him free from his engagement with the lover. But for the beautiful and high-born not to have lovers is disgraceful, since this neglect would be attributed to a bad disposition.

The *parastathentes*, for this is the name which they give to

those youths who have been carried away, enjoy certain honours. They are permitted to wear the *stole*, which distinguishes them from other persons, and which has been presented to them by their lovers; and not only at that time, but
in mature age, they appear in a distinctive dress, by which
each individual is recognised as *kleinos* [praised], for this
name is given to the object of their attachment, and that of
philetor to the lover.

➤   ➤   ➤

Ancient accounts of Ganymede are quite brief. The story is cited
often, but with few elaborations. Here are two versions by Roman
authors. The first is from Ovid's *Metamorphoses*, told in the voice of
Orpheus; the second is from the *Thebaid* by Statius.

➤   ➤   ➤

"The king of the Gods above was once inflamed with a passion for Ganymede, and something was found that Jupiter
preferred to be, rather than what he was. Yet into no bird
does he vouchsafe to be transformed, but that which can
carry his bolts [i.e., an eagle]. And no delay is there. Striking the air with his fictitious wings, he carries off the youth
of Ilium; who even now mingles his cups for him, and, much
against the will of Juno, serves nectar to Jove."

From here the Phrygian hunter [Ganymede] was swept
    away on bronze wings.
Rising up, Gargara [Mt. Ida] sinks below, and Troy
    recedes,

S   P   I   R   I   T   S

his friends stand sadly by, and in vain the noisy hounds
    tire their voices
baying at the cloudy sky and chasing after his shadow.
Thereupon, pouring his flowing wine, he calls in order
on all the gods of heaven. . . .

➤ ➤ ➤

Once in Olympus, Ganymede becomes immortal. As cupbearer to the gods, he is identified with the constellation Aquarius. The following poem by Theognis is typical of the way in which ancient writers used the image of Ganymede to stand for homosexual love.

➤ ➤ ➤

The love of youth has been a delight ever since Ganymede
was seized by the son of Cronos, king of the immortals,
snatched away and brought to Olympus, and made
a god, a charming flower in his boyhood.
So be not astonished, Simonides, that it has come out—
I, too, am overpowered with the love of a beautiful youth.

➤ ➤ ➤

The myth of Zeus and Ganymede became an important wellspring for images of homosexuality in Western culture. The story itself, since the time of the Greeks, has been interpreted both erotically and spiritually. Plato, for example, gives the myth a spiritual reading in the *Phaedrus*, describing how "the fountain of that stream, which Zeus when he was in love with Ganymede named Desire, overflows upon the lover" and how it fills the beloved with love as well so that he becomes a mirror in whom the lover sees himself. But elsewhere Plato claims that the Cretans had invented the myth of Ganymede only to

SPIRITS

justify their sexual preferences. This double reading of Ganymede, erotic and spiritual, is not paradoxical in the context of gay sexuality, however. As Harry Hay argues, sexuality for us is often the gateway or trigger to our spirituality.

The terms *ganymede* and *catamite* (which is derived from *ganymede*) have been used since medieval times to refer to individuals who are objects of same-sex desire and, more generally, to all homosexuals. John Boswell found that, in the late Middle Ages, *ganymede* was regularly used as a nonjudgmental term for same-sex love, an alternative to *sodomite*. It "evoked connotations of mythological sanctions, cultural superiority, and personal refinement which considerably diminished negative associations in regard to homosexuality."

Ganymede was especially popular in the Italian Renaissance. Art historian James Saslow has identified some two hundred works of art from this period depicting the winsome shepherd. Dante used the imagery of Ganymede's capture to describe his ascent to the gates of purgatory: "In a dream methought I saw an eagle poised in the sky, with plumes of gold, with wings outspread, and intent to swoop." Ganymede figures even more prominently in the writings and art of Michelangelo. Saslow argues that Michelangelo identified equally with the position of the young beloved, who is literally swept off his feet, and the older lover, who bears his loved one to heaven and makes of him a god. I think this is an important clue to the workings of the Initiation archetype—it eventually leads to experience with *both* roles, father/son, master/apprentice.

Images from the Ganymede story continually reappear in Michelangelo's sonnets. The following was translated by the early gay liberationist John Addington Symonds.

S   P   I   R   I   T   S

With your fair eyes a charming light I see,
    For which my own blind eyes would peer in vain;
    Stayed by your feet the burden I sustain
Which my lame feet find all too strong for me;
Wingless upon your pinions forth I fly;
    Heavenward your spirit stirreth me to strain;
    E'en as you will, I blush and blanch again,
Freeze in the sun, burn 'neath a frosty sky.
Your will includes and is the lord of mine;
    Life to my thoughts within your heart is given;
    My words begin to breathe upon your breath:
Like to the moon am I, that can not shine
    Alone; for lo! our eyes see naught in heaven
    Save what the living sun illumineth.

➤ ➤ ➤

By the end of the Renaissance, church disapproval of pagan themes
had led to Ganymede's disappearance from the visual arts but not from
the Western imagination. Archetypes have a way of living on in the
unconscious, even when they lack social expression. In the nineteenth
century, Ganymede continued to show up, often in unexpected ways.
Here is Paul Verlaine's playful ode to the god, written in 1889.

➤ ➤ ➤

What? in this resort, even here,
Truce, repose, peace, retreat,
You again, from the front or from the rear
Handsome Ganymede, my sweet?

The eagle carries you, seemingly
With regret, from the flowers;

Q U E E R

He flaps his wings begrudgingly,
As if to wish you elsewhere

Than in tyrannical Jupiter's house
So said Revard
And his eye makes fun of us
Glancing at you with queer regard.

Shucks, stay with us, good boy,
Distract us a little from our bothers
Give us a bit of joy.
Are you not our little brother?

TEXTS *The Geography of Strabo*, vol. 2, trans. H. C. Hamilton and W. Falconer (London: George Bell & Sons, 1913), 10.4.21, pp. 205–6; Ovid, *Metamorphoses*, trans. Henry T. Riley (London: George Bell & Sons, 1876), 10.162–219; Statius, *Thebaid*, 1.548–53 (my translation); Theognis, 1345–50 (my translation); Michelangelo, "Veggio Co' Bei Vostri Occhi," trans. John A. Symonds, in *Renaissance in Italy: The Fine Arts* (New York: Henry Holt, 1888), p. 522; Paul Verlaine, "On a Statue," in *Femme/ Hombres* (my translation).

OTHER SOURCES Robert Koehl, "Ephoros and Initiatory Homosexuality in Bronze Age Crete" (paper delivered at the meeting "At the Frontier: Homosexuality and the Social Sciences," City University of New York, 2 December 1993); K. J. Dover, *Greek Homosexuality* (Cambridge, Mass.: Harvard University Press, 1978); Edward Brongersma, "The Thera Inscriptions—Ritual or Slander?" *Journal of Homosexuality* 20, nos. 1/2 (1990): 31–40; Jan Bremmer, "An Enigmatic Indo-European Rite: Paederasty," *Arethusa* 13, no. 2 (1980): 279–98; John Boswell, *Christianity, Social Tolerance, and Homosexuality: Gay People in Western Europe from the Beginning of the Christian Era to the Fourteenth Century* (Chicago: University of Chicago Press, 1980), p. 253; James M. Saslow, *Ganymede in the Renaissance: Homosexuality in Art and Society* (New Haven, Conn.: Yale University Press, 1986); Dante Alighieri, "Purgatorio," in *The Divine Comedy* (New York: Modern Library, 1950), canto 9, p. 243.

S P I R I T S

He Fell in Love

When the Mountain Rose

Was in Bloom

In Japan, samurai warriors who followed *wakashudō*, "the way of loving boys," were called *nenja* and their youthful lovers *wakashu*. As this story from Ihara Saikaku's 1687 collection *The Great Mirror of Male Love* reveals, their affairs were governed by rules and conventions just as formal as those for heterosexual relations. The *nenja* was an adult samurai, who had completed his training and undergone the coming-of-age ceremony in which his forelocks are shaved off and he begins to wear adult male dress. His relationship with a *wakashu* generally lasted until the young man underwent this ceremony himself, usually at the age of nineteen. Then the former *wakashu* might seek a relationship of his own with a younger man. This was the ideal, anyway. In practice, as Saikaku's stories reveal, relationships sometimes lasted long beyond the younger man's coming of age. In a story called "Two Old Cherry Trees Still in Bloom," the partners are sixty-six and sixty-three years old!

Although Saikaku wrote primarily to entertain Japan's newly emerging urban middle classes, his tales draw on archetypal images and themes of same-sex love. In fact, by constantly refering to actual places, people, and dates, Saikaku creates the sense that archetypal lovers and their heroic gestures could be a part of anyone's life.

The following story has a lot to say about what happens when we become infatuated with another person. For the samurai, Tagawa Gizaemon, the young page, Okukawa Shume, is an irresistibly attractive figure that beckons him to follow. The samurai, as Saikaku writes, "walked the path of dreams." Figures like Okukawa Shume are, indeed, dreams—projections of unknown parts of ourselves. Following them always leads us into trouble. The phrase "falling head over heels in love" is an apt one. These affairs turn our lives upside down. I think that we are most susceptible to them when we are young and, again, as we approach the middle years, when younger men suddenly take on a god-like quality.

One of the pitfalls for gay men is that, in our terrific need to love and be loved, to feel good about ourselves, we fall obsessively in love, wishing not merely to cherish and be cherished by another man but somehow actually to be that person—because he has the beauty, intelligence, social skills, and so forth that we find lacking in ourselves. Love on this basis is doomed to fail because it's based not on love of a real person but on love of an image. The image is really something within ourselves. Its lesson has to do with giving ourselves permission to believe that we are beautiful and to love ourselves for it.

➤ ➤ ➤

EXHAUSTED BY FOUR YEARS OF FOLLOWING
A LORD'S RETINUE.
PARTING WITH LIFE FOR LOVE'S SAKE.
A PETITION PROMPTED BY LOVE.

Seeking relief from life in the barracks, he made his way from Toranomon to a village called Shibuya at the edge of the endless plain of Musashi. The Konnō cherry tree was at its peak of bloom, not unlike this spirited young samurai named Tagawa Gizaemon. Years ago in his youth he had been the most handsome young man in all four provinces of Shikoku and enjoyed considerable fame in Matsuyama. Due to certain circumstances he became a masterless samurai but before long was fortunate enough to get a new position at this original stipend of 600 koku. Grateful that things had gone smoothly for him this spring, he decided to visit the temple in Meguro dedicated to Fudō.

There, at the base of the waterfall where people wash to purify themselves, stood a handsome youth wearing a jewel-rimmed sedge hat tied with a pale blue cord. Below the hat his hair gleamed rich and black. His long-sleeved robe was dyed in a morning-glory pattern, and at his slender hips he sported two swords, long and short, sheathed in a polished shark skin. He held a lovely branch of mountain rose in his left hand. His quiet, untroubled beauty made it hard for Gizaemon to believe that he was human. Surely he was like the holy men of Mt. Ku She who could transform themselves into peonies at will. In a daze, Gizaemon followed after him. It appeared that the boy was a treasured possession of some great daimyo [lord], for he led a horse behind him and was attended by a host of young samurai and two watchmen-monks. Gizaemon knew that this was no ordinary personage. He forgot everything else and followed after him. The two monks had enjoyed some wine on the outing and began singing songs. Shortly, at the edge of Koroku's Shrine, they entered a gate bearing the paulownia crest.

At the crossroads nearby was a daimyo guard post. There Gizaemon asked about the boy and learned that his name was Okukawa Shume, a page in personal attendance to the lord. Gizaemon went home and that night could think of nothing but those lovely forelocks parted in the middle. Early the next morning he went back to the gate where he had last seen the boy and stood there for the rest of the day. He lost all interest in his official duties, so he claimed sudden illness and received permission to take a leave of absence. He rented lodgings in an alley south of Kojima Nichōme and lived there without employment, going every day from the 24th day of the third month to the beginning of the tenth month in the same year to wait outside the gate. He never glimpsed the boy's face again, however. To plead his case by letter was out of the question, so he was condemned to suffer from dawn to dusk the torments of unrequited love.

In the midst of his torment came word that the boy's lord had been granted leave to return to his domain. He and his retinue would depart from Edo on the 25th day of the tenth month. Gizaemon decided that he would follow the boy no matter where he might go and immediately gave up his rented lodgings. He sold off his belongings, settled his debts with the sake shop and the fishmonger, and dismissed his servant. Completely alone now, he set out in secret after the daimyo's retinue.

That night, the lord and his entourage stopped at Kanagawa. The following day darkness overtook them at Ōiso. At the edge of a marsh where sandpipers rose, the lovely boy he so longed for brought his palanquin to a halt and partially opened the door facing the cove. He recited an old poem, "Even the heartless soul feels moved. . . ." Intently, Gizaemon looked at him, and the boy returned his glance. They parted there and Gizaemon had no opportunity to see him again. Though wide awake, he walked the path of dreams.

Later, on the road cut through Mt. Utsu, he hid himself among some low boulders and peeked into the window of the palanquin as it passed. His eyes filled with tears despite himself. Perhaps the boy he loved had begun to take note of him, for Shume looked back with a gentle expression of sympathy on his lovely face. This increased Gizaemon's ardor for the boy even more, but days passed and he failed to catch another glimpse of him. He finally saw the boy one last time at Toyama in Mimasaka and then entered Izumo Province where he painfully shouldered a carrying pole in order to make a living. Thus the year came to an end.

In the beginning of the fourth month of the following year, the lord was again required in attendance at Edo. Gizaemon saw the boy three times on the way to Musashi, first at the Kuwana River crossing, again at Shimozaka, and last at Suzunomori. During the year-long residence in Edo, Gizaemon went every day to yearn for him outside the mansion compound. By now Gizaemon's appearance was quite strange. He was in love, to be sure, but no samurai should so disgrace himself in society. That he should have allowed himself to fall so low could only be attributed to a remarkable karmic bond.

The following year he once again followed the boy to his native province. Three years had now passed since he first saw the boy and gave up his position as a samurai. By now his sleeves were torn, his collar threadbare, and his only remaining possession was a single short sword. Outside the waystation at Kanaya, Gizaemon was watching the boy mounted on a horse in the distance when Shume noticed him and suddenly seemed to realize how much Gizaemon loved him. His heart went out to the man in compassion.

"Perhaps I can speak to him when the guards are not looking. If we could but exchange a few words, it might relieve his yearning," the boy thought, and secretly waited for him in the shadow of some pines at Nakayama Pass. Yet Gizaemon never appeared. Soon afterwards, the boy lost track of him completely. At odd moments when at rest he would sometimes wonder what had become of the man. He was indeed a tender-hearted youth.

Ten days after the daimyo returned to his province, Gizaemon straggled into Izumo. He had injured his foot and was now totally unrecognizable as his former self and apparently on the verge of death. His yearning for the boy, however, made him cling to his useless life, and for survival he turned to begging. He warded off the morning frosts with his straw hat and tucked his legs under him against the fierce wind at night. During the day he avoided notice by staying in the far-off corners of fields, appearing late at night to wait outside the castle gate for the pleasure of seeing Shume on his way home from night duty.

One cold and rainy winter night Shume spoke sadly to Kyūzaemon, a young samurai assigned to his service.

"I was born a warrior but have yet to kill a man with my own blade. If I should ever have to do so, I am not confident I could succeed. Please, allow me to try out my swordsmanship on someone tonight."

"From what I have seen in your regular practice, your skill with the sword is excellent," Kyūzaemon replied. "To kill without purpose would invite heaven's displeasure. Please wait until the right opportunity presents itself."

"I am not talking about killing someone for no reason. Earlier, I was looking at the big drainage ditch outside the mansion facing ours. There was a filthy beggar there who looked like he would be better off dead. Do you think if I fed and clothed him for a time he would then let me kill him? Go and ask him, please."

"I don't know. All he has left is life, and he may want to keep it," Kyūzaemon remarked dubiously, but he went anyway to where the beggar lay.

"Excuse me. I have something to ask," he began. "It is impossible to guarantee that a person's life will last until the rain, now falling, clears. Look at yourself, debased and without any purpose in life. It is the desire of the young master I serve to satisfy your wishes for thirty days, and after that to practice his swordsmanship on you in exchange. If you agree, he will see that you are properly mourned afterwards," Kyūzaemon explained.

To his surprise, the man replied without a hint of sadness. "I know I will not last till spring; I am completely worn out trying to survive the freezing nights. I have no family. Therefore, no complaints could arise after my death. Yes, I think it would be a splendid way to die." So saying, he rose and was led into the house.

After Kyūzaemon had reported this to his master, the man was made to wash and given a change of clothes. He lived in the central chamber for ten days, the period shortened by his own request. During that time he received good food and was well cared for in every way. The promised day arrived, and after midnight the man was led to a large garden.

"When you said you would give me your life, was it the truth?" the boy asked.

The beggar thrust out his neck and said, "I beg the honor of death at your hands."

The boy hitched up his trousers and jumped down to where the beggar sat, slashing at him with his sword. The man did not even wince, however. The sword had no edge on the blade!

The boy's attendants were all amazed to see this, but he chased them beyond the middle gate and locked them out. Seating himself in the waiting room, he asked the man to show his face.

"I recognize you," the boy said. "You were once a samurai, were you not?"

Gizaemon denied it, insisting that he came from a long line of merchants.

"Come now, do not hide it. I know that you love me deeply. If you do not tell me now, when will you have another chance? Or, am I mistaken?"

When the boy said this, the man reached inside his robe and from against his skin took out a package wrapped in bamboo bark. It was a persimmon weave purse of brocade. He presented it to the boy and said, "I beg you to look inside. It contains the proof of my love." Even as he spoke, tears like a string of jewels streamed from his eyes.

The boy untied the purple cord binding the purse and looked inside. It was a scroll made of 70 sheets of thin paper glued end to end. In it, the man had written every detail of his love for the boy from the day he first saw him standing in the field at Meguro up to the present. Shume was able to read only four or five pages of the scroll before he rolled it up again. Asking Kyūzaemon to look after the man, Shume went at dawn directly to the castle and appeared before the lord.

"A certain man has fallen in love with me," he said. "If I refuse him, I betray my honor as a follower of the way of boy love. If I act freely, it means breaking my lord's laws and is tantamount to rejecting your long-standing benevolence toward me. Please kill me so that I may escape this quandary."

"Explain yourself," the lord demanded.

Shume produced the scroll mentioned above and gave it to him. In private, the lord spent over one hour reading the scroll from beginning to end. When he finished, he called Shume to him.

"First, I order you to return home," the lord said. "I will discuss the matter with my advisers, and when I reach a decision you will be informed."

"If you send me home now, I will act improperly with the man," Shume protested. "Allow me to commit seppuku [ritual suicide] here instead." This was his second request to die.

The lord thought for a moment and then called his chief agent, ordering him to place the boy under house arrest.

Shume returned home and from that day the masterless samurai was presented with two swords and given new clothes befitting his rank. They spent their nights together, knowing full well it would cost them their lives. Never in previous ages was there boy love like this. Shume meanwhile made preparations for his funeral. Waiting in this way for death, however, must have had its pleasures.

Q U E E R

Twenty days later Shume's house arrest was lifted. In addition, he received five sets of robes with rounded sleeves and a gift of 30 *ryō* of gold. It was a most unexpected conclusion to the affair.

As for the masterless samurai, he was ordered to leave for Edo at an appropriate hour the next day. The man was overwhelmed with gratitude.

"How can I ever repay the lord's kindness?" he said.

That very night he reluctantly parted from Shume and set out on the trip home by horse. It was the 27th day of the twelfth month. At Hyōgo he sent those who were to accompany him back to their province and, instead of proceeding to Edo, secretly went to live in Izumi near Mt. Katsuraki, in the town where the Enohai well is found. He cut off his hair and took the monk's name of Mugen. There he lived, saying nothing and going nowhere. He took comfort in the flow of water that never ceased pouring from a pipe buried deep within the rocks beyond his bamboo fence and found pleasure in the words of the Chinese sages.

Without even fanning himself with one of the gaudy fans so popular nowadays, his heart grew pure and cool.

TEXT From Ihara Saikaku, *The Great Mirror of Male Love* (Stanford, Calif.: Stanford University Press, 1990), pp. 151–57.

S P I R I T S

And He Remained
with Him That Night
(Jesus)

Sometime in the late second century C.E., Clement, the bishop of Alexandria in Egypt, sat down to write a letter to a follower in Palestine. Clement's correspondent had encountered members of the Carpocratian sect, an early gnostic group that believed in communalism and sexual freedom. Apparently, the Carpocratians were quoting passages from a "secret" version of the Gospel of Mark. At that time, written copies of Christian texts were rare, and few believers were allowed to see those that existed, including Clement's disciple, who was, therefore, unable to respond to the heretics. The Carpocratians were claiming that the secret gospel endorsed a practice called *gumnos gumnō*, or "naked man with naked man." Clement wrote to reassure his friend that he had seen the secret gospel of Mark and that it contained nothing of that sort in it. Clement went on to quote directly from the secret gospel.

The discovery of this text in the 1950s by Morton Smith (it was part of an ancient book that had been recycled into endboards for another book and stashed in a desert monastery) triggered a lively debate. The passage that Clement quotes in his letter is no longer part of the Gospel of Mark. Indeed, the very existence of a "secret gospel" in the early church is something of a scandal as far as Christianity is concerned, which does not like to have to revise its history and certainly not the teachings of Jesus.

In any case, whatever the Carpocratians were saying about their version of Mark, Clement's own quote from it is quite surprising. He relates a version of the Lazarus story that appears to include a mystical baptism in which a scantily clad initiate is taught "the mystery of the kingdom of God." Although previously unknown, this passage helps explain the mysterious young man who is with Jesus in the garden of Gethsemene in Mark 14:51. He wears the same kind of white linen baptismal cloth worn in Clement's story. Later, he flees naked from the scene.

The Carpocratians were claiming that part of Jesus' secret initiation included something called *gumnos gumnō*. What did this actually involve? Smith cites a passage from Aelian, who describes a technique used by Libyans for curing snake bites: "He lies down beside the sick man, naked man with naked man [*gumnō gumnos*], and applying to him by friction the innate power of his own skin, renders the man free of the poison." The ancients also knew techniques for reviving the dead in which the healer pressed his naked body against that of the afflicted and breathed into his or her mouth. Perhaps this was the method Jesus used here and in the Lazarus episode to raise the dead.

Smith speculates that, like other early Christians, the Carpocratians performed baptism in the nude, in a rite that served to induct the initiate into the "mystery of the kingdom of God." Part of this process may also have involved a symbolic negation of gender. A well-known saying to this effect is attributed to Jesus in several early texts. According to the gnostic Gospel of Thomas, "When you make the two one, and when you make the inside like the outside and the outside like the inside, and the above like the below, and when you make the male and the female one and the same, so that the male not be male nor the female female . . . then will you enter the Kingdom."

Here is Clement's quote from the "secret" Gospel of Mark.

➤ ➤ ➤

To you, therefore, I shall not be slow in answering your questions, refuting falsifications by proclaiming the very words

S P I R I T S

of the gospel. For instance, after "And they were in the road going up to Jerusalem," and the following, up to "After three days he shall arise," the secret gospel counters word for word: "And they come to Bethany. And there was in that place a woman whose brother had died. And coming forward she prostrated herself before Jesus and said to him, 'Son of David, be merciful to me.' But the disciples admonished her.

"And being angered, Jesus went with her into the garden where the tomb was, and immediately a great cry was heard from the tomb. And coming near Jesus rolled back the stone from the door of the tomb and entering immediately where the young man was he extended his hand and raised him up, holding his hand. But the young man, looking at him, loved him and began to implore that he might be with him and going away from the tomb they came into the house of the young man, for he was rich. And after six days, Jesus instructed him. When evening arrived, the young man came to him, having wrapped a linen cloth around his naked body, and he remained with him that night. Jesus taught him the mystery of the kingdom of God. Rising from that place, he returned to the other side of the Jordan."

After this follows, "And James and John come to him," and all that section. But "naked man with naked man" and the other things you wrote are not found.

TEXT Morton Smith, *Clement of Alexandria and a Secret Gospel of Mark* (Cambridge, Mass.: Harvard University Press, 1973), 2.20–3.14 (my translation).

OTHER SOURCES Aelian, *De Natura Animalium*, 28.16; James M. Robinson, ed., *The Nag Hammadi Library in English* (San Francisco: Harper & Row, 1977), p. 121; Robert Murray, *Symbols of Church and Kingdom: A Study in Early Syriac Tradition* (Cambridge: Cambridge University Press, 1975).

S P I R I T S

You Will Now Perhaps

Be Less Angry

(Kolhamana)

Although many psychologists and mythographers speak of the role of the initiator as always being masculine, in the following myth from the Zuni Indians of New Mexico this figure is female—a powerful, undomesticated goddess whose name, Cha'kwen 'Oka, literally means Warrior Woman.

According to the Zuni origin myth, the original two-spirit, called at first Kokk'okshi, was born from the incestuous union of a brother and a sister. Kokk'okshi has nine brothers, sacred clowns with supernatural powers. The clowns are assigned to live in the region between the village of Zuni and "Zuni heaven," a small lake southwest of the village where the spirits of the dead, the *kokko,* live. The clowns are mediators of life and death, young and old. The two-spirit, on the other hand, is assigned to live with his mother at Zuni heaven, overseeing the dances of the *kokko.*

Meanwhile, the ancestors of the Zunis, who've been migrating eastward toward the Sun Father, encounter another people, the Kan'akwe. The Zunis kill two of their women, and this triggers a war. Kokk'okshi joins the other Zuni gods in fighting the Kan'akwe. In the process, he is captured by their leader, the Warrior Woman. Following this episode, he is known as Kolhamana, or "supernatural two-spirit." Every four years, when these events were commemorated in a major ceremonial, the god Kolhamana entered the village with the masked dancers who represented the enemy people, carrying not only male and female symbols but those of hunting and farming as well, thereby uniting the key oppositions of Zuni society.

This myth offers a viable alternative to the story of Oedipus as a model of psychological growth for gay men. Freud and his followers believed that the development of homosexuals was somehow "arrested." It was not possible, in their view, to be an adult *and* a homosexual. But in the Zuni story we see that the two-spirit *leaves* the home of his mother, the classical gesture of psychological independence, and joins the male gods in a male activity—warfare. In the course of this adventure, he undergoes an initiation, receiving a new name and new clothes from the Warrior Woman.

This kind of initiation is possible because of the complex images of women in Zuni mythology, from the benevolent Kachina Mother to the scary Warrior Woman, who has the authority and power to tame Kolhamana's unsocialized behavior and teach him the self-control that the Zunis expected of all adults. The episode ends with the entrapped game animals being released to roam the world—an apt symbol for the final, liberatory phase of initiation.

➤ ➤ ➤

PLAYERS AND PLACES

Middle Place   the present village of the Zunis, which they
   believe to be the center of the world
Hanlhibinkya   a ruin west of Zuni village
Divine Ones   twin gods who lead the original Zunis out of
   the underworld
Newekwe   Galaxy society, a religious society with both
   healing and hunting magic

S P I R I T S

Kan'akwe   a god people who block the progress of the migrating Zunis, famous for their skill as hunters

Cha'kwen 'Oka   "Warrior Woman," leader of the Kan'akwe

Kokko   also called *kachinas*, the gods of the Zuni, portrayed in masked dances

Kokk'okshi   "Good God," the original name of the two-spirit kachina

Kolhamana   "Two-Spirit God"

'Itsebasha   one of the sacred clowns

Sayalhi' 'a   a warrior kachina

During their migrations in search of the Middle Place, the Zunis settled at a place called Hanlhibinkya. But they were not alone. When smoke was spotted coming from the east, the rain priest of the north exclaimed, "Ha! There is a village. I wonder who these people are?"

"We will see," said the Divine Ones, the supernatural twins who had led the Zunis out of the underworld. They asked two members of the Newekwe society to go ahead and "hunt" a trail. At first the clowns refused. "We are fighting men," they said, "and we may meet some one and kill him, and thus get you into trouble." But the Divine Ones insisted, and the two left as instructed.

Proceeding a short distance, the Newekwe spotted two women from a nearby village washing buckskin on the bank of a stream and without provocation killed them both. Discovering the murders, the people of the village—the

Kan'akwe—were enraged and attacked the Zunis. Their leader was the giantess Cha'kwen 'Oka. The Kan'akwe and the Zunis fought for two days, but neither side was able to win. Everything was at a standstill.

Each night, in their village, the Zunis danced and prayed for rain—so that their bowstrings, made of yucca fiber (because they were farmers), might be made strong, while the bowstrings of the Kan'akwe, made of deer sinew (because they were hunters), might be weakened. On the third morning, the Zunis' prayers brought heavy rains as they sallied forth to meet the enemy. Their ranks were swelled by the presence of the *kokko*. But Cha'kwen 'Oka again appeared before her army, shaking her rattle and stamping back and forth. She captured three of the Sacred Lake kachinas: Kokk'okshi, a *lha'ma*, the Koyemshi clown called 'Itsebasha, and one of the Sayalhi"a warrior kachinas.

Back in the Kan'akwe village, the prisoner gods were required to appear in a dance held in celebration of their capture. Kokk'okshi was so angry and unmanageable that Cha'kwen 'Oka had him dressed in female attire, saying to him, "You will now perhaps be less angry."

Meanwhile, the rain continued to fall, and on the fourth morning the bowstrings of the Kan'akwe became so weak that most of their shots failed. At the same time, after many prayers to the Sun Father, the knowledge came to the elder War God that Cha'kwen 'Oka carried her heart in her rattle. Carefully aiming his arrow, he pierced the rattle, and Cha'kwen 'Oka fell dead. The Kan'akwe retreated, and the Zunis captured their village, freeing the three captive gods.

Then the Zunis opened the gates of the corral in which Cha'kwen 'Oka had kept all the game animals, telling them, "We have opened for you the doors of the world; now you may roam where you will, about the good grass and springs, and find good places to bear your young; you will no longer be imprisoned within the walls, but have the whole world before you."

TEXT Based on Matilda C. Stevenson, "The Zuni Indians: Their Mythology, Esoteric Societies, and Ceremonies," *Bureau of American Ethnology Annual Report* 23 (1904): 34–38.

OTHER SOURCES Will Roscoe, *The Zuni Man-Woman* (Albuquerque: University of New Mexico Press, 1991).

The
Ecstatic
Body

The myths and stories in this collection have opened up a broad and varied psychic landscape. Scanning history, we've found our presence in unexpected times and places. Stretching our imaginations, we've encountered gay gods and a few demons. Everywhere we have seen the evidence of the myriad powers that are part of our ways of living and loving.

In the introduction, I distinguished the paths of the Queen, the Divine Twins, and Initiation, noting that each has its own historical tradition. But now I want to talk about a place where the spiritual and psychological impulses of these patterns converge. There seems to be a way that, when carried out to their fullest expression, all these patterns of same-sex love reach a similar state—the psychological condition known as *ecstasy*. Traditionally, ecstasy can take two forms: the shamanic type, in which the soul temporarily leaves the body to travel in the realm of the spirits, and the Dionysiac type, in which the god temporarily "possesses" the individual. Both types involve a suspension of the boundaries of the individual ego.

The radical Queen becomes ecstatic by wantonly transgressing the limits of gender. The way of Initiation produces ecstasy through ritual and by refined manipulation of the body. The Divine Twins escape ego boundaries when, mirroring each other's souls, they slip into the ecstasies of subject-SUBJECT love.

This inner potential of same-sex love to produce ecstatic consciousness is guarded, however, by some fearful images. If you want to enter this ground, you'd better have a strong stomach. The techniques of ecstasy can be extreme, the experience chaotic and disorienting. We stand at the threshold of a realm where monstrous hybrids of gender and sexuality and violent transformations of the body are the rule.

What is ecstasy? What does it mean to say that, in ecstasy, the boundaries of the ego are erased?

What I have in mind is that sensation of being "one" with everything around you. It's not really so rare. If you've ever found yourself writhing for hours on end on a disco dance floor feeling united with the music and the people around you—and everyone looks beautiful, including yourself—well, you've been there. If you've ever felt, in the heat of sexual passion, merged with your lover, or wishing to be so; if you've ever felt, in the fleeting moments after orgasm, as if you were floating on air, or, for a moment, forgot where you were—you've been there. And if you've ever put on a wig for Halloween and suddenly found a whole other personality emerge from within you—you've been there.

These are all experiences of ecstasy. Suddenly we feel at one with everything around us. Everything is accepted. Everything is pleasurable. Like a beautiful Gay Day parade that stretches out to include everyone from lesbian bikers to gay fathers, pagans to Christians, and men and women of every race and nation. Ecstatic consciousness makes room for everyone. If you keep it going, it becomes a carnival. There are, of course, more extreme forms of ecstasy—losing consciousness, having visions, being "possessed." The forms that ecstasy take are shaped by customs and individual differences, but its basis lies in the capacity that all humans have for multiple modes of consciousness.

Another way of defining ecstasy would be to distinguish it from the consciousness that Christianity and patriarchy endorse. Official Judeo-Christian consciousness requires individuals to be making moral judgments at all times, distinguishing between good and evil, not in a state of communion with the universe. Above all, it requires that sex be limited to genital contact for the purpose of procreation; there is no place for the indiscriminate sharing of touches that erases social distinctions. There have been ecstatic movements within all monotheistic traditions—prophets, self-flagellators, whirling dervishes—but they have always been marginal. Western societies as a whole have chosen Apollo over Dionysus, Oedipus over Attis.

Of course, all societies seek to create not only a certain kind of consciousness among their members but a specific kind of body as well. In patriarchal societies, the ideal male body is one that has never been penetrated or "used" by other men, but rather, using its erect penis, only penetrates others. Everything is narrowed down to the penis. The penis alone is the source of pleasure at the same time that it becomes a symbol of social power in general. All this requires a great deal of concentration on the part of men, an exercise of "mind" over "body." A psychic axis is forged between the head and the penis so that one symbolizes the other. In the oedipalized female body, on the other hand, all erotic energies are centered around the *lack* of a penis, the "empty" vagina, and the woman's need to fill this "lack" by having sex with men.

These are the bodies created by "oedipalization," by being raised according to the model of the ancient myth of Oedipus. The story of Oedipus unfolds within a world dominated by the concerns of the father and organized according to his values. Laius, the king, must have a son to preserve and extend his rule of Thebes. Everything hinges on a certain function of his penis: its ability to produce another penis. To symbolize the identification of the son with the father, the father gives him his name. But the extension of the father ends up replacing him. After all, sons can't be versions of their fathers without acting like patriarchal males themselves. They must be their "own men." If fathers resist, the sons will kill them. Thus, in the imagination of the father, giving the son his name signifies his own death. Laius tries to avoid this fate by abandoning his infant son Oedipus at birth. But Oedipus grows up and kills Laius anyway. Then Oedipus marries his mother, which, according to Freud, is what all heterosexual men do in psychological terms. The succession of fathers and their sons invariably perpetuates the founding acts of violence on which patriarchal male psychology is based.

The oedipalized body is centered on the penis as both organ and symbol. It is the body of the father. Norman O. Brown describes the oedipalized body in his classic book *Love's Body*:

> What the psychoanalytically uninitiated call "sex," psychoanalysis calls "genitality," or "genital organization," seeing in it an arrangement, a *modus vivendi*, a political arrangement arrived at after stormy upheavals in the house of Oedipus. *The arrangement is to concentrate sexuality in one part of the body, the genital; this concentration, or organization, establishes the "primacy" of one "component-impulse" which is now the "dominating" or "supreme" component-impulse in the sexual life of the body.* It is, says Freud, a well-organized tyranny, of a part over the whole. (italics mine)

What Freud and his followers did not and could not imagine, however, was that there might be other bodies than this one. Or, if they did imagine them, they assumed that they had to be the bodies of psychotics and schizophrenics. But, in fact, there are functioning nonpatriarchal cultures and healthy nonpatriarchal bodies in many parts of the world and in history. European folk traditions, for example, often project alternative and unauthorized images of the body as part of their resistance against the church. As the literary critic Mikhail Bakhtin points out, the novels of Rabelais are filled with folk characters whose bodies transgress all boundaries. Bakhtin calls this the *grotesque body*, but it is also a good example of the de-oedipalized body as well:

> The grotesque body, as we have often stressed, is a body in the act of becoming. It is never finished, never completed; it is continually built, created, and builds and creates another body. Moreover, the body swallows the world and is itself swallowed by the world. . . . This is why the essential role belongs to those parts of the grotesque body in which it outgrows its own self, transgressing its own body, in which it conceives a new, second body: the bowels and the phallus. These two areas play the leading role in the grotesque image, and it is precisely for this reason that they are predominantly subject to positive exaggeration, to hyperbolization; they can even detach themselves from the body and lead an independent life. . . .
>
> The artistic logic of the grotesque image ignores the closed, smooth, and impenetrable surface of the body and retains only its excrescences (sprouts, buds) and orifices, only that which leads beyond the body's limited space or into the body's depths.

Whereas the patriarchal male body is "closed" and "sealed," the de-oedipalized body is "open." This is the key to understanding the symbolic meaning of castration in the stories that follow—it produces a radically de-oedipalized body permeable to its environment.

The spiritual meaning of de-oedipalization is indicated in the Hindu story of the god Shiva at the beginning of the world. Brahma and Vishnu asked Shiva to create the world. Shiva agreed, but plunged himself into the water for a thousand years to meditate. Impatient, Vishnu gave Brahma the female power of creation, and Brahma created the gods and other beings. When Shiva finally emerged, he found the universe already filled, so he broke off his phallus and threw it to the earth, saying, "There is no use for this *linga*." This did not render him asexual, however. His detached phallus became an object of worship in the cult of the *linga*, and through this cult his sexual power continues to enter the world.

But what about the body that no longer has a phallus? In the case of the *hijra*, the flow of blood during their castration is believed to empty them of both desire *and* gender. They describe themselves as "broken vessels." A broken pot, of course, holds nothing; rather, anything that is put in it is immediately passed on. In a similar sense, *hijra* receive and transmit the erotic energy of their goddess. If the *linga* stone represents the detached phallus of Shiva, then the *hijra* are, in effect, the detached phallus of the goddess, *her* vehicles for extending erotic energy and fertility into the world. The underlying hostility of self-castration must also be acknowledged. This is an intensely antagonistic gesture against the primary symbol and instrument of patriarchy—although, as Freud once observed, the removal of a part is often a metaphor of birth.

Of course, these are *myths*, and castration is symbolic. From the patriarchal point of view, we gay men castrate ourselves every time we give up male privilege, every time, especially, that we allow our bodies to be penetrated by other men. For us, penetration is a key to ecstasy because it erases the distinction between inside and outside. Most heterosexual men find this distinction indispensable to their sense of ego, which they tend to think of in terms of metaphors of fortification. Indeed, for most heterosexual men, sexuality *is* penetration. This is why, in the early days of the AIDS epidemic, when gay men first asked doctors what they should do to protect themselves, the typical answer was, "Stop having sex." As heterosexual men, sex to them meant penetration and, therefore, an exchange of bodily fluids. Mutual masturbation, an extremely safe form of sex, never occurred to them as an alternative because it wasn't "sex" in heterosexual terms. Gay men had to discover nonphallocentric sex on their own. In this regard, it should be noted that many of the pioneers of safe sex were gay men who had been active in the radical faerie movement, where alternatives to depersonalized gay sex had been explored since the 1970s.

In short, there are less radical methods of de-oedipalizing the body. To the extent that safe sex directs erotic focus away from penetration, it can be delightfully nonphallic. Piercing, tattooing, bodybuilding, and costuming are also ways of reclaiming the body, of making it something of our own choosing and remapping our erotic zones in the process. All these practices interrupt the head-crotch axis and direct attention away from the penis to other parts. Eventually, the entire surface of the body becomes a sex organ. Over time, the oedipalized body of the father sloughs off like an old skin, revealing a distinctly gay body, capable of responding on emotional and sensual levels unimaginable to those locked within the rigid roles and inhibitions of patriarchal sexuality.

To erase the inside/outside boundary is the first step toward a complete sensory and symbolic disassemblage of the body along shamanic lines. The devotees of leathersex constantly report ecstatic and out-of-the-body sensations similar to those of shamans. What is too often missing from their accounts are the reasons why these extreme experiences are to be valued: not as an end in themselves, but because they heal and teach us lessons that we can use to heal others. As Mark Thompson writes, "Radical sexuality helps clear out the psychic basement, that place deep within where things that trouble us most are kept hidden. Long-held feelings of inferiority or low self-esteem, grief and loss, familial rejection and abandonment, come to surface during S/M ritual." But having discovered such potent medicine, do we need to keep taking dose after dose? Merely because we *can* unleash ecstatic energies in ourselves and others does not mean that everyone needs to or should. Such states of being are only good or bad depending on what they're used for. Healing does seem to me to be one of those desirable ends.

It's obvious that many gay men are experimenting with these ancient magics. In fact, I see gay men creating ecstasy all the time, erasing boundaries, stretching the limits of their sense of self, re-creating their bodies. But we're doing so unconsciously, haphazardly, inefficiently. We think it's all for fun, when what we're really looking for, weekend after weekend, is connection with something larger than ourselves.

Understanding that it is archetypes and myths we are seeking contact with makes the difference between purposive and compulsive behavior. If we work consciously with the symbols associated with these experiences, we can use the symbol, instead of the experience, to achieve the states of awareness we desire. But we can no longer put off answering the question that sex keeps asking us. The myths that follow offer guideposts for this journey, a journey to the worlds beyond the body of the father.

SOURCES Norman O. Brown, *Love's Body* (Berkeley: University of California Press, 1966), pp. 126–27; Mikhail Bakhtin, *Rabelais and His World* (Bloomington: Indiana University Press, 1984), pp. 317–18; Mark Thompson, *Leatherfolk*, p. xvii.

The Power
of the
Hijras

The image of the *hijra* holding up his bloody parts in the following story is one of the most disturbing in this collection. But the story underscores the social, political, and magical dimensions of this act. The phallus symbolizes the source of power for men. Precisely for this reason, the individual who is indifferent to this symbol, who does not care if he is powerless in the way men define power, acquires a frightening and awesome power of his own. He can no longer be manipulated by other men.

As this story suggests, the *hijra*'s power of refusal makes her more potent than the king. Holding up his parts, he exposes the fragility of gender identity, especially that of men. His act bespeaks defiance and even hostility toward the male symbol. By treating it as a gesture of religious devotion, Indian society softens its threat to the gender order. Even so, the power is there. It is a power we gay men can seize when we refuse the standard male role and when we refuse to be intimidated by the charge of being unmasculine.

➤ ➤ ➤

There once was a king who asked a hijra to show him her power. The hijra clapped her hands three times and immediately the door of the king's palace opened automatically, without anyone touching it. Then the king said, "Show me your power in some other way." By the side of the road there was a thorny cactus. The hijra just took the thorn of the cactus and emasculated himself. He showed the king that he had the power. The hijra just stood there with the blood oozing out and raised his hand with his penis in it. Then the king realized the power of the hijras.

TEXT Serena Nanda, *Neither Man nor Woman: The Hijras of India* (Belmont, Calif.: Wadsworth, 1990), p. 24.

He Ceased to Be

What He Was

(Attis)

Attis, the patron of the *galli* priests, also commits self-castration. As the various stories about him reveal, this shepherd boy from Phrygia was caught in a web of social and psychological dilemmas, trapped between the demands of the patriarchal male role, which requires that men marry and reproduce, and the possessive attachment of Cybele, the Mother of the Gods, who refuses to let him grow up.

To understand the symbolic significance of Attis's self-castration, however, we need to keep in mind the context of these myths, the world of ancient Greece and Rome. These were male-dominated societies, in which men and women were sharply differentiated and socially separated. At the same time, even as women were degraded in social terms, men honored and revered archetypal images of women in the realm of religion. The worship of Cybele, for example, was an official religion of the Roman state. This contradiction between men's idealization of women and their often brutal treatment of them was the source of deep psychological conflicts.

The various versions of Attis's myth show him unable to meet the demands of either father or mother figures. The implicit message is that neither of these roles is in his nature. As Arnobius remarks, the Phrygian shepherd is "safe" only if he remains "free" of marriage. At the same time, the story of Attis warns against the danger of resolving this dilemma by repressing the feminine. In the following selection from Ovid, Attis suffers a violent return of the repressed, represented by the Stygian goddesses, the feminine deities of fate. Self-castration resolves his dilemma by disqualifying him from *either* set of demands. Since he can't reproduce, he is ineligible to inherit a male role, nor can he reciprocate the sexual demands of the mother figure. In this sense, it is an act of liberation, and, because it founds the *galli* priesthood of Cybele, it is also a creative act.

The earliest versions of the Attis myth emphasize his relationship with the father figure, either his own or in the form of Zeus. The following example was recorded by the Greek author Pausanius, who credits Hermesianax (born around 300 B.C.E.) as his source. Significantly, Attis does not survive the father god's jealous wrath.

➤   ➤   ➤

> As to Attis, I could learn no secret about him, but Hermesianax, the elegiac poet, says in a poem that he was the son of Calaüs the Phrygian, and that he was born from the womb a eunuch [*ou teknopoios*, "not child begetting"]. On growing up, continues the account of Hermesianax, he migrated to Lydia and observed for the Lydians the rites of the Mother; and he rose to such great honor that Zeus was made angry and he sent a boar upon the fields of the Lydians. And there certain Lydians, with Attis himself, were put to death by the boar. . . .

➤   ➤   ➤

Another account of the Attis myth comes from the Roman poet Ovid, who wrote at the beginning of the common era. Like most later versions, it emphasizes Attis's relationship to Cybele.

➤   ➤   ➤

PLAYERS AND PLACES

Attis   a young shepherd of Anatolia (ancient Turkey), in
some accounts the son of a Phrygian or Lydian king

Cybele   called the "tower-bearing goddess" because of the
crown she wore

Sagaritis   a nymph or *Naiad*, identified with a Phrygian
river of the same name or with a fruit-bearing tree

Mount Dindymus   a mountain in Anatolia sacred to
Cybele

Stygian goddesses   also called the Furies or Moirai

Attis, a Phrygian boy of handsome appearance who lived in
the woods, bound himself with a chaste love to the tower-
bearing goddess. She wished him to be kept for herself to
guard her temple, and she said, "Resolve that you will always wish to be a boy." Having been commanded, he gave his
word. "If I lie," he said, "may the love for which I break faith
be my last."

But he broke faith with the nymph Sagaritis and ceased to
be what he was, and for this the angry goddess exacted pen-
alties. By wounds made on the tree she cut down the Naiad,
who thereby perished, for the fate of the Naiad was in the
tree. Attis went mad, and, believing the roof above his marriage bed to be falling in, he fled, and running to the top of
Mount Dindymus, he pleaded at one moment, "Take away
the torches!" and at another he shouted, "Remove the
lashes!" And often he swore that he could see the Stygian
goddesses approach him.

And so, with a sharp stone, he mangled his body and

dragged his long hair in the unclean dust, and his cry was, "The blame! With blood I pay the penalty I deserve. Ah! Perish the parts that were my ruin! Ah! Let them perish," he kept saying. He cut away the burden of his groin, and suddenly none of the signs of manhood remained.

His madness is an example, for unmanly ministers [the *galli*] cut their virile members while they wildly toss their hair.

TEXTS Pausanias, 17.9–12 (my translation); Ovid, *Fasti* 4.223–44 (my translation).

S   P   I   R   I   T   S

The Ecstatic Body

Blue

Light

In the following excerpt from Steven Saylor's short story "Blue Light," Bill is a cocky topman, newly arrived in town. He rents a room in a rambling old Victorian occupied by two women and a mysterious and irresistibly attractive man named Michael. Michael keeps to himself; his lifestyle appears to be largely nocturnal. When Bill finally manages to initiate a sex encounter with him, he discovers he that has taken on more than he can handle.

Michael invites Bill to his loft at the top of the house. At first, Bill takes his usual dominant role, but Michael quickly reverses the situation. Bill finds himself handcuffed and helpless. Then things take a real twist. Using a glowing neon hoop, Michael envelops Bill's body in a strange blue light. He places a choker around Bill's neck and slowly pulls on the chain until Bill's head lifts free from his body. Bill has been decapitated, but he's still alive and still conscious. Mind and body completely split, he is able to witness what follows with a literal sense of detachment. Saylor's story incorporates all the themes of ecstasy, gender transgression, and the de-oedipalized body that we've seen in the previous examples of more traditional myths.

➤ ➤ ➤

Michael picked up the riding crop and walked with long slow strides to the crouching, trembling body. He raised the leather high above his head and slashed it across my shoulders.

My body jerked, spun, rolled away—staggered to its feet,

tripped over my pants on the floor, rose desperately, ran blindly into a wall—turned and took a defensive stance, hiding its stinging shoulders against the wall. Tits clamped and cock hard. I couldn't understand that, the way my cock stayed so stiff the whole time—not yet.

Michael followed slowly. He looked at the crop. Looked at my chest, muscles in high relief, tense with pain. He touched the crop to my cock. My body flinched. Michael squeezed his hard-on. Then he raised the crop and slashed it backhanded across my stomach.

I saw my body double over and run, reeling with pain and confusion, trying to escape. Michael followed it patiently around the room, taking his time, stroking his thick white cock and wielding the crop. Like a hunter, exhausting his trapped game. Playing with me.

At last the pain-wracked body collapsed kneeling in the center of the room. Shoulders against the floor, heaving—ass thrust in the air.

Michael stood over the broken body. He slowly masturbated as he beat my ass with the crop, blow after blow, until the pale buns were red and blistered.

Michael discarded the crop, grabbed my body by the clamps and forced it to stand. In the reflections I could see every mark—the long red stripes across my shoulders, the back of my legs, my stomach. My cock—a slave's cock, rock hard after the beating, veins pulsing, dribbling from the tip. I suddenly knew why—the body craved it, but so did my head, watching, crazy with excitement at the spectacle. Two places at once. Masochistic victim and sadistic observer of my own humiliation, wanting more.

S   P   I   R   I   T   S

Michael played with the clamps—twisted, pulled the hard flat muscles into sharp peaks, watched my body twitch and heave. He pulled the clamps off, one at a time, and tossed them away. He caressed my body, watching the skin writhe when his fingertips brushed over the tender stripes.

He cocked his head and flashed me a cryptic smile. "Good slave body. Takes it well. Ready for whatever's next. Shall I fuck it?"

He rubbed his hard cock against mine. "Sure. Give him what he wants. But do it my way."

He hooked his finger through the dangling cock choker and pulled it taut. Tighter and tighter. The chain sank into the gathered flesh, my cock bulged until I thought the skin would burst. I knew what was about to happen, and my mind plummeted deeper into the numb stupor that was its only protection.

Michael licked his free hand. His saliva seemed to glow with blue light. He worked his wet fingers mysteriously around my cock and balls. I saw his lips move, as if he were whispering inaudibly. The thin chain flashed with blue flame—

Then the chain slipped through. He dropped it quickly and raised his hand to lift the genitals free. He held the nine inch shaft by the testicles in his right hand. In its place there was a smooth hairless swelling of flesh between my legs.

Again I tried to scream, though I knew it was hopeless. "I said, don't twist your face up like that," he growled. He swung the disembodied cock and slapped me across the face with it. My eyes welled with tears, making the candlelit room swim and sparkle.

My mind was sinking. I longed for unconsciousness. But his voice pulled me back.

"It'll stay hard," he said. He was rubbing thick lubricant over my cock. There was a dim sensation of pleasure somewhere below me. "All the energy of the spell holding you is focused in your cock, like a powerful conductor. But I have a warning for you. When you come—when your cock ejaculates—you'll break the spell. You'll remain in whatever condition you're in at that instant. So unless you want to stay in three pieces, you'd better hold off." He smiled and slid my cock through his fist. "Of course, you won't have much control."

He returned to my body and struck it with the cock, wielding it like a blackjack. The body jumped like a startled animal.

He dug the nails of his left hand into my right nipple and pulled the body, headless, sexless, up onto tiptoes. He stepped forward and rubbed his cockhead against the denuded stump where my cock had been. My body responded instantly—thighs parted, hips rocking back and forth. The body rubbed its groin against the blunt tip of Michael's cock.

He bent at the knees, lowering his cock and breaking the contact. My body followed blindly. The hairless groin sank down and searched for Michael's cock, found it, rubbed itself on the silky knob. Humping, like a bitch in heat.

Michael folded smoothly to his knees and settled his ass on his ankles, his hard cock pointing up like a missile. The handcuffed body spread its knees and squatted deeply, craving more contact.

Michael licked his middle finger and rubbed it against the

sleek spot between my legs. My body squatted, swayed back and forth, barely kept its balance. Once again, I sensed what was about to happen. The unbelievable. The unthinkable.

There was no sign of an opening in the place where my genitals had been. Just a bald swelling, like the ball of a shoulder. But as I watched, Michael slowly, gradually buried his finger in the flesh. He began to slide it in and out. My body begged for more.

He turned his head and shot me a quick glance. His face was slack, lips parted, eyes flashing with triumph. As if to say, see what I can make you into? See how badly you want it?

As he finger-fucked me, he reached around with his right hand and began to push the disembodied cock—my cock—into my squatting ass. All nine inches, all the way to the balls in one steady shove. He pressed his palm over the crack to hold it in.

My hips squirmed on his finger, pushed back onto my cock. Michael removed the finger and my groin tried to follow, ready to abandon the cock up its ass for more of his hand. Again, I could see no opening there.

But when he grabbed my tit to pull my body forward and down, his cockhead slipped inside. And my body squatted, deeper, desperate for it, until Michael's thick shaft was completely swallowed.

Michael gasped and rolled his big shoulders with pleasure. Closed his eyes and hissed inaudible obscenities. Or incantations.

And my body—the body he had handcuffed, beaten,

The Ecstatic Body

clamped—decapitated, emasculated—subjected to something unspeakable and inhuman—it rode his fat cock and
screwed back onto the shaft he held up its ass. Mindless but
hungry. More a whore than a slave. More animal than human. A creature of dark magic. His creation.

I was thankful that body had no head. It gave me a way to
fool myself. To say that it wasn't me.

There was a sudden ghost sensation, more vivid than the
others—a flash—as if I felt my cockhead rubbing against
his deep inside my bowels. It jolted me, like two charged
wires touching. I felt feverish. The lights dimmed.

For a long time my consciousness came and went. My
eyes would flicker open, glimpse grappling bodies, hear Michael's sex-charged groans. Scenes in the mirrors: Michael's
beautiful ass, fucking wildly, my legs wrapped tight around
his hips, Michael on his back on the bed, my body on its
knees above him, fucking itself on his cock while he pulled
on my tits—my body, shoulders on the bed, Michael standing between my drawn-back legs fucking with long strokes
while he used my hard cock like a truncheon across my
stomach and chest—

After a long blackness, I felt Michael slapping me awake.
I opened my eyes and saw a cock before my face. But not Michael's cock. A bigger, coarser instrument, knotted with
thick veins and streaked with rectal mucus. My throat filled
with fresh saliva. I opened my mouth—

—then realized it was my cock held before me. I closed
my mouth, recoiling from the insanity of it.

"Go ahead." I heard Michael's voice above me. "It's not as

pretty as mine, but it'll give you what you need. Go ahead. What's wrong? Don't wanna taste shit? Come on, you've made plenty of guys suck it after you've screwed 'em. Besides, it's your shit, man."

I looked hard at the cock. I had seen it in mirrors of course, even in photographs. But now I saw it as my slaves had. Huge and pulsing, inches from my lips. And I knew why men had groveled for it. Knew the power that made them crave it. I opened my mouth and moaned silently.

Michael laughed and shoved it down my throat. Rammed it in and out, the way I would have. I discovered how it felt— exactly how it felt. I remembered the riding-crop trick in New York—the sweltering afternoon with the six-pack when I tied his face to my crotch and kept my cock down his throat for hours—coming, pissing, coming, pissing. Now I knew why four hours hadn't been enough for that cocksucker.

I felt pleasure in my cock as I sucked. Almost like sixty-nining, sucking and being sucked. Two places at once.

I squeezed my throat around the huge dick, milking it, savoring the pleasure I was giving and receiving. Then Michael spoke.

"Remember, Bill. When it shoots, the spell breaks. And if that happens while you're still in pieces—there's nothing I can do to put you together again." He kept sliding it in and out of my throat.

My blood froze. I stopped the undulations in my throat. "Come on, Bill." His voice was low and evil. "Your cock's close. Been close for hours. The balls are way up in the sack. Come on," he teased, ramming it hard and fast, "make it come. Work your throat like a good cocksucker. Don't you wanna know how it feels when you shoot in some guy's mouth? Must be good—I bet they always come back for more. Don't you wanna taste your own come?"

I looked up at him and pleaded with my eyes. He kept sliding the big dong in and out—I felt it expand, the way I always do when I'm on the verge—

I clamped my teeth down on it, hard, to stop the stroking.

Michael laughed. "Okay. I believe you." He whipped the spit-streaked plunger from my throat and tossed it on the floor. I heard it land with a heavy thud and felt ghost pain in my balls.

He picked up my head and carried it to the center of the room. My body was lying on its side on the floor, exhausted. Michael squatted, placed my head on my shoulders, wet his fingers with glowing blue saliva and stroked the connection. I felt warmth flow from my neck to my chest, my hips, my legs. Thank god, whole again—almost.

I spent a few minutes coughing and swallowing convulsively, clearing the juices that clogged my throat. Michael undid the handcuffs and pulled me to my feet. My legs were shaky, there was pain everywhere. But it was wonderful to feel anything beneath my neck.

Michael stretched and yawned. "Shit, I'm beat," he said. "Been fucking you for hours, baby." He pinched one of my nipples, making me throw my head back in pain. "Came in you twice while you were out. Once in your ass, and once— well, you saw. Think I'll take a shower and hop right in bed."

"But—" I looked at my cock on the floor and quickly looked away.

"Oh, yeah," Michael said. "That. Go ahead and take it. It's yours."

My chest knotted with horror. "Please," I whispered.

"What did you say? I couldn't hear you."

I lowered my eyes—caught a glimpse of the bare flesh between my thighs—shut my eyes tight.

"Oh please, Michael. Let me have it back. Oh please, for god's sake—"

I felt a heavy slap across my face and knew it wasn't his hand. His voice was deep and unctuous above me. "That's no way to beg."

I kept my eyes shut.

"Get on your knees and beg with your mouth."

I knelt and took his soft meat between my lips. My face was wet with tears.

"Make me come again, Bill. It won't be easy. Three times is usually my limit. Show me how good you are. Show me how good you suck cock. Make me come, and I'll let you have it back. That is—if you don't shoot first." I heard and felt the slick crackle of flesh on flesh above my head. He was holding my hard cock and stroking it.

I sucked and tried to think of nothing but his cock. Slowly, slowly it hardened, until the beer-bottle thickness gorged my throat. It wasn't so easy this time. I choked, gagged, felt my gorge rise—but I never let go. I forced my throat onto him over and over, strangling myself.

"Better than your cock, isn't it, Bill?"

Yes, he was right. His cock, so thick, so flawless; it *was* better.

The Ecstatic Body

He began to moan and twist. He was close. I was going to make it.

Then he pulled out. Held my face off, fought off his orgasm. "Not yet," he whispered, "not yet."

He tortured me that way. I brought him close over and over, sucking desperately, using every trick I could remember. Then he would pull out and make me start over, all the while working my cock.

"Think about it," he crooned. "What happens if I make you shoot first. You'll be what you are now, forever. Might not be so bad." He reached down and stroked a finger over my sexless groin. I felt an incredible flash of pleasure, unearthly. I jerked back and whimpered around his shaft.

"You'd be my slave, Bill. Really my slave. You've been playing that game for years, but this is real. I'd own you—or own your cock, which is the same thing. You'd be mine. You could never show yourself to another man like that. Think about it. Have to come crawling to me for sex. Maybe I'd be in the mood. Maybe not. And you've seen the kind of games I like to play."

With that nightmare in my head, I gave him my last ounce of energy. Worshipped him like the primal force he was. Sucked and sucked and *sucked—*

—and finally heard his roar above me. Felt his meat stiffen and pump. Tasted bitter semen—and at the same instant, my own hips began to jerk. I was coming, in response to him. *Too late—*

I felt his hands on my crotch—blue fire—

And when it was over, I was whole again. Michael pulled

his shaft from my throat with a pop and collapsed onto his throne, chest heaving. He looked worn out and happy. I was too drained even to hate him. Too exhausted to stand. He forced me to lick my cum from the floor. Made me kiss his feet.

I looked up at him. After long minutes I caught my breath. The numbness seeped out of my head. Even as wrecked as I was, I had to know how.

"Michael, what you did—what you do . . . I don't know what it's called, I don't even know if it has a name . . . but what . . . what—"

"Something you're born with," he said. "There are others. I've met three in my lifetime, heard of more. We keep our distance from each other. Don't get ideas about learning it. I've studied, learned the ancient laws, found new ways to focus my power. But either you have it—and you know it—or you don't. I knew that you didn't when I first saw you. The tan is a giveaway. You like sunlight far too much. I can't teach it. I can only share it."

He pushed his big toe into my mouth. "So if you ever want it again, you know where to come. You'd be crazy to ask for it, though. I like danger. The possibilities—the games—are endless. Sooner or later. . . ."

He pulled his toe from my mouth and pushed my face to the floor with his foot. "Now get out. I'm tired of you."

I staggered naked to my room. It was dark outside. I looked at the clock. I had spent eight hours in his room. I closed the door and crawled into bed. I saw the leather strap

The Ecstatic Body

on my right arm. I wanted to put it back on my left, but I was afraid he would know somehow.

I heard Michael in the hallway, then in the shower. He was singing happily, basso profundo, as I dropped off to sleep.

TEXT Steven Saylor writing as Aaron Travis, "Blue Light," in *The Flesh Fables* (New York: Masquerade, 1994).

Their

Beastly Customs

and Inordinate Desires

In the ancient world, the *galli* were one of several cult groups, such as
the Corybantes, Curetes, and Idaean Dactyli, whose rites were based
on wild dancing and music. These groups of religious devotees were all
believed to have originated in Phrygia or Crete, and all were associated
with the goddess Cybele (or Rhea, as she was known to the Greeks).
They are said to have been guardians at the birth of Zeus and also of
Dionysus, clashing their swords and shields to hide the sounds of birth
from a father determined to destroy his offspring. According to Strabo,
the Corybantes and Curetes were "inspired people . . . subject to
Bacchic frenzy," who provoked terror "by means of war-dances,
accompanied by uproar and noise and cymbals and drums and arms,
and also by flute and outcry." The purpose of these *teletai*, or "ritual
techniques," was not to honor the gods as such but to directly benefit
the participants. They were healing rites.

According to Plato, the purpose of the rites of the Corybantes was to
cure obsessive fear caused by an unhealthy state of mind and emotions
that the Greeks called *mania*. Dancing frantically about the patient
while playing loud music induced a trance-like state, during which the
patient was believed to be possessed by the gods. Sometimes the
patient uttered prophecies while in this condition. When the trance
ended, the patient felt a sense of inner calm and repose, a condition
Strabo calls "restored, corrected." In others words, as is often the case
in Greek religion, a dose of the poison was part of the cure—good
mania drives out the bad. I believe that the public rites of the *galli* had
a similar purpose: to induce catharsis on the part of bystanders and

observers. Theirs was a public ministry—and herein lies the source of their popular appeal, which lasted until the final days of paganism in the Roman Empire.

When I began reading about the *galli* priests of Cybele and Attis and the way that they shocked the sensibilities of elite Greeks and Romans—and horrified early Christians—I couldn't help but think of a more recent band of gender guerrillas, the Sisters of Perpetual Indulgence. The "Sisters" were a group of gay men in San Francisco in the late 1970s and early 1980s who dressed as nuns and practiced a campy form of street theater. Their founders—Sister Missionary Position, Reverend Mother the Abbess, Sister Hysterectoria, and Sister Vicious Power Hungry Bitch—combined interests in theater, dance, politics, and spirituality to create a group that became an icon for gay San Francisco.

The Sisters' humor was cutting edge, but most people in San Francisco delighted in their appearances. Bobbi Campbell, the early AIDS "Poster Boy," was a member of the Sisters, and the group put out one of the first safe-sex brochures in 1982. Beneath the hilarity, many of the Sisters were quite serious about the spiritual side of their calling. "Our mission is much bigger than we could ever have imagined," they declared in a tongue-in-cheek statement of purpose. "Our ministry is one of public manifestation and habitual penetration. Our motto is 'Give up the guilt.'" The Sisters sought to expiate guilt through laughter, to lift the yoke of repression and self-recrimination that an anti-sexual culture places everyone. That this should be done while garbed in some outlandish version of a nun's habit only made it more powerful. Even for non-Catholics, nuns stand for sexual repression and authority through guilt. The Sisters reversed all this, offering on-the-spot catharsis.

The following account of the priests of Dea Syria, the Syrian God-

The Ecstatic Body

dess, whose cult was closely related to that of Cybele and whose priests were also called *galli*, comes from Apuleius's comic novel *The Golden Ass*, written around 150 C.E. Although Apuleius exaggerates for comic effect, the practice of these priests traveling through the city and countryside to beg for alms is well documented.

➤   ➤   ➤

The day following I saw them apparelled in divers colours, and hideously tricked out, having their faces ruddled with paint, and their eyes tricked out with grease, mitres on their heads, vestments coloured like saffron, surplices of silk and linen; and some wore white tunics painted with purple stripes that pointed every way like spears, girt with belts, and on their feet were yellow shoes; and they attired the goddess in silken robe, and put her upon my back. Then they went forth with their arms naked to their shoulders, bearing with them great swords and mighty axes, shouting and dancing like mad persons to the sound of the pipe. After that we had passed many small villages, we fortuned to come to a certain rich man's house, where at our first entry they began to howl all out of tune and hurl themselves hither and thither, as though they were mad. They made a thousand gests with their feet and their heads; they would bend down their necks and spin round so that their hair flew out in a circle; they would bite their own flesh; finally, every one took his twy-edged weapon and wounded his arms in divers places . . . so that you might see the ground to be wet and defiled with the womanish blood that issued out abundantly with the cutting of the swords and the blows of the scourge:

which thing caused me greatly to fear to see such wounds and effusion of blood, lest the same foreign goddess should likewise desire the blood of an ass for her stomach, as some men long for ass's milk. After they at last were weary, or at least satisfied with rending themselves, they ceased from this bloody business: and, behold, they received from the inhabitants, who offered eagerly, into their open bosoms copper coins, nay silver too, vessels of wine, milk, cheese, flour and wheat. . . .

At length they came to a certain town, purposing to make good cheer there, being glad at a great gain they had gotten, where, under colour of divination, they brought to pass that they obtained a fat ram of a poor husbandman for the goddess' supper, and to make sacrifice withal. After that the banquet was richly prepared, they washed their bodies, and brought in a lusty young man of the village to sup with them; and when he had scarce tasted a few herbs before the supper they began to discover their beastly customs and inordinate desires. For they compassed him round about as he sat, to abuse him,[1] but when mine eyes would not long bear to behold this horrible fact, I could not but attempt to utter my mind and say, "O masters," but I could pronounce no more

1. The original Latin here might be more literally translated as "and here and there surrounding the young man, stripped and lying on his back, they abused him [*flagitore*] with their foul mouths." The term *flagitore* originally referred to a legal proceeding in which creditors verbally harangued their debtors. It eventually became a euphemism for sexual solicitation. The implication is that the priests performed oral sex on the young rustic whom they had invited for dinner.

but the first letter, "O," which I roared out very clearly and valiantly and like an ass. . . .

TEXT Apuleius, *The Golden Ass: Being the Metamorphoses of Lucius Apuleius*, trans. W. Adlington, rev. S. Gaselee, Loeb Classical Library (Cambridge, Mass.: Harvard University Press, 1915), 8.27–30.

OTHER SOURCES Strabo, 10.3.7–23; Ivan M. Linforth, "The Corybantic Rites in Plato," *University of California Publications in Classical Philology* 13, no. 5 (1946): 121–62; Plutarch, *Amatorius* 758E–763B.

Dionysus

at the

Disco

When I first visited San Francisco in 1975, I was just twenty years old and had to sneak my way into the city's countless gay bars. By the time I moved there three years later, I considered myself a veteran of gay life. I had come out in my hometown, where I made myself infamous as president of a gay student group. I had made expeditions to the bars and baths of Seattle and Portland, and I had spent a summer in New York, absorbing gay politics, the West Village, and Cherry Grove. Patti LaBelle was my goddess, David Bowie my god, and the song "San Francisco" by the Village People my anthem. And so, on a cold, rainy morning on the last day of 1977, I stuffed all my possessions and my dog, Steve, into my Mazda and drove south from Eugene, Oregon, where I had been attending college, for the fabled city of San Francisco. I was following the trail of several of my friends; soon I would be drawing others after me.

Almost none of those friends are alive today—even as I write this, February 1994, I learn that my first lover, Mitch, has died. They died, not only from AIDS, but from cancer and suicide and drinking and bullets. What makes me saddest in remembering them now is thinking about all their half-finished, just-about-to-get-it-together projects— their writings, paintings, and precious collections—all piled up some- where, in the garages of their families, or worse, simply tossed out by friends or relatives overwhelmed by the incredibly depressing process of cleaning out a dead person's apartment. I guess it's the historian in me that should think of their words and their images as much as their faces and their touches. But this was how they reached me, by inspiring me to be creative and bold and to dream that in some way I, too, could live the life of an artist.

In thinking about these times now, the years that immediately followed Stonewall, I'm struck at how aggressively we moved to seize our freedom. If the police no longer arrested us for holding hands in bars, we insisted on doing it in the streets, in and out of drag. Like Patti Smith, we claimed "the freedom to be intense . . . to defy social order and break the slow kill monotony of censorship . . . to break from the long bonds of servitude—ruthless adoration of the celestial shepherd. Let us celebrate our own flesh—to embrace not one's race mais the marathon—to never let go of this fiery sadness called desire." And when Sylvester, San Francisco's homegrown disco diva, sang "you are a star," we believed him. Stars are bright but way-out.

Were we secretly hoping someone or something would impose a limit, restore a sense of containment? We, the Stonewall Generation, overthrew every constraint ever imposed on homosexuality. We shattered the social contract based on denial, silence, and secrecy. We sailed off the end of the map following our Eros. Some have said that all this—our sexuality, our dancing through the night, our flamboyance—is just typical "male" behavior, competitive, betraying a fear of intimacy. My work with gay myths gives me another perspective.

How can we ignore the Dionysiac elements of gay male experience in the 1970s? We were discovering/recovering the arts of ecstasy, our lost heritage from the history of radical queens and gender transgressors, from the *hijra*, *galli*, and all the two-spirits of the world. It wasn't merely rebellion. We had stumbled into the powerful and ancient magics of music, dance, eroticism, and gender transgression. We learned how to erase the father ego, to neutralize gender, to experience epiphanies—on the dance floor, in the bathhouses, up and down Castro Street and Christopher Street in the finest drag we had. We soared like Saint Nijinski, on the wings of ecstasy: "I am not a fakir and a magician. I am god in a body. Everyone has that feeling but no one uses it. I do make use of it, and know its results. People think that this feeling is a spiritual trance, but I am not in a trance. I am love, I am in a trance of love."

And, yes, we seized on sexuality because it is one of the few domains in modern life where ecstasy is possible—that is, not criminalized or labeled insane. Sex is the only place where the average person can play with the unconscious, to allow some of its images and fantasies to escape, to relax the terrific strain of ongoing repression, and sometimes to touch the divine. This is, finally, why we do these things—because they heal us in profound ways.

As Judy Grahn says, gay people like to "go first." Sometimes that means paying the most. So it seems important now not to lose what was gained from the experiments of the 1970s, first and foremost being an understanding of the inherently *spiritual* impulse underlying all these behaviors; or else, all is merely conspicuous consumption, the privatized "pleasures" of a market economy. If you ask me why we took such terrific risks with drugs and sex and our bodies, I can only say that we were trying to create a new reality founded on beauty. Like Arjuna, we were "a son or daughter without father or mother." No one had been where we were going. And where we were going was down and in, a descent much like Asushunamir makes in search of Ishtar.

When I arrived in the Bay Area, I lived in Berkeley for several months and completed an internship at a gay social service agency. Berkeley was wild enough I suppose by middle-American standards, but San

Francisco was even wilder, and that's where I plunged myself every weekend. Friday or Saturday nights (often both), I made the rounds of the city's bars and bathhouses with my friend Andy, wherever a friendly guy with happy pills was welcome. I was amazed and fascinated by the cross section of humanity that I saw. And at the center of it all, or so it seemed, was Andy and his pills, the common ground for this nocturnal democracy.

Meanwhile, during the dull weekdays back in Berkeley, I started the habit of taping large pieces of poster paper to my walls and writing journal-like entries about my experiences on them. Sometimes I illustrated them with what I considered to be avant-garde "sissy-punk" graphics, inspired by my friend Roan Pony (who at the time was somewhere in London absorbing the punk movement firsthand). I'm including the following example of this writing not so much for its literary value but as an ethnographic document from a lost time, a time in which gay archetypes came out of centuries of hibernation and blazed forth like fireworks.

➤ ➤ ➤

And this is when I came onto the scene, totally game for Andy's routine, new in town from the hinterlands, etc. Each weekend, wide-eyed off the Bay Bridge and into the city breathless, here I am, show me around, I'm lost don't know who I am what I want to be, etc., etc. And immersing myself into Andy and his trip, going wherever he was going, just following and going along. And Andy, gradually, after two or three weekends, finding companionship in having such a willing victim to go with him, take into his trip, trust with his dealing, and get into places through his infinite contacts.

Weekend after weekend, ricocheting through the maze of
San Francisco, crawling up to terrible heights, careening
into the gulches, valleys, sloughs, basins, whipped around
skirts of hills, avenues, alleys, freeway exits—South San
Francisco, the long wait in the car while Andy is in a house,
behind a window half covered by a green army blanket, the
mysterious exchanges of dealers and countings and check-
ing out and measured, casual conversation, while I'm in the
car, getting high (and Andy comes out and I say, "So what
took you so long . . . don't tell me you counted every one of
those pills" "Oh don't give me your old dirt, I saw you sitting
out here smoking pot in her little pipe"—and he pulls the
door shut and tosses me a giant, empty pharmaceutical bottle for Quaaludes, a thousand at a time, a souvenir for Andy
from his connection)—the Castro, the Polk, the Haight,
parties in the Mission with flashes of rock stars, drunks falling out of windows—food at late-night Zim's or I-HOP or
the Grubstake in the Polk, the baths on Post Street or Ritch
Street. And each weekend I can see the subtle changes in
Andy—during the week, for whatever reason or cause,
something affects him, he slips through these shifting images—he's a hippy at the Stud, he's a clone in the Castro,
he's carrying a purse on Polk Street—then he discovers the
Trocadero, the now famous Trocadero, but in its earliest
days, before they started memberships, the new monster ul-
timate disco in a warehouse after hours club and giant fantasy dance floor, a huge magic carpet to transport 1200
people, a disco machine pumping out night perpetual—and
Andy is a disco queen with slacks and polyester shirts and

gold chains, he meets a couple guys who work there and they sneak us in so Andy can sell his pills to the masses—and you're instantly part of this scene, this dance, these hundreds of people, a swirling human glob of release and expression, everything is happening, dancing, talking, cruising, puking, falling down, muffled shouts, people collapsed on risers while bass sound radiates through their limp bodies, queens sitting in the middle of the dance floor holding their spinning heads, giggling on MDA, LSD, quacks, perks, barbs, val-yums, preludins, crystal meth, black beauties, mesc, coke, tuinals, talwins, dust, Quaaludes, Quaaludes, Quaaludes—sex, grabbing, rubbing, sex-looking, sex-feeling—longing, crying, hysterical laughter, birth and death of all forms of human contact, now, here, all on one tribal, pounding dance floor for thousands, bathed in all-brain encompassing disco beats like great pounding waves and all eye-filling lights, initiates we surrender our senses to the disco temple—it's a *scene*: *the* scene::1978::San Francisco::WE MADE IT—twelve hundred people struck dumb and transcended, stand stunned, stumble about, forgot something, seek eyes of others, the doors are locked, we bump into each other spinning different directions—*you make me feel, you make me feel, you gotta feel*—SNAP:: men in leather swishing great gold lamé fans, men with mustaches and round muscles and poppers and skin wet, chest shining and whistles, glowlights, scarves, tambourines, veils, bells, chains, tubes, bandages, plastic, dressed like Arabs, like Indians, like cowboys, like construction workers, like bikers, like cycle sluts, like disco stars, like somebody, like nobody,

Q U E E R

with slips over jeans and Jimmy Carter masks, with shiny gym shorts in spiked boots, in jockstraps, with bandannas to catch sweat, pumping iron boys, pounding flesh, killing time, the weekend—this is the universe—disco heaven, paradise promised, the heart, the dream, and there is no past, no future, time stopped—*you make me feel, you make me feel, oh make me feel*—I've never been hurt, I've never been alone, I've never hated myself, I'm apart of this, a/part, of this, apart, a part, apart—*you::you make::you make me::you make me feel::you make me feel so mighty real!*

TEXT Will Roscoe, *Hollywoe* (1978).

S P I R I T S

The Ecstatic Body

Our

Spiritual

NEITHERNESS

Harry Hay, one of the founders of the modern gay movement, deserves credit for first seeing lesbians and gay men as a cultural minority—as a group with shared values based on a unique window on the world and an important, if hidden, history. Harry has been exploring all the implications of this idea for over forty years now. The following passage comes from an essay he wrote in 1986, originally called "Radical Faerie Proposals to the 'March on Washington' Organizing Meeting." Harry was especially concerned that the gay people gathering at this event project a distinct identity, not stage events in which they seemed to imitate heterosexual forms. Here he speaks eloquently of gay powers and pinpoints their source in our ability to escape the rigid confines of gender.

➤ ➤ ➤

As adults, though similar to our hetero counterparts physiologically, we Gay folk differ emotionally, temperamentally and intellectually, or, in a word that subsumes all three, SPIRITUALLY. Some of us may be a combination of both hetero masculine and hetero feminine, but mostly we are a *combination of neither*.

· It is from this *spiritual NEITHERNESS*, evident in our capacity to fly free from historical conformities and prejudices, evident in our capacity to invent in the very

teeth of nullifying rules and regulations—that our contributions come.

· It is from this *spiritual NEITHERNESS* that we draw our
capacities as mediators between the seen and the
unseen—as berdache priests and shaman seers; as artists and architects; as scientists, teachers, and as
designers of the possible; mediators between the make-
believe and the real—through theater and music and
dance and poetry; mediators between the spirit and the
flesh—as teachers and healers and counselors and
therapists.

· It is from this *spiritual NEITHERNESS*, as the sissies and
the tom-boys of the schoolyard, the kids who grew up
(each the only one of her/his kind he/she thought) on
the outside of the chain-link fence looking in and
observing both sides of the hetero social experiences of
boy/girlhood, teenhood, and adolescence that they had
thrust us away from and then shut us out from . . . it is
from this spiritual neitherness we draw our capacities to
see them as they can never see themselves, to be to them
a nonjudgmental mirror, to give this back to them
through theatre, dance, music, poetry and—*above
everything else*—through the affectionate mockery of
camp, which expresses itself in healing laughter.

When we begin to truly love and respect Great Mother Nature's Gift to us of gayness, we'll discover that the bondage

of our childhood and adolescence in the trials and tribulations (dark forests with no one to guide us) of *neitherness* was actually an apprenticeship she had designed for teaching her children new cutting edges of consciousness and social change. In stunning paradox our *neitherness* is our talisman, our faerie wand, the gift we bring to the hetero world to

—*transform their pain to healings;*
   —*transform their tears to laughter;*
      —*transform their pumpkins to coaches;*
         —*transform their hand-me-downs to visions of*
         loveliness.

TEXT Harry Hay, "Radical Faerie Proposals to the 'March on Washington' Organizing Meeting," published as "A Separate People Whose Time Has Come," in *Gay Spirit: Myth and Meaning*, ed. Mark Thompson (New York: St. Martin's, 1987), pp. 284–85.
OTHER SOURCES Stuart Timmons, *The Trouble with Harry Hay: Founder of the Modern Gay Movement* (Boston: Alyson, 1990).

The Circle

of Loving

Companions

It seems incredible to me that the AIDS epidemic is now over a decade old. How long can a nightmare last? For me, living in San Francisco, it seems as if time stopped around 1983 with the horrible realization that a disease was spreading among gay men, that it was sexually transmitted, and that there was no treatment for it.

I guess it's a measure of my own continuing denial that I'm still grappling with the very idea of the AIDS epidemic. And it's true, I've done all I can to keep this alien force from taking over my life completely, stealing my future, dehumanizing me, turning me and my friends into statistics. Early in the epidemic, I made a more or less conscious decision to continue my work in gay history and culture and not become an AIDS activist or a professional service provider. I would help any and all friends, and that turned out to be several. But I would not let this damn disease take away what was emerging at that point in my life as the work I was most interested in doing. As time went on, this work became my escape. I learned to cherish every moment free enough of crisis and grief that I could continue researching and writing about gay history and culture. Buried in books, sitting at my computer, "Thoth," my imagination slips far away, to the possibility of worlds without homophobia and dreams I could manage—not the out-of-control nightmare of AIDS.

In the midst of this crisis, I've witnessed countless responses to the virus, from complete denial to total immersion. I've learned to accept each person's response as valid for him. Who is to say what is the proper way to react to meaningless, random death and how to be human in an inhuman situation, to witness inconceivable suffering and the loss of friend after friend after friend? I have a hard time grieving because I can't allow myself to normalize this crisis. To go through gestures and to mouth words designed somehow to make what has happened all right, a lesson, a blessing in disguise—I just don't have the stomach for it. Any world that treats the massive dying of young people as normal is sick and cannot itself survive.

I still remember thinking that the AIDS epidemic was not going to affect me because I and most of my friends had dropped out of fast-lane gay life by 1980—or we had never been admitted to its ranks in the first place. After all, those parties, drugs, bathhouses, and gay resorts cost lots of money that many gay men I knew didn't have. Slowly, the real nature of the disease and its long incubation period unfolded. As we now know, the government's response to the epidemic ensured that it would spread far and wide before the right changes were made. When my lover and I went to get tested in 1986, we did it mostly out of a sense of being politically correct and socially responsible. We had never defined our relationship as monogamous, but since becoming lovers in 1980 we practically had been. Actually, we had both spent plenty of time in bathhouses. Brad was working at the Ritch Street baths in San Francisco when I first spotted him and we began cruising each other. I used to go on Friday afternoons to take advantage of a discount rate on lockers.

But I was the bottom, and I had been sexually active on both coasts. If either of us were going to get AIDS, it should have been me.

Yet it was Brad who tested positive and I who was negative. How? Why? Everything about AIDS remains mind-boggling to me.

And one by one my other friends got tested, and so many of them were infected, too.

So my efforts to keep AIDS at an emotional and psychological distance failed. Between myself and all those who have not been touched by the epidemic, a great chasm has emerged. They have a future and a past. My life is focused on the present only; both past and future are too frightening to think about. I live in the pure pleasure of every day that doesn't involve a health crisis, and on those days that do I keep my thoughts on the humble, so often futile tasks of bringing comfort. Eight years have gone by since the day Brad and I got those test results. We've lived in a kind of suspended animation ever since, punctuated by medical emergencies and funeral services. Brad suffers but with an incredibly bright spirit, his dignity unscathed by the horrendous tortures his doctors call treatment. I do my best to keep up with him.

On any given day now the majority of conversations I have in my mind are with dead people. Their spirits crowd my little apartment, along with their bittersweet mementos, reminding me of the joys we'll never share again, of the horrifying images of their dying faces I'll never forget. There is little solace knowing that their lost lives are but one stream flowing into the rivers of blood that crisscross the American landscape, the blood of millions of native people, Africans, working people, women, and children, all sacrificed to the New World principle of Holy Profit. Their angry, tortured spirits crowd the land. I see them everywhere, seeking vengeance by driving people crazy with voices of guilt—crazy with violence, crazy with addictions, crazy with hatred. No one can escape *this* epidemic, the disease of a sick nation and of a society grown insensitive to suffering.

What are the mythical dimensions of HIV? This is hard for me to think about because I still can't accept the horror of the AIDS epidemic as a growth experience. Certainly, one effect of an epidemic is to freeze-frame the image of those who die young. Incomplete lives always have a mythical dimension. Like Icarus, a whole generation donned wings and took flight for new and unimaginable lands. But we flew out of the shadows too fast and got too close to the searing rays of the sun—one after another we crashed, spectacularly, in mid-flight, swallowed up by the waters below.

When I think of my friend Pony, less than five feet tall but a spitting image of David Bowie, who introduced me to the world of punk music and New Wave art, to Brian Eno and Patti Smith—or Nona, always on the verge of getting her life together so that she could write, who managed, in the middle of the HIV epidemic, to come up with an old-fashioned killer like leukemia—or Dennis, nicknamed Murder Boy because of his reckless disregard for polite behavior, who managed to mount at least one art show and spray paint his name on the streets of San Francisco before he died—or Mitch, my first lover, who made AIDS his mission in life and, in five years of HIV living, inspired thousands of people around the country, most of all his family and neighbors back in our home state of Montana—when I think of them now, they are all mythical figures. Who knows what they might have become?

As Franklin Abbott suggests, we need to honor our lost friends in the same way that so many traditional societies honor their dead—as ancestors. We need to find the small gestures and shared rituals that not only preserve their memory but help as well to convert those guilty feelings we have as survivors into positive affirmations of what we learned from our friends while they were alive.

Gays have always had a special relationship to death, even before AIDS. This is not merely because society imagines us linked to death because we don't biologically reproduce or, because of homophobia, so many of us have thought about suicide. The arts of healing, mediation, and transformation that we have seen linked again and again to two-spirit personalities and same-sex love regularly bring us into contact with death and dying. As the account "Don't Look Back" shows, burying the dead was a common function of two-spirits in native California. We saw earlier in the story of Asushunamir how the figure who is neither male nor female is able cross the boundary between living and dead. In our own lives, we gain knowledge of death through the soul-searching of our years in the closet, through the shamanic experiences of ecstasy described earlier, and through the process of continually coming out, allowing old skins to slough off so that new facets of ourselves can keeping emerging.

When I first tried to think of a name for this chapter, the phrase "closing the circle" came to mind. But what was the circle in the case of gay men? What images of closure and continuance do we have, compared to the scene of the heterosexual funeral, with family members surrounding the casket, each promising continuance by the shared features of their faces? What takes the place of this for gay men?

At this point the phrase "the circle of gay love" came to my mind. I thought of the networks we form of friends, gay and sometimes straight, of boyfriends, former boyfriends, and those very special friends we call *sisters*. Our ties in these networks are nothing like the mandatory obligations of family relations. They may even seem flaky in comparison. Best friends are likely to move across the country at a moment's notice or disappear whenever they find a new boyfriend. Still, I've seen the resilience of gay friendships again and again in the AIDS epidemic. There are always those who disappear in a crisis, but there are always others who appear, often from afar and at great sacrifice, when they are most needed. While the heterosexual family stumbles and hesitates, unable to decide whether to comfort their gay child or maintain the facade of their Puritan values, gay friends step in and take over, overseeing the passage of their tortured friends as they also manage the homophobia of family members.

Now, I thought of the phrase I wanted, "the circle of loving companions." The Circle of Loving Companions was originally an affinity group started by Harry Hay and John Burnside in the 1960s to provide an alternative voice within what was then a very cautious gay movement. Groups and concerns not normally represented (such as gay youths) were invited to use the Circle of Loving Companions as an organizational identity so that they would be recognized at meetings of the more conservative groups. Later, Harry and John used this name for the small but politically minded network of gay people they formed in New Mexico in the 1970s. The Circle of Loving Companions also became a working name for the collective of gay men that Harry and John long dreamed of forming—a dream that eventually gave rise to the faerie sanctuary operated today by Nomenus at Wolf Creek, Oregon. Although the collective has never come together, they have still managed to draw around them a genuine circle of loving companions.

In May 1993, Harry and John were burned out of their home in Los Angeles. Once again a circle of gay love took care of its own, as friends looked after the couple's housing, financial needs, and the tremendous amount of backbreaking, heartbreaking work involved in sorting through the singed remains of one's life. Writer friends wrote press releases and articles to alert the community, artist friends organized benefits, and others came forward to offer hours of time and bottomless concern.

What redeems our lives, what makes of death a living, is this circle of loving companions—bonds based on true caring, not the unthinking obligations of blood relation. Our loving friends lend grace and humor to the transformations of age and death. Their caring keeps our memory alive, ensuring that our life's work will not be forgotten. Although a part of me rebels at the idea of attributing anything positive to HIV and its epidemic, it is clear that the disease has brought the circle of loving companions to the forefront of gay life. It has given us the true and tested bonds that only a shared experience of trauma can forge. If it has taught us to love and respect each other better, to cherish our gay circles, then it has indeed given us something we can nourish and pass on to future generations.

Don't
Look
Back

The person who can bridge genders can often bridge other oppositions as well—including that of life and death. Among the Yokuts Indians of California, two-spirits, or *tono'chim*, were traditionally chosen for the role of burying the dead. Because these corpse handlers have dreams that come from the dead, they can risk contact with the spirit world. Their dreams protect them.

➤   ➤   ➤

At death the corpse was washed with cold water and a piece of old deerskin. The hair was washed with soaproot, dried, brushed, and arranged. All the best clothing and ornaments were put on it, and it was laid on deerskins in the center of the house, behind the fireplace, with the head toward the west or northwest. The corpse was flexed, tied, and wrapped in deerskins at this time, and left in the same place and position. Anyone who wished might visit it and join in the wailing which was carried on all night. After the corpse was removed for burial, the house was burned. . . .

Meanwhile two men and two "women" (the latter transvestites, *tono'chim*) had dug the grave, using digging sticks and baskets. If, while digging, they came upon another burial, it was necessary that they crush the skull, remove the brains and taste a bit of them, otherwise they would die.

The following morning at dawn, the strongest of the four

buriers carried the corpse in a net on his back to the grave. He walked around the grave three times before lowering his burden. Then he addressed the deceased, saying, "You're going where you're going; don't look back for your family." Then they filled in the earth. They were paid for this work, and cleansed themselves by bathing.

TEXT Ana Gayton, "Yokuts and Western Mono Ethnography," *University of California Anthropological Records* 10, nos. 1–2 (1948): 46.

The Circle of Loving Companions

Thou Shalt Ever

Be with Me

(Apollo and Hyacinthus)

One of the most moving accounts of the loss of a lover in any mythology is that of Apollo and the Spartan youth Hyacinthus. The god Apollo lives with the mortal youth Hyacinthus as an equal while they roam the mountains together. But, in a contest of skill, Apollo "unintentionally" kills Hyacinthus—that is, his motives are repressed or unconscious. In his grief, Apollo commits himself to memorializing Hyacinthus in song and words. As Freud describes the process of mourning, "an object which was lost has been set up again inside the ego." In other words, Apollo devotes a part of his self to Hyacinthus, and Hyacinthus lives on. Freud believed that this was the only way in which the ego could survive the loss of emotional ties to others.

Hyacinthus's relationship with Apollo was a model of Sparta's version of age-based homosexuality. The male population of Sparta, organized like a permanent standing army, all lived in barracks. Every young man of good character had a lover, who was referred to as his "inspirator" (*eispnēlas*, literally, "breather into"), while the youth was referred to as his "listener" (*aitas*). The inspirator had the responsibility of a parent for the behavior of his beloved. The pair stood together in battle. This pattern is similar to that found on Crete and described in the last chapter. A festival in honor of Hyacinthus and Apollo was celebrated annually at both Amyclae and Sparta.

Although the accident occurs while the two lovers are engaged in military games, the rebirth of Hyacinthus as a purple flower seems distinctly nonmilitaristic. As Judy Grahn notes, "Purple represents, brings about, and is present during radical transformation from one state of being to another. Purple appears at twilight and at predawn. It stands at the gate between the land of the material flesh in one world and the land of the spirit or soul in another and is present in the envelope of energy that surrounds the body, usually called the 'aura.'" It's also interesting to note how the rebirth of Hyacinthus as a flower places him and same-sex love in the world of nature. (Many years later, Proust would also use the imagery of flowers to locate homosexuality within nature in *Remembrance of Things Past*.)

Here is Ovid's account of the death of Hyacinthus, told in the voice of the bard Orpheus, who addresses the youth directly.

➤ ➤ ➤

PLAYERS AND PLACES

Phoebus   "Bright" or "Pure," an epithet of Apollo

Hyacinthus   according to one tradition he was the son of Amyclas, founder of *Amyclae* near Sparta; according to another he is the son of the Spartan king Oebalus and therefore called *Oebalides*; he is also called the "Taenarian youth" after a promontory in his native land

Eurotas   a river that passes by Sparta

Titan   there are several Titans, this being a reference to Helios, the sun

"Phoebus would have placed thee too, descendant of Amycla, in the heavens, if the stern Fates had given him time to place thee there. Still, so far as is possible, thou art immortal; and as oft as the spring drives away the winter, and the

Ram succeeds the watery Fish, so often dost thou spring up and blossom upon the green turf.

"Thee, beyond all others, did my father [Apollo] love, and Delphi, situated in the middle of the earth, was without guardian Deity, while the God was frequenting the Eurotas, and the unfortified Sparta; and neither his lyre nor his arrows were held in esteem by him. Unmindful of his own dignity, he [Apollo] did not refuse to carry the nets, or to hold the dogs, or to go, as his companion, over the ridges of the rugged mountains; and by lengthened intimacy he augmented his flame [of love].

"And now Titan was almost in his mid course between the approaching and the past night, and was at an equal distance from them both; when they stripped their bodies of their garments, and shone with the juice of the oily olive, and engaged in the game of the broad quoit [discus].

"First, Phoebus tossed it, well poised, into the airy breeze, and clove the opposite clouds with its weight. After a long pause, the heavy mass fell on the hard ground, and showed skill united with strength.

"Immediately the Taenarian youth [Hyacinthus], in his thoughtlessness, and urged on by eagerness for the sport, hastened to take up the circlet; but the hard ground sent it back into the air with a rebound against thy face, Hyacinthus.

"Equally as pale as the youth does the Divinity himself turn; and he bears up thy sinking limbs; and at one moment he cherishes thee, at another, he stanches thy sad wound; and now he stops the fleeting life by the application of herbs.

His skill is of no avail. The wound is incurable. As if, in a well-watered garden, any one should break down violets, or poppies, and lilies, as they adhere to their yellow stalks; drooping, they would suddenly hang down their languid heads, and could not support themselves; and would look towards the ground with their tops. So sink his dying features; and, forsaken by its vigour, the neck is a burden to itself, and reclines upon the shoulder.

"'Son of Oebalus,' says Phoebus, 'thou fallest, deprived of thy early youth; and I look on thy wound as my own condemnation. Thou art the object of my grief, and the cause of my crime. With thy death is my right hand to be charged; I am the author of thy destruction. Yet what is my fault? unless to engage in sport can be termed a fault; unless it can be called fault, too, to have loved thee. And oh! that I could give my life for thee, or together with thee; but since I am restrained by the decrees of destiny, thou shalt ever be with me, and shalt dwell on my mindful lips. The lyre struck with my hand, my songs, too, shall celebrate thee; and, becoming a new flower, by the inscription on thee, thou shalt imitate my lamentations. The time, too, shall come, at which a most valiant hero shall add his name to this flower, and it shall be read upon the same leaves.'

"While such things are being uttered by the prophetic lips of Apollo, behold! the blood which, poured on the ground, has stained the grass, ceases to be blood, and a flower springs up, more bright than the Tyrian purple, and it assumes the appearance which lilies have, were there not in this a purple hue, and in them that of silver.

"This was not enough for Phoebus, for 'twas he that was the author of this honour. He himself inscribed his own lamentations on the leaves, and the flower has 'ai, ai' [alas, alas] inscribed thereon; and the mournful characters there are traced.

"Nor is Sparta ashamed to have given birth to Hyacinthus; and his honours continue to the present time; the Hyacinthian festival returns, too, each year, to be celebrated with the prescribed ceremonials, after the manner of former celebrations."

TEXT Ovid, *Metamorphoses*, trans. Henry T. Riley (London: George Bell & Sons, 1876), 10.162–219.

OTHER SOURCES Sigmund Freud, *The Ego and the Id*, trans. Joan Riviere, ed. James Strachey (New York: Norton, 1960), p. 18; Judy Grahn, *Another Mother Tongue: Gay Words, Gay Worlds* (Boston: Beacon, 1984), pp. 6–7.

Sweet to Me
above All
Sweetness

As I looked for material that expressed how I felt about death and loss, I was somewhat surprised to find the following passage in the writings of St. Augustine, an early Christian father. In his mature years, Augustine propounded deeply antisexual doctrines and wrote diatribes against the *galli* and other elements of pagan culture. For all that, love, including passionate love, between members of the same sex was not a problem in the church as long as it remained nonsexual. The assumption that churchmen were celibate made the expression of love between them seem innocent. The church even fostered these relationships through the practice of separate living for religious men and women. Thus, it is part of the mixed nature of the Christian tradition that it gives us passages like this one from St. Augustine, describing his emotions following the loss of a friend while he was still a young man (and before his conversion to orthodox Christianity). As a literary expression of grief, it deserves comparison with the account of Gilgamesh mourning the death of Enkidu.

Augustine finally turns to his circle of friends and there finds distraction from his sense of loss. Hasn't our circle of friends, our support groups and networks and whatever you want to call them, been the one thing that has gotten us through this epidemic? They help us find ways to laugh again; they draw our attention back to the world of the living; they remind us that the best answer to grief is community, making "but one out of the many."

➤　➤　➤

In those years when I first of all began to teach rhetoric in the town where I was born, I had gained a very dear friend, upon the occasion of the nearness of our studies; one who was about mine own age [twenty-one], now springing up with me in the flower of youth. He had grown up of a child with me, and both school-fellows and play-fellows we had been. . . . But behold thou, ever at the back of thy runaways, the God of revenge, and fountain of mercies, both at the same time, who turnest us to thyself by most wonderful means, tookest that man out of this life, when he had scarce continued one whole year in my friendship, sweet to me above all sweetness of this life. . . .

At the grief of this, my heart was utterly over clouded; and whatsoever I cast mine eyes upon, looked like death unto me. Mine own country was a very prison to me, and my father's house a wonderful unhappiness; and whatsoever I had communicated in with him, wanting him turned to my most cruel torture. Mine eyes roved above everywhere for him, but they met not with him; and I hated all places for that they had not him; nor could they now tell me, Behold, he will come shortly, as when he was alive they did whenever he was absent. I became a great riddle to myself, and I often asked over my soul, why she was so sad, and why she afflicted me so sorely: but she knew not what to answer me. And if I said, "Put that trust in God," very justly she did not obey me; because that most dear man whom she had lost, was both truer and better than that fantastical god she was bid to trust in. Only tears were sweet to me, for they had now succeeded in my friend's place, in the dearest of my affections.

And now Lord, are these things well passed over, and time

hath assuaged the anguish of my wound. May I learn this from thee who art Truth, and may I apply the ear of my heart unto thy mouth, that thou mayest tell me the reason, why weeping should be so sweet to people in misery?

Hast thou (notwithstanding thou art present everywhere) cast away our misery far from thee? And thou remainest constant in thyself, but we are tumbled up and down in divers trials: and yet unless we should bewail ourselves in thine ears, there should no hope remain for us. How comes it then to pass, that such sweet fruit is gathered from the bitterness of life, namely to mourn, and weep, and sigh, and complain?

Is it this that sweetens it, that we are in hope thou hearest us? This may rightly be thought of our prayers, because they have a desire to approach unto thee. But may it be so said too concerning that grief and mourning for the thing lost, with which I was then wholly overwhelmed? For I did not hope he should revive again, nor did I pray for this with all my tears: but bemoan him only I did, and weep for him: seeing a wretch I was, and had utterly lost all my joy. Or is weeping a truly bitter thing, pleasing to us only from a distaste for the things we once enjoyed and only while the distaste remains keen?

But why speak I of these things? For 'tis no time to ask questions, but to confess unto thee. Wretched I was; and wretched is every soul that is bound fast in the friendship of mortal beings; who becomes all to pieces when he forgoes them, and then first he becomes sensible of his misery, by which he is already miserable even before he forgoes them. This was my case at that time, I wept full bitterly, and yet was best at quiet in that bitterness. Thus was I wretched enough, and that wretched life I accounted more dear than my friend himself. For though I would gladly have changed it, yet more unwilling I was to lose that, that I had been to lose him; yea I know not whether I would have forgone that, even to have enjoyed him. Like as the tradition (if it be not a fiction) goes of Pylades and Orestes [two sworn lovers], who would gladly have died one for another, both together, it being to them worse than death not to live together.

But a strange kind of affection prevailed with me which was clean contrary to theirs, for both grievously tedious to me it was to live, and yet fearful was I to die. I suppose that how much the more affectionately I loved him, so much the more did I both hate and fear (as my cruellest enemy) death, which had bereaved me of him: and I imagined it would speedily make an end of all other men, because it had the power to do of him. Even thus I remember, stood I then affected.

Behold my heart, O God, yea, search it thoroughly; search it because I remember it well, O my Hope, who cleanest me from the impurity of such affections, directing mine eyes towards thee, and plucking my feet out of the snare. For I much marvelled that other mortals did live, since he whom I so loved, as if he never should have died, was now dead: yea, I more marvelled that myself who was to him a second self, should be able to live after him. Rightly has a friend been called, "thou half of my soul": for I still thought my soul and his soul to have been but one soul in two bodies: and therefore was my life a very horror to me, because I would not live by halves. And even therefore perchance I was afraid to die, lest he should die, whom so passionately I had loved.

O Madness, which knowest not how to love men, as men should be loved! O foolish man, which so impatiently endurest the chances Mortality is subject unto! Thus mad and foolish was I at that time. Therefore I stormed, and puffed, and cried, and chafed, being capable neither of rest nor counsel. For I was fain to carry my shattered and bleeding soul, which yet had not patience enough to be carried by me; yet a place where to dispose of it, I could not light upon. Not in the delightful groves, not where mirth and music was, nor in the odoriferous gardens, nor in curious banquetings, nor in the pleasures of the bed and chambering; nor, finally, in reading over either verse or prose, took it any contentment. Everything was offensive, yea, the very light itself; and whatsoever were not he, was alike painful and hateful to me, except groaning and weeping. For only in those found I a little refreshment. But so soon as I had retired my soul from these, a huge misery overloaded me, which thou only could ease and lighten, O Lord. . . . And yet after all this, out of my country I fled: for so should mine eyes less look for him there, where they were not wont to see him. And thus I left the town of Thagaste, and came to Carthage.

Time loses no time: nor does it idly go by and return about these senses of ours; but through them it causes strange operations in our minds. Behold, it came and went day by day, and by going and coming to and again, it brought into my mind other notions, and other remembrances, and by little and little pieced me up again with my old kind of delights, unto which my present sorrow gave some way. And to that again there succeeded, though not other griefs, yet the causes of other griefs. For how came that former grief so easily and so deeply to make impression in me, but even from hence, that I had spilt my soul upon the sand, in loving a man that must die, as if he never had been to die? For the comfortings of other friends did mostly repair and refresh me, with whom I did love, what afterwards I did love. . . .

They were other things which in their company did more fully take my mind; namely, to discourse, and to laugh with them, and to do obsequious offices of courtesy one to another; to read pretty books together; sometimes to be in jest, and other whiles seriously earnest to one another; sometimes so to dissent without discontent, as a man would do with his own self, and even with the seldomness of those dissentings, season our more frequent consentings; sometimes would we teach, and sometimes learn one of another; wish for the company of the absent with impatience, and welcome home the newcomers with joyfulness. With these and the like expressions, proceeding out of the hearts of those that loved and repaired one another's affections, by the countenance, by the tongue, by the eyes, and by a thousand other most pleasing motions, did we set out souls ablaze, and make but one out of many.

TEXT *Saint Augustine's Confessions*, trans. William Watts (Cambridge, Mass.: Harvard University Press, 1912), 4.4–8.

S P I R I T S

His Mind Became Healthy

(Dekanawida and

Hayonhwatha)

Sometime in the 1500s (or perhaps earlier), the Iroquoian-speaking tribes of the Northeast and Great Lakes areas forged a powerful political alliance. Once surrounded by their traditional enemies, the Algonkians, the confederated Iroquois established themselves as the most powerful force in the region, driving out whole tribes from their homelands, adopting and absorbing others. For the American revolutionaries, the Iroquois confederacy provided a model of a confederation based on checks and balances and consensus decision making, and some scholars have argued that this had an influence on the American Constitution.

According to Iroquois oral tradition, the confederacy was founded by a Huron Indian named Dekanawida and a Mohawk named Hayonhwatha (Longfellow mistakenly used this Iroquois name for his unrelated Ojibway character Hiawatha). Together, these two leaders brought peace to the nations of the Oneida, Onondaga, Seneca, Cayuse, and Mohawk (and, later, the Tuscarora). Their story provides an excellent example of how the bond between two men can become a potent source of healing, unification, and innovation. It seems especially fitting to include it in this chapter since the issue of grieving is a central theme.

The story begins with the birth of Dekanawida. Like other heroes in this collection, he has no father but is born miraculously—outside normal heterosexual reproduction and outside heterosexual kinship roles. His only personal relationship is with Hayonhwatha, an Onondaga adopted by the Mohawk, and this relationship is the key to the realization of Dekanawida's mission: bringing peace to the warring Iroquois nations. By healing Hayonhwatha's grief, Dekanawida enables him to fulfill his own vision of instituting a condolence ceremony. This ceremony, in turn, becomes the basis for healing the wounds that have kept the five nations at war for so long. Following this, the two heroes become friends, fulfilling the Divine Twin archetype.

The key episode of the myth involves the efforts to heal the monster Adodarhoh. Adodarhoh was a chief of the Onondaga people who acquired witch-like powers and began to kill men and animals. In time, his whole appearance changed. Snakes encircled his head, and the people became afraid to look at him. He is described as having a "crooked" mind. In Indian sign language, the gesture for a person suffering mental and emotional distress is "crooked mind." It was the "twisted minds" of the Iroquois that kept them locked in patterns of violence. Bringing about peace required healing on all sides, by healers who could cross social boundaries. To include the story of Dekanawida and Hayonhwatha here is not to label them gay or to imply that their relationship was erotic when we simply don't know—only that their story speaks to those of us living gay lives today. We, too, are often unrecognized at first and rejected by our families and communities; we, too, must learn how to break the cycle of abuse we grew up in.

Dekanawida's encounter with the cannibal monster Tahdodaho (probably a version of Adodarhoh) offers a remarkable illustration of the powers of magickal twinning. The monster, peering into pail of water, sees the face of Dekanawida, who is looking down through a hole in the roof, and he mistakes it for his own. Suddenly, where he had seen only evil and ugliness, Tahdodaho sees beauty—beauty in himself that he had not known. This causes him to reevaluate his entire existence. Healed, he returns to his people as an emissary of peace.

This is what we gay men can do for each other when we tap the energy of the Divine Twins. In our gender sameness, we are mirrors to each other. If what we reflect is the beauty we see in the other, we can facilitate a profound transformation, a self-realization, a new level of self-respect and self-esteem—and he will do the same for us. Given this great power to heal each other, which seems to work in nonsexual as well as sexual relationships, why don't we share it more often?

The following excerpts come from three manuscripts prepared at the turn of the century: "The Dekanawida Legend," collected and translated by a Mohawk named Seth Newhouse and later revised by an Onondaga-Tuscarora named Albert Cusick; "The Traditional Narrative of the Origin of the Confederation of the Five Nations," prepared by the Chiefs of the Six Nations in 1900; and "The Hiawatha Tradition," related by an Onondaga named Baptist Thomas.

➤   ➤   ➤

PLAYERS AND PLACES

Wyandots   "Crooked Tongues," a branch of the Huron or
   neutral tribe
Oneida   "People of the Stone"
Mohawks   "People of the Flint"
Cayuga   "Great Pipe People"
Seneca   "People of the Great Hill"
Onondaga   "Many Hills People"
Tuscarora   "Hemp gatherers"
Ongwe-oweh   "Original People," the Iroquois

S   P   I   R   I   T   S

Dekanawida   (Dekanahwideh in Chiefs' version), founder
of the Iroquois Confederacy, his name has been
translated as "two water currents flowing together,"
"double row of teeth" (referring to a speech impediment
that led him to appoint Hayonhwatha as his
spokesman), and "master of things"

Hayonhwatha   adopted member of the Mohawk tribe, his
name has been translated as "he has misplaced
something but knows where to find it," "he who combs"
(a reference to combing the snakes out of Adodarhoh's
hair), and "he who seeks the wampum belt" (in
reference to his role in making the first wampum belt)

Tahdodaho   a cannibal wizard in the Chiefs' version,
Thadodaho in the Thomas version

Adodarhoh   Onondaga chief in the Newhouse version
whose mind has become "twisted," turning him into a
monster

THE BIRTH AND JOURNEY OF DEKANAWIDA (NEWHOUSE)

North of the beautiful lake (Ontario) in the land of the
Crooked Tongues, was a long winding bay and at a certain
spot was the Huron town, Ka-ha-nah-yeh (Tkahaánaye).
Near by this was the great hill, Ti-ro-nat-ha-ra-da-donh. In
the village lived a good woman who had a virgin daughter.
Now strangely this virgin conceived and her mother knew
that she was about to bear a child. The daughter about this
time went into a long sleep and dreamed that her child
should be a son whom she should name Dekanawida. The

messenger in the dream told her that he should become a great man and that he should go among the Flint people to live and that he should also go to the Many Hill Nation and there raise up the Great Tree of Peace. It was true as had been said the virgin gave birth to a boy and the grandmother greatly disliked him and she rebuked her daughter.

"You refuse to tell me the father of the child," she said, "and now how do you know that great calamity will not befall us, and our nation? You must drown the child."

So then the mother took the child to the bay and chopped a hole in the ice where she customarily drew water and thrust him in, but when night came the child was found at his mother's bosom. So then the mother took the child again and threw him in the bay but at night the child returned. Then the third time the grandmother herself took the child and drowned him but in the morning the child nestled as before on its mother's own bosom.

So the grandmother marveled that the child, her grandson, could not be drowned. Then she said to her daughter:

"Mother, now nurse your child for he may become an important man. He can not be drowned, we know, and you have borne him without having marriage with any man. Now I have never heard of such an occurrence nor has the world known of it before."

Beginning with that time the mother took great care of the child and nursed him. She named him Dekanawida in accord with the instruction of her dream.

The child rapidly grew and was remarkably strong and

healthy. His appearance was noticed for its good aspect and his face was most handsome.

When Dekanawida had grown to manhood he was greatly abused by the Huron people because of his handsome face and his good mind. He was always honest and always told what he believed was right. Nevertheless he was a peculiar man and his people did not understand him.

Many things conspired to drive him away, for the Crooked Tongues had no love for such a man. Their hearts were bitter against a man who loved not war better than all things.

➤   ➤   ➤

Traveling alone and unarmed, Dekanawida arrives in the land of the Flint Nation. When he is taken before the chiefs, he tells them:

➤   ➤   ➤

"The Great Creator from whom we all are descended sent me to establish the Great Peace among you. No longer shall you kill one another and nations shall cease warring upon each other. Such things are entirely evil and he, your Maker, forbids it. Peace and comfort are better than war and misery for a nation's welfare."

➤   ➤   ➤

To prove his power, Dekanawida climbs a tall tree perched at the edge of a precipice. The people cut the tree down, and Dekanawida disap-

pears into the depths below. The next morning the warriors spot a column of smoke rising from an empty cabin—it is Dekanawida.

➤   ➤   ➤

DEKANAWIDEH HEALS TAHDODAHO
(CHIEFS' VERSION)

Dekanahwideh continued his journey and came to where
the great wizard Tahdodaho lived. This man was possessed
with great power as a wizard and no man could come to him
without endangering his life, and it is related that even the
fowls of the air whenever they flew directly over his place of
abode would die and fall down on his premises, and that if
he saw a man approaching him he was sure to destroy him or
kill him. This man was a cannibal, and had left the settle-
ment to which he belonged for a long time and lived by himself in an isolated place.

Dekanahwideh came and approached the abode of the
cannibal and saw him carrying a human body into his house
and shortly he saw him come out again and go down to the
river and draw some water. Dekanahwideh went closer and
when he had come to the house he went up onto the roof and
from the chimney opening he looked in and saw the owner
come back with a pail of water, put up a kettle on the fireplace to cook his meal and after it was cooked he saw him
take the kettle from the fire and place it at the end of the fireplace and say to himself, "I suppose it is now time for me to
have my meal and after I am finished I will go where I am
required on business."

Dekanahwideh moved still closer over the smoke hole and

looked straight down into the kettle. The man Tahdodaho was then moving around the house and when he came back to take some of the meat from the kettle he looked into it and saw that a man was looking at him from out of the kettle. This was the reflection of Dekanahwideh. Then the man Tahdodaho moved back and sat down near the corner of the house and began to think seriously and he thought that it was a most wonderful thing which had happened. He said to himself that such a thing had never occurred before as long as he had been living in the house. "I did not know that I was so strange a man," he said. "My mode of living must be wrong." Then he said: "Let me look again and be sure that what I have seen is true." Then he arose, went to the kettle and looked into it again, and he saw the same object—the face of a great man and it was looking at him. Then he took the kettle and went out and went toward the hillside and he emptied it there.

Then Dekanahwideh came down from the roof and made great haste toward the hillside, and when Tahdodaho came up the hill he met Dekanahwideh.

Dekanahwideh asked Tahdodaho where he came from and he said, "I had cooked my meal and I took the kettle from the fire and placed it on the floor. I thought that I would take some of the meat out of the kettle and then I saw a man's face looking at me from the kettle. I do not know what had happened; I only know such a thing never occurred to me before as long as I have been living in this house. Now I have come to the conclusion that I must be wrong in the way I am and the way I have been living. That is why I carried the kettle out of my house and emptied it over there by the stump. I was returning when I met you."

> ➤ ➤ ➤

Dekanawida declares him healed and repented and sends Tahdodaho back to his village to promote peace and friendship.

The following version opens with a description of the strife-torn Iroquois nations and the cannibal monster Adodarhoh.

> ➤ ➤ ➤

THE STORY OF HAYONHWATHA (NEWHOUSE)

In those same days the Onondagas had no peace. A man's life was valued as nothing. For any slight offence a man or woman was killed by his enemy and in this manner feuds started between families and clans. At night none dared leave their doorways lest they be struck down by an enemy's war club. Such was the condition when there was no Great Law.

South of the Onondaga town lived an evil-minded man. His lodge was in a swale and his nest was made of bulrushes. His body was distorted by seven crooks and his long tangled locks were adorned by writhing living serpents. Moreover, this monster was a devourer of raw meat, even of human flesh. He was also a master of wizardry and by his magic he destroyed men but he could not be destroyed. Adodarhoh was the name of the evil man.

Notwithstanding the evil character of Adodarhoh the people of the Onondaga, the Nation of Many Hills, obeyed his commands and though it cost many lives they satisfied his insane whims, so much did they fear him for his sorcery.

> ➤ ➤ ➤

The Onondaga, led by Hayonhwatha, try many times to "clear the mind of Adodarhoh and straighten his crooked body," but every attempt is foiled by the monster's witchcraft. At this point, "a certain great dreamer" has a vision that Hayonhwatha must leave Onondaga for the land of the Flint People. There he will meet with another, and the two of them together will prevail over Adodarhoh. A terrible plot is devised to force Hayonhwatha onto this odyssey—all seven of his daughters are killed by witchcraft.

> ➤ ➤ ➤

The grief of Hayonhwatha was terrible. He threw himself about as if tortured and yielding to the pain. No one came near him so awful was his sorrow. Nothing would console him and his mind was shadowed with the thoughts of his heavy sorrow.

"I shall cast myself away, I shall bury myself in the forest, I shall become a woodland wanderer," he said. Thus he expressed his desire to depart. Then it was known that he would go to another nation.

Hayonhwatha "split the heavens," Watanwhakacia, when he departed and his skies were rent asunder.

> ➤ ➤ ➤

In the Thomas account, Hayentwatha (= Hayonhwatha) leaves the Mohawk people in grief over the death of his only sister. "When his great sorrow came he went away. He took a canoe and went upstream. He paddled up the Mohawk river and when he landed to camp he talked to himself about his sorrow. 'I would comfort others in sorrow,' he said, 'but no one comforts me.'"

As Hayentwatha wanders about despondent, he discovers that a monster named Thadodaho appears before him wherever he goes. Snakes writhe in his hair and cover his shoulders. A single, huge snake curls up from his thighs.

HAYONHWATHA IS HEALED (NEWHOUSE)

During his travels, Hayonhwatha makes a vow to introduce a condolence ceremony for anyone afflicted like himself. "This would I do if I found anyone burdened with grief even as I am. I would console them for they would be covered with night and wrapped in darkness. This would I lift with words of condolence and these strands of beads would become words with which I would address them." Hayonhwatha does not want to impose his wish, however. Instead, he waits until he is asked for his help, and he visits various people before this happens. Finally, a messenger arrives reporting a dream in which two great men meet and establish the Great Peace. Hayonhwatha is escorted to Dekanawida.

➤   ➤   ➤

Dekanawida arose when Hayonhwatha had entered and he said: "My younger brother I perceive that you have suffered from some deep grief. You are a chief among your people and yet you are wandering about."

Hayonhwatha answered, "That person skilled in sorcery, Osinoh, has destroyed my family of seven daughters. It was truly a great calamity and I am now very miserable. My sorrow and my rage have been bitter. I can only rove about since now I have cast myself away from my people. I am only a wanderer. I split the heavens when I went away from my house and my nation."

Dekanawida replied, "Dwell here with me. I will represent your sorrow to the people here dwelling."

So Hayonhwatha had found some one who considered his distress and he did stay. Then Dekanawida told of his suffering and the people listened. . . .

➤   ➤   ➤

Dekanawida heals Hayonhwatha, using the sacred objects Hayonhwatha has collected during his wanderings. Dekanawida says, "My younger brother, it has now become very plain to my eyes that your sorrow must be removed. Your griefs and your rage have been great. I shall now undertake to remove your sorrow so that your mind may be rested." Dekanawida addresses Hayonhwatha with eight ceremonial condolence speeches, handing him a string of shell beads after each speech. Then "the mind of Hayonhwatha was made clear. He was then satisfied and once more saw things rightly." Thus is established the Iroquois condolence ceremony and the use of wampum, the small shell beads threaded in symbolic designs on sashes and belts.

Dekanawida then invites Hayonhwatha to assist him in healing Adodarhoh, and he says, "My younger brother, since you have agreed I now propose that we compose our Peace song. We shall use it on our journey to pacify Adodarhoh. When he hears it his mind shall be made straight. His mind shall then be like that of other men." But first Dekanawida and Hayonhwatha negotiate peace among the warring nations, establishing the Iroquois confederacy. All the nations agree to join except the Onondaga, still under the sway of Adodarhoh. So Dekanawida, Hayonhwatha, and the people march to the lodge of Adodarhoh. Dekanawida himself heals the giant, singing before his lodge and then rubbing has hand over the monster's body, "to know its inherent strength and life. Then Adodarhoh was made straight and his mind became healthy." Other accounts refer to Hayonhwatha "combing the snakes" out of Adodarhoh's hair.

Dekanawida declares, "We have now overcome a great obstacle. It has long stood in the way of peace. The mind of Adodarhoh is now made right and his crooked parts are made straight. Now indeed may we establish the Great Peace."

TEXT Arthur C. Parker, "The Constitution of the Five Nations or the Iroquois Book of the Great Law," *New York State Museum Bulletin* 184 (Albany, 1916).

OTHER SOURCES Horatio Hale, *The Iroquois Book of Rites* (New York: AMS, 1969); Paul A. W. Wallace, *The White Roots of Peace* (Philadelphia: University of Pennsylvania Press, 1946); Shirley H. Witt, *The Tuscaroras* (New York: Crowell-Collier, 1972).

S   P   I   R   I   T   S

The Circle of Loving Companions

The Moth
and the
Star

In the course of compiling this collection, I asked friends for examples of stories or myths that had a special appeal to them or simply stuck in their minds for some reason. John Burnside suggested the following tale from James Thurber's collection *Fables for Our Time*. I have to admit I was doubtful at first that Thurber, whose humorous writings are largely based on the "plight" of the middle-class, henpecked, suburban husband of the 1950s, could have written a story that spoke to gay men. But, as John related it to me, his eyes filled with tears when he came to the part about the old moth who had outlived everyone else and was still trying to reach the star. "And that's Harry," John said, "the old moth, still trying to reach the star."

John was referring to his long-time lover and comrade, Harry Hay. Truly, Harry is the moth: the gay boy who would not settle for the street lamps of the other boys or the house lamps of the girls but sought his own star, which he (foolishly, innocently) believed was just in reach. (Of course, John, too, is a great old moth whose dreams have become only brighter with time.)

We gay men know quite a bit about the little moth boy who defies conventions, but we rarely get a glimpse of the old dignified moths we can become if we hold on to our dreams. Our culture denies us images of gay maturity and gay wisdom. My friendships with older gay men like Harry and John have taught me that, whether or not you achieve your dreams, being true to yourself is the secret of a rich and rewarding life.

➤　➤　➤

A young and impressionable moth once set his heart on a certain star. He told his mother about this and she counselled him to set his heart on a bridge lamp instead. "Stars aren't the thing to hang around," she said; "lamps are the thing to hang around." "You get somewhere that way," said the moth's father. "You don't get anywhere chasing stars." But the moth would not heed the words of either parent. Every evening at dusk when the star came out he would start flying toward it and every morning at dawn he would crawl back home worn out with his vain endeavor. One day his father said to him "You haven't burned a wing in months, boy, and it looks to me as if you were never going to. All your brothers have been badly burned flying around street lamps and all your sisters have been terribly singed flying around house lamps. Come on, now, get out of here and get yourself scorched! A big strapping moth like you without a mark on him!"

The moth left his father's house, but he would not fly around street lamps and he would not fly around house lamps. He went right on trying to reach the star, which was four and one-third light years, or twenty-five trillion miles, away. The moth thought it was just caught in the top branches of an elm. He never did reach the star, but he went right on trying, night after night, and when he was a very, very old moth he began to think that he really had reached the star and he went around saying so. This gave him a deep and lasting pleasure and he lived to a great old age. His par-

ents and his brothers and his sisters had all been burned to
death when they were quite young.

    *Moral: Who flies afar from the sphere of our sorrow is here to-
day and here tomorrow.*

TEXT James Thurber, *Fables for Our Time and Famous Poems Illustrated*
(New York: Harper & Row, 1990), p. 17.

Future

Spirit

Being able to see ourselves in the past is linked to our ability to imagine ourselves in the future. As we've found in this collection, censorship may have cut us off from our heritage, but it has not succeeded in erasing our presence, then or now. Gay traditions may be broken, but they are not missing. Of course, the roles and identities based on same-sex patterns vary over time and from place to place. But there are a core set of *cultural forms* associated with homosexuality that are remarkably similar wherever they occur—we've seen them in the guise of the Two-Spirit, the Twins, and the figures of Initiation, among others. Times have changed, but these images still show up in our psychology, in our dreams, and in the mythologies being spun out every day in popular culture. Same-sex love has diverse, sometimes conflicting meanings, but it also has certain intrinsic meanings in almost any culture in which it occurs—as mediation, as a source of interpersonal powers, as a symbol of gender unity, as the ideal of a voluntary relationship—themes we've encountered throughout this book.

If "we," meaning those of us living in the Western world, have forgotten where we came from, the living representatives of two-spirit traditions have not. Although alternative gender roles around the world have suffered under the impact of Western political and cultural imperialism, some have tenaciously survived. It seems appropriate to draw this collection to a close with reports of their presence and the sounds of their voices.

➤   ➤   ➤

THREE THOUSAND EUNUCHS

BHOPAL, INDIA. Three thousand eunuchs [*hijras*] wearing garish makeup, gaudy saris, bangles, and bells are holding their national convention here. They have gathered for a ten-day festival to proclaim their cult's new national guru. Their former guru died as a result of the Union Carbide gas leak in 1984.

TEXT AP news item, cited in Serena Nanda, *Neither Man nor Woman: The Hijras of India* (Belmont, Calif.: Wadsworth, 1990), p. 38.

➤   ➤   ➤

BEAUTICIANS FOR DEMOCRACY

During the massive demonstrations for freedom in Rangoon, Burma, with almost 1 million marchers, onlookers saved their loudest cheers for a group of transvestites and gays parading behind a banner which proclaimed: "Beauticians for Democracy." However, the hard-nosed military crackdown that followed the anti-government demonstrations has sent gays underground once again.

At one time, transvestite males were popular, just to entertain people. They still ply their trade, dancing and selling sweets and snacks. . . .

TEXT *Passport*, no. 23 (July 1989): 2.

S   P   I   R   I   T   S

> ➤ ➤

IN A SPIRITUAL SENSE

When asked the difference between a Mahu and a gay identity, Kehao explains: "Mahus hold on to the traditional Hawaiian spirituality and value our feminine ways. The Hawaiian gays, and also the transvestites, are modernized.
They're too involved with other things, they're not realizing
where their heritage is. For Hawaiians, Mahu is part of the
culture, it's natural. I guess for the *haoles* [whites] who find
out they're gay—it's harder for them. You don't get that kind
of isolation with Hawaiians, because we've always existed
here. . . . Gays have liberated themselves sexually, but they
have not yet learned their place in a spiritual sense."

TEXT Michael Kehao in Walter Williams, "Sex and Shamanism: The
Making of a Hawaiian Mahu," *Advocate*, no. 417 (2 April 1985): 48–49.

> ➤ ➤

THEY KNEW WHO THEY WERE

In the old days, groups of berdaches lived on the outer edge
of the camp. They lived together in a tipi, or a group of tipis,
that were usually the best made and decorated in camp. The
old time berdaches had a pride in their possessions and in
themselves. They knew who they were and what place they
had in Plains Indian society.

I believe this is exactly what needs to happen again with
gay Indians today. There is a need to take pride in one's self
and to respect other gay Indian people. There is a need for a
resurgence of that old pride and knowledge of place. Tradi-

tions need to be researched and revived. If traditions have
been lost, then new ones should be borrowed from other
tribes to create groups or societies for gay Indians that would
function in the present.

TEXT Clyde Hall/M. Owlfeather (Shoshone-Bannock) in *Living the
Spirit: A Gay American Indian Anthology*, ed. Will Roscoe (New York: St.
Martin's, 1988), p. 104.

➤   ➤   ➤

ANYBODY CAN DO ANYTHING

In our culture, in our little gay world, anybody can do anything. I mean, you find some very good mothers that are
men. And you find very good fathers that are women. We
can sympathize, we can really feel how the other sex feels.
More so than the straight community. The straight community is so worried about staying within their little box and
making sure that I look like a female when I'm out there, or
that I really play the role of the male image.

I think that society is ready for that kind of atmosphere
where we don't have to compete against each other over sexual orientation, or we don't have to feel like the men play a
bigger role in society than women do. I think it's time for that
neutralness, where people can understand just how to be
people. . . .

It seems to be that gay people are a lot more intense about
life in general. They're a lot more keen on feelings, other
peoples' feelings. I don't know why that is but it just seems
that way to me.

There's a lot of caring in gay people that is towards all lifestyles, from children, all the way up to grandparents. Society is getting used to it now because of this sensitivity. I think it might wear off after a while—we'll get everybody thinking like us. . . . Yeah, we are special, because we're able to deal with all of life in general. It's very special.

TEXT Erna Pahe (Navajo) in *Living the Spirit: A Gay American Indian Anthology*, ed. Will Roscoe (New York: St. Martin's, 1988), pp. 112–14.

Sun

and

Flesh

The Sun, the hearth of tenderness and life,
Spills burning love over the enraptured earth,
And, when one is reclined in the valley, one senses
That the earth is nubile and pulsing with blood;
That its immense breast, stirred up by a spirit,
Is made of love like God, of flesh like woman,
And that it contains, great with both pith and rays,
The grand teeming of all the embryos!

And all grows, and all ascends!

                —O Venus, O Goddess!
I miss those times of ancient youth,
Of lascivious satyrs and hairy fauns,
Gods who chew, out of love, the bark of saplings
And in the water-lilies kissed the blonde Nymph!
I miss the times when the pith of the world,
The water of the river, the rose-red blood of the
    green trees
Placed a universe into the veins of Pan!
When the earth palpitated, green, under his goat-feet;
When his lips, gently kissing the luminous syrinx,
Warbled under the heavens a grand hymn of love;
When, standing up on the plain, he heard all about
Living Nature reply to his appeal;

When the mute trees, cradling the bird who sings,
The earth cradling man, and all the blue Ocean
And all the animals were in love, loved in God!

I miss the times of great Cybele
Whom they said traversed, with her enormous beauty,
In a great chariot of bronze, splendid cities;
Her two breasts pouring into the immensities
Pure streamings of infinite life.
Man suckled joyfully at her consecrated breast,
Like a small child, frolicking upon her knees.
—Because he was strong, Man was chaste and sweet

Woe! Today he says: I know things,
And goes on, eyes shut and ears closed.
—And still, no more gods! no more gods! Man is King,
Man is God! But love, behold the great Faith!
Oh! if man only drew from your breast,
Cybele, Great Mother of gods and men;
If he had not deserted immortal Astarte
Who of old, emerging into the immense splendor
Of blue waves, flower of flesh that the billow perfumes,
Showed her rose navel whence the foam came to snow,
And set to singing, that Goddess who conquers with
    great black eyes,
The nightingale in the wood and love in our hearts!

TEXT Arthur Rimbaud, "Soleil et Chair," in *Rimbaud: Complete Works,
Selected Letters*, ed. Wallace Fowlie (Chicago: University of Chicago Press,
1966), pp. 27–29 (my translation).

S   P   I   R   I   T   S

Afterword

I hope this collection inspires you to search for myths on your own, in other cultures and in the culture around you. Here are some things to keep in mind.

Few recorders of gay-related myths were able to imagine why these figures behaved as they did and what they might have *gained* by doing so. They saw only what was *lost*—the status and privilege of the heterosexual male. Consequently, myths often come to us distorted and exoticized, their relevance and their messages obscured, with only faint clues to signal their gay themes. But with patience one can learn to zero in on them. The following are some of the touchstones I use when reading myths:

- Question single-dimensional labels—*homosexual, transvestite, transsexual, hermaphrodite.*

- Imagine the *rewards* and *inner motives* for being different; imagine gayness as a multidimensional constellation of traits.

- Look for multiple genders and gender "neitherness," for "nonheterosexual" as well as homosexual figures, for sons without fathers, and for males identified with the moon

- In the battle of the sexes, who stands with the mother?

· Who are the innovators, the creators, the originators?

· Above all, what feelings and images are evoked within you? What myth are *you* living?

Credits

Index by Region

Specific tribe, author, or place appears in parentheses.